STUDIES IN GDR CULTURE AND SOCIETY 2

KV-240-771

Proceedings of the Seventh International Symposium on the German Democratic Republic

Editorial Board:

Margy Gerber, Chief Editor
Christine Cosentino
Volker Gransow
Nancy A. Lauckner
Duncan Smith
Alexander Stephan
W. Christoph Schmauch

UNIVERSITY
PRESS OF
AMERICA

Copyright © 1982 by

University Press of America, Inc.

P.O. Box 19101, Washington, D.C. 20036

ISBN (Perfect): 0-8191-2525-3
ISBN   (Cloth): 0-8191-2524-5

Library of Congress Catalog Card Number: **81-43512**

TABLE OF CONTENTS

iv

Preface

The twenty-two articles collected in this volume
are the revised versions of papers read at the Seventh
International Symposium on the German Democratic Republic, which was held from June 19 - 26, 1981 on the
rustic grounds of the World Fellowship Center near
Conway, New Hampshire.

The International Symposium on the German Democratic Republic, which has been held annually since
1975, is an interdisciplinary gathering of academi-
cians and others with expertise in the many varied
aspects of GDR culture and society. The week-long
program is comprised of papers and presentations,
extensive informal discussion, and other events such
as films, music, and art exhibits. The Symposium is
pluralistic in its approach and philosophy; it has no
particular political or ideological basis and welcomes
a variety of viewpoints.

The collecting and publishing of the papers presented at the Symposium is intended as a means of fur-
thering the understanding of the culture and society
of the German Democratic Republic, about which--still
today--relatively little is known in the West.

Margy Gerber (Bowling Green State University)
Chief Editor

Christine Cosentino (Rutgers University)
Volker Gransow (Universität Bielefeld/FU Berlin)
Nancy A. Lauckner (Univ. of Tenn., Knoxville)
Duncan Smith (Brown University)
Alexander Stephan (Univ. of Calif., Los Angeles)
W. Christoph Schmauch, ex officio (World Fellow-
ship Center)

The Rediscovery of Romanticism: Revisions and Reevaluations

Patricia Herminghouse

Almost as suddenly as it began, the romance of western readers and critics with GDR literature seems to have fizzled out. The fascination which blossomed in the early 1970s, animated by Willy Brandt's Ostpolitik and sustained by the appeal of literary works such as Christa Wolf's Nachdenken über Christa T., culminated in a chronique scandaleuse: the Biermann affair and its seemingly endless sequels. Awkward as the early enthusiasm to explore the newly discovered literary landscape of the GDR may have been, it was no less naive than the simplistic tendency in the post-Biermann era to categorize almost everything which is published by GDR authors as either (good) dissident or (bad) non-dissident literature. By focusing our attention on writers who have been surrounded by controversy or marketed onto bestseller lists in the West—which is often the same thing—we risk overlooking significant developments within the cultural life of the GDR, developments in which dissident as well as non-dissident writers may participate. The rediscovery of Romanticism in the GDR is just such a development, one which has called major premises of literary history, cultural theory, and aesthetic principles into question, which has involved scholars and artists alike in rethinking the function of literature in contemporary socialist society, addressing the contradictions, and revising the tenets of previous cultural dogmas.

Although some aspects of this internal discussion, particularly the emphasis on subjectivity, seem to pick up on the themes of dissidence, it is important to keep the GDR context in mind. Here critics and writers are engaged in a process of reflecting

1

qualitatively new modes of perception and experience, of critiquing the dominant traditions which have thus far shaped the meaning of and possibilities for literature in socialist society. What is new is not only the way in which both scholars and writers are seizing upon the Romantic heritage, often with markedly different emphases, but the fact that the writers themselves have become engaged to an unprecedented extent in activities which were previously the province of the professional critics and scholars: presenting papers at conferences, publishing essays on and editions of Romantic writers, even providing appendices and glosses to their own creative works which feature Romantic writers as central figures.

Although it has long been accepted that an author's involvement in the issues of the day need not be confined to the problems of factory and agricultural workers and quite legitimately includes questions of his/her own artistic work and relationship to society, those questions have, until quite recently, been posed in contemporary settings. No matter how controversial the depiction of GDR literary life in some of these works--such as Wolf's Christa T., Hermann Kant's Impressum, Günther de Bruyn's Preisverleihung, or Jurek Becker's Irreführung der Behörden--may have been, it was nonetheless relatively conventional in comparison to the bold poetic experiments of recent years which explore the significance for writers in the present of writers of the Romantic period, particularly Friedrich Hölderlin, Heinrich von Kleist, E.T.A. Hoffmann, and the women Romantics. In terms of their ability to establish affinities between the situation of these Romantic writers and their own contemporary reality, GDR writers have been far more perceptive and bold than their scholarly colleagues. From Stephan Hermlin's radio play Scardanelli (1970) to Christa Wolf's short novel Kein Ort. Nirgends (1979) at the end of the decade, the trace which has led writers of the 1970s to writers of the Romantic era has been less the vision of a better future than dissatisfaction with present reality, a belief in certain ideals which makes it impossible to affirm the present as being in harmony with them. Not coincidentally, this dissatisfaction also connects them to most of their fellow writers who have left the GDR, writers who have employed western media rather than the medium of the past to articulate their criticism of the present.

If the GDR celebrated its birth as a state in the sign of the Goethe bicentennial of 1949, it ended the 1970s with a decided switch in emphasis, discovering in German Romanticism much more that seemed to speak to contemporary needs than in Goethe, who is viewed much more critically, not only for his readiness to adapt to the values of the Weimar court, but also for his quickness to condemn many of his contemporaries. It becomes obvious that much more than the German penchant for centennial celebrations is at work here when one compares the flurry of conferences, articles, editions, and literary works which marked the 200th birthdays of Caspar David Friedrich (1974), E.T.A. Hoffmann (1976), Friedrich von Kleist, Philipp Otto Runge, and even so obscure a figure as Carl Wilhelm Salice-Contessa (1977) to the way in which bicentennials of somewhat older Romantic figures were allowed to slip by in the immediately preceding years. The current preoccupation with Romanticism is part and parcel of a larger effort to break with certain aspects of previous aesthetic theory and to define a "socialistic national literature." The old, prescriptive dogmas of Socialist Realism, which excluded--among other things--the use of symbolism, the fantastic, and formal experimentation, are now held responsible for the abandonment of significant portions of literary territory to the bourgeois camp. Likewise, Erbetheorie is being rethought and the concept enlarged to include almost any work from the past which, consciously or unconsciously, might be regarded as relevant to the present. Minimizing the value judgment which adhered to the word Erbe--so that describing a work as belonging or not belonging to the Erbe was tantamount to tagging it as "recommended" or "not recommended"--and loosening the constraints of cultural conventions which had consigned vast bodies of important literature to the margins of respectability has resulted in opening up entire literary traditions, such as Romanticism, for examination and appropriation. It simultaneously has freed writers and critics to be much more critical of traditions which had oppressed them, such as the cult of German Classicism and Goethe, in particular. Clumsy, repetitious, and tedious as much of the discussion about the question of Erbe has tended to be, the literary works which reflect this debate are fascinating and provocative. My own interest in this topic actually began with the astonishing use of the fantastic and the reappropriation of Romanticism by a number of GDR women writers: Anna Seghers, Sarah Kirsch, Irmtraud Morgner, and

3

Christa Wolf.[1]

In order to understand the complexities of the current reception of Romanticism in the GDR, it is easiest to begin with the relatively simple explanations of why, until recently, it was at best neglected and more often maligned. Fraught as the term "Romantik" had become with negative political implications, it is not surprising that the GDR waited for some three decades before attempting to recover the movement from the distortions of the National-Socialistic cult of Romanticism, which emphasized nationalistic and irrational aspects of the movement. Instead, the GDR based its literary canon on a "progressive" tradition, which stretched from the Reformation and Peasant Wars through the Enlightenment and Classicism to Vormärz and Bourgeois Realism as the predecessors of Socialist Realism. Without going into detail, one need only recall how many of the most important figures in this progressive canon had damned the emotional excesses and formal experimentation of Romanticism as the antithesis of healthy action-oriented Realism—Goethe, Hegel, Heine, Marx, and most especially Georg Lukács—to realize how inherent the disregard for Romanticism was in the very premises. Admittedly, there were a few timid admissions of single writers, such as E.T.A. Hoffmann, Eichendorff, and Hölderlin, who were often legitimized by emphasizing their affinities to Classicism or Realism, thus as exceptions to the decadence and formalism which were considered characteristic of the period as a whole. Likewise, Achim von Arnim and Clemens Brentano as well as the Grimm brothers were praised for the social quality (Volksverbundenheit) of their various anthologies of folk literature.

The greatest obstacle to any serious consideration of the period as a whole was the theory advanced by some of the most respected anti-fascists of the post-war years that Romanticism was a precursor of fascism. The very status in cultural and political circles of figures such as Lukács, Heinrich Mann, Alfred Kurella, Friedrich Wolf, and Alexander Abusch lent such credence to their point of view that other voices and other opinions faded away without an echo until very recently. In order to understand their disregard for Romanticism as well as their insistence on Goethe as a model upon which German society would rebuild in the post-war years, one must remember that these men spent the years after 1933 in exile—many of

4

them in Stalin's Soviet Union--with the memories of the misuses the National Socialists had made of Goethe and the centennial of his death in 1932 still painfully fresh. For them, Goethe, with his clear rejection of "sick" Romanticism, came more and more to represent the "good," humanistic Germany, the banner under which all varieties of anti-fascism could unite in the post-war years. They also recognized that "Mit Goethe vorwärts" was an idea sure to have more popular appeal than the slogans of Marxism-Leninism.[2]

Of course, there were other obstacles to a positive reception of Romanticism and its integration into GDR literary history besides Lukács' influence and the pre-fascism theory. Not the least of them was the very state of bourgeois literary historiography, which clung to ahistorical existentialism and Geistesgeschichte in its approach to Romanticism long into the post-war era. Until quite recently, western scholarship afforded few alternatives to the views of Haym, Gundolf, Korff, Lion, and Unger--to name a few--from which the GDR was determined to dissociate itself. Yet, paradoxically, it was the unfortunate "pre-Romanticism" theory advanced by many of these scorned critics--a theory which sees the origins of Romanticism in opposition to the tenets of Enlightenment--which inhibited the GDR from seeking its own access to the period and heeding other voices in its own tradition which offered another view of the matter. Only recently, in connection with both the critical reconsideration of the legacy of Lukács and the seventy-fifth birthday of Anna Seghers have there been reexaminations of her "dialogue" with Lukács in the 1930s, when she cautioned against a one-sided orientation toward Goethe which excluded other writers whose lives and work reflect the crisis of their more critical encounter with society. For her, figures such as Kleist, Büchner, Hölderlin, Lenz, Karoline v. Günderrode--the problematic writers of a transitional era--are more relevant than Goethe, whose work was, she points out, "erkauft durch eine starke Anlehnung seines Schöpfers an die bestehende Gesellschaft, eine Auflehnung hätte vermutlich dieses Werk gefährdet."[3] But it was not until the 1970s that the positions of Goethe critics such as Brecht and Seghers were taken seriously, despite the superficial rejection of Lukács in 1956.

In 1977, a memorial conference following the death of Werner Krauss paid tribute to the work of this man, who had received more appreciation abroad than in his own country.[4] Krauss' historical analysis of Romanticism as the attempt of some of the most progressive thinkers of the period to carry out the implications of the French Revolution in literature had been almost ignored during his lifetime, since it conflicted with the prevalent view of Romanticism as counter-revolutionary restoration. With the use of Krauss' analysis, it became possible to establish a direct line from the Enlightenment to the Revolution to the literature of Romanticism, thus integrating it into a dialectical continuum of emancipatory movements which lead from the eighteenth century into Vormärz. Not very much is said even today about the organizer of the 1962 colloquium at which Krauss read his now highly regarded paper: it was Hans Mayer, whose opening lecture, "Fragen der Romantikforschung," made the same point and argued for a conception into which Hölderlin, Kleist, and Jean Paul could be integrated as key figures of literary history rather than anomalies. Mayer's analysis of the way in which a movement conceived of both as a continuation of emancipatory impulses and as protest against post-revolutionary reality contained within it the seeds of its evolution into "revolutionäre Romantik und romantische Restauration"[5] did not prevail after his move to the West. Rather than examine the function of various literary movements which co-existed in the late eighteenth and early nineteenth centuries, GDR literary history continued to draw on them—in the formulation of one annoyed critic from within the ranks—as a kind of "self-service store," where every critic could pick and choose among those literary products which served to support or legitimate his own position.[6]

The long and troubled history of the attempt to produce the seventh volume (1789-1830) of the GDR's national literary history can be traced by comparing versions of parts of it which were published in the early 1970s with the book, which finally appeared in 1978.[7] But an even more striking insight into the reservations that had to be overcome and the revisions of literary judgment that were involved can be gained from newer articles on Romanticism published by members of the book's collective authorship since 1977. Hans-Dietrich Dahnke, the leader of the collective, rejected in 1971 the utopianism of what he called the "revolutionary-democratic tendency" in favor of the realism of the reformers Goethe and Schiller, who pursued improvement through evolution "im Bündnis mit einsichtigen Vertretern der herrschenden Klasse der Gesellschaft."[8] Dahnke saw a clear danger in Romantic individualism and opposition to capitalism--a necessary stage in the historical process outlined by Marx --since it could lead to neglect of the anti-feudalism and realism of Classical humanism. But at the end of the decade, Dahnke is calling for the elimination and correction of undialectical and illusionary views of literary history, polemicizing against normative postulates and admitting that people are growing tired and suspicious of enlightened didacticism, classical objectivity and "vormärzliche Operativität."[9] Romanticism has come of age. In the words of Claus Träger, it has become an "unveräußerlicher Bestandteil der sozialistischen Nationalkultur."[10]

Träger has certainly been among the most outspoken critics in his calls for theoretical and methodological re-evaluations of concepts of realism and literary heritage that have been too narrow to encompass Romanticism. Instead of mere patchwork, Träger insists that critics finally develop a dialectical view of history and abandon their undifferentiated use of the terms "Realism" and "Classicism." Realism, he laments, has been wrongly transformed from a period designation into a standard of judgment.[11] Träger also denounces the dogmatic opposition of Classicism and Romanticism as a German national peculiarity which has more to do with Weimar provincialism than with the sort of internationalism to be expected of the contemporary GDR: "Unseren Begriff der Klassik verstehen nur wir--wenn überhaupt."[12] Träger's emphasis on the contemporary relevance of the Romantic preoccupation with the problem of the artist reflects the current willingness to recognize the importance of the subjective factor, described by one writer as "die konsequente Suche nach den eigenen Möglichkeiten zu literarischer Mitteilung über wesentliche menschliche Verhaltensweisen und Zeitumstände."[13] His argumentation makes the appropriation of Romanticism not only possible, but also proper, by relating it to present-day needs and interests.

Besides the work of the literary historians, another important factor in the rehabilitation of Romanticism has been the widespread discussion of the function of literature at the present stage of the GDR's development. Changed attitudes derived from two major factors: firstly, the emergence of a new generation of writers whose literary careers have developed

entirely in the GDR and who are thus able to articulate the subjective needs and experiences of individuals in socialist society; and, secondly, developments
in literary criticism, which has begun to shift from a
production-oriented to a reception-oriented stance.
In the 1970s the tiresome vocabulary of "Bewahrung,"
"Pflege," "Aneignung" yielded to much more critical
reflection on the actual function of this heritage in
socialism. In an official statement, "Zu Fragen der
Kulturpolitik der SED," in 1972, Kurt Hager sealed the
already established rejection of the slogan "Kunst ist
Waffe" with the imprimatur of party policy, calling
for an end to all forms of restrictions on the function of art, especially those which degrade it to mere
illustration of ideas which can be developed in other
contexts.[14]   Through the 1970s this sentiment was
echoed in various formulations which, despite differences of nuance, all indicated rejection of what Horst
Redeker refers to as "einseitige gnoseologische Betrachtungsweise"[15] and Dieter Schlenstedt as "Wissen-
schaftsorientierung" which is all too inclined to
regard literature as the execution of ideological
guidelines, the fulfillment of cultural-political
programs, and as illustration for glorious history.[16]
Instead of this rhetorical relationship between author
and reader, which formerly characterized the literary
process, Schlenstedt describes an emerging partnership
which has its parallel in a changing conception of
"Literaturwissenschaft" from "Leitwissenschaft" of
literary production to a partner offering reflections
in a process of social self-analysis. [17]

     The current emphasis on communication through and
about literature reflects a changed understanding of
the function of art, the process of influence (Wirkung), and the meaning of reception. The movement is
away from knowledge and representation, toward experience and evaluation, acknowledging that regardless of
whether the work of art reproduces the objects of
empirical reality, the recipient appropriates the work
for him/herself in terms of identification, rejection,
imitation, or reinterpretation, comparing it with
his/her own subjective experience and options.[18] Thus
what the reader does with the artist's creation is
itself a creative act.

     When the reader--of a Romantic work, for example
--is at the same time a writer, this process of appropriation is a special one, for the reception will be
based on the specific needs, experience, and interests

of a writer. Thus, not surprisingly, the affinity of
contemporary writers with writers of the Romantic
period--writers in an uncertain period whose lives
often ended in despair and tragedy, in the madness or
suicide of the disillusioned and disappointed--is far
more personal than the more abstract occupation of the
scholars with a neglected period, a gap to be filled
in literary history. Not coincidentally, their sympa-
thies for these writers are linked to emphatic criticism of Goethe and the Goethe cult. Instead of being
used as a model, Goethe is held up as a paradigm of
all that they find wrong in contemporary cultural
policies. By casting Goethe in the role of antag-
onist, these writers provoke a more historical analysis of his relevance and the falsifications of the
Goethe myth which have persisted in the GDR. In every
case, it is the writer's distance, not attachment, to
Goethe which is emphasized.

A few examples from the literature of the last
decade will serve to illustrate the process I have
been describing here. In 1970, the 200th birthday of
Friedrich Hölderlin, who was generally accepted as a
"Classical" writer, was observed with myriad traditional activities celebrating him as the "ewig jungen
Genius deutscher Poesie . . . Dichter der Menschheit,"[19] but also with a radio play, Stephan Hermlin's
Scardanelli, which was in pointed disharmony with the
tenor of official encomiums.[20] For while the GDR
celebrated with ceremonies and symposia, linking
Hölderlin to the humanistic tradition of German Classicism, Hermlin insisted instead on portraying the
post-Jacobin Hölderlin, alienated and estranged. The
poet gone mad of Hermlin's play was a bold challenge
to the claims which were being advanced in regard to
his belonging to the humanistic heritage, as was
Hermlin's indiscreet reminder of Hölderlin's treatment
at the hands of the self-centered Hofrat and Minister
who advised him to stick to writing short poems (p.
18). The radio play is a somewhat uneven montage,
constructed of quotations from Hölderlin and his
contemporaries, many of whom Hermlin must explain to
the non-expert in an appended glossary of persons and
places. Yet despite this gesture in the direction of
comprehensibility, the work is clearly directed at
people in the know, the cultural politicians and
literary critics who are confronted with the unanswered questions Hermlin raises in the play. Whether
or not one wishes to read remarks on the situation of
Hölderlin as a parallel to that of the contemporary

writer, the political implications of Hermlin's work are unmistakable: Hölderlin is an inappropriate choice for those who are trying to legitimate their own cultural policies.

Two years later, Gerhard Wolf's Der arme Hölderlin picked up where Hermlin left off: the poet is now confined to an asylum because his freedom, as Sinclair writes to Hölderlin's mother, could be dangerous to the public.[21] Wolf makes a great point of emphasizing that the poet is kept in a straitjacket and gag in order to keep him in line. He also draws attention to the devastation of the poet in a sphere dominated by Geheimrat Goethe and his circle in Weimar, repeating Goethe's uncomprehending reception of the poet, conveyed in a letter to Schiller: "Rät diesem Hölterlein, kleine Gedichte zu machen" (p. 104), going farther than Hermlin in pointing out the insensitive trivialization of the poet's name.

The fact that Wolf decided to append a chronology of Hölderlin's life to aid the reader does little to make the complex and subtle confrontation of Wolf's own reflections with the objective historical material of Hölderlin's life and times accessible to a popular audience. The chapter-by-chapter juxtaposition of Wilhelm Waiblinger's 1831 Aufzeichnungen über Friedrich Hölderlins Leben, Dichtung und Wahnsinn with Wolf's own text unmasks the apparent objectivity of the "historical" account as highly subjective, even unintentionally deceptive. Wolf's narrative tone is pensive and fragmented, marked by the tentativeness and hesitation of his attempt to reconstruct the tragic process of the poet's devastation--something which Christa Wolf again attempts at the end of the decade in Kein Ort. Nirgends.

Günter de Bruyn's Das Leben des Jean Paul Friedrich Richter (1975) is far less recondite, but no less political than the Hölderlin works we discussed thus far. De Bruyn, whose works have often dealt with the compromises artists and academics make in the name of success, or even survival, is at his best when examining this aspect of Jean Paul, too. Jean Paul is certainly not the only author to have pilloried prevailing societal conditions in his works, only to deny everything he stands for in a subservient petition for a "Präbende . . . ein Gehalt ohne Arbeitsleistung, ein Honorar für Ehrenmitgliedschaft, wie es heute, aus ähnlichen Motiven (nämlich um einen bedeutenden Mann zu verpflichten) zum Beispiel noch Kunstakademien zahlen. Man kann das, je nach Standpunkt, Korruption oder Förderung der Künste nennen."22

The chapter on Jean Paul's "Freiheitsbäumchen," a satirical pamphlet against censorship, is a splendid example of the way in which the Jean Paul material is transformed into a paradigm for fundamental questions of the relation of the author to society and authority. De Bruyn quotes directly from Jean Paul's satirical proposal to undermine the practice of censorship: to increase the number of censors until it equals the number of readers and then make the process more efficient by providing each censor with a freshly printed copy of the work instead of an untidy manuscript. But the remainder of his summary of Jean Paul's pamphlet is constructed in such a way that one who is not familiar with it cannot discern whether the thoughts not inside quotation marks are de Bruyn's or Jean Paul's. The technique is so refined that it is worth citing at some length here:

> "Warum glaubt man überhaupt, daß
> verderbliche Bücher so großes Unheil
> stiften können? Ich wünschte, sie
> könnten dies stark und schnell; dann
> brächten gute desto leichter Heil."
> Und wenn in Schriften Regierungsformen
> kritisch untersucht werden, sollen die
> Herrschenden doch froh sein, Wahrheiten
> über sich zu hören. Wem nutzt denn die
> Freiheit, den Herrscher zu loben, wenn
> die, ihn zu tadeln, nicht besteht?
> Am wenigsten ihm selbst, der doch irren
> kann wie jeder und falsch handeln auch.
> "Muß ein Staat erst tot sein, ehe man
> ihn zergliedern darf, und ists nicht
> besser, durch dessen Krankheitberichte
> die Sektionsbericht abzuwenden?"
>
> (p. 273)

De Bruyn's personal involvement becomes even more apparent when he summarizes the conclusion of "Das Freiheitsbäumchen," where Jean Paul retracts his idea of making every reader a censor and offers to become his own censor:

> Er ahnt dabei nicht, wieviel Ernst sich
> in diesem Spaß verbirgt. Denn mit dem,
> was er 'Selber-Zensierung' nennt, be-

> schreibt er, was zur wirklichen Gefahr
> für den Wahrheitsgehalt von Literatur
> werden könnte: den unter Zensurdruck
> und geistiger Manipulation einsetzenden
> Vorgang, der aus einem sozialen Hemmnis
> ein psychisches macht, äußere Grenzen
> vorverlegt ins Innere des Schreibenden
> und damit zwar den Zensurbeamten ent-
> lastet, die Literatur aber von Wirk-
> lichkeit entleert.   (p. 275)

De Bruyn emphasizes that his attempt to bring Jean Paul's life and work closer to our times is based on a very personal fascination with another of those poets who did not enjoy the favor of the poet prince of Weimar. Here, too, Goethe's intolerance of those whose positions differ from his, his readiness to condemn them as "sick" is termed a "fauler Trick" (p. 157) and provokes de Bruyn's sharpest criticism: "Der dichterischen Größe Goethes und Schillers entspricht leider auch die Größe ihrer Unfähigkeit, andersgear-tetes Talent erkennen zu können und gelten zu lassen" (p. 159).

But de Bruyn's work is mellow in comparison with Günter Kunert's bitter depiction of the relationship between Kleist and Goethe, both in the controversial "Pamphlet für K.," published in Sinn und Form in 1975, 23 and in his radio play, Ein anderer K., 24 (Kunert's self-identification with the K. of both ti-tles is analogous to that of Kafka to his K.) The radio play is a scurrilous allegory which superfi-cially deals with the attempts of state authorities to cover up the motives for Kleist's suicide, denounced as an affront to the state. "Das klügste ist jetzt, die Affäre K. gar nicht mehr anzurühren, das würde ihr nur wieder neue Publizität verschaffen . . . rigides Druckverbot" (p. 111). In Ein anderer K., Goethe is made to share, if only indeliberately, some of the guilt for Kleist's suicide through the devastating effects of his shabby production of Der zerbrochene Krug and his reneging on promised contributions to Kleist and Müller's Phoebus.

The play can be fully understood only by reading it against the background of the events surrounding the expatriation of Wolf Biermann in late 1976 and of Kunert's much more explicit comments on Goethe in the 1975 pamphlet, where he had unleashed a harsh polemic against Goethe which included terms such as "archaischer Big Brother," "denunziatorisch," "der 'Olympier' in seiner hintervotzigen Art," "der Vielzuvielschreiber" (p. 1092). Like de Bruyn, Kunert takes as his point of departure Goethe's readiness to dismiss that with which he disagreed as "sick." It is not Goethe's position in itself which provokes Kunert's rage, but its pernicious persistence as a way of dealing with art and artists to the present day: "Wenn nämlich die Ausrottung 'krankhafter' Erscheinungen zur Staatsräson wird" (p. 1094). Kunert proves his point with a quotation from the <u>Lexikon deutschsprachiger Schriftsteller</u> (1972), which describes Kleist's work as an "eigentümliche Vermischung von . . . Gesundheit und Krankhaftigkeit" (p. 1093). Kunert asks:

> Doch wer rehabilitiert Kleist? . . .
> Es ist tatsächlich nötig, denn an sei-
> nem Fall exemplifiziert sich ein
> schein-wissenschaftliches Vorurteil,
> welches, um es verkürzt zu sagen, zur
> Vernichtung von Intellektuellen, von
> Künstlern führte und dessen Fortwirken
> bis heute nicht aufgehört hat und das
> weiterhin die gleichen Argumente für
> seine 'Endlösungen' benutzt wie die
> gegen K. angeführten. (p. 1092)

One might think that Kunert is attempting to substitute "Goethe" for "Romanticism" in the old pre-fascism theory. No doubt he is alluding to it, but only to mock such a simplistic theory and put the blame not on the artists of the past, but on those in the present who would misuse them for their own purpose.

Finally I would like to turn to the much more subtle and diffused allusions to the relationship between Kleist and Goethe in Christa Wolf's most recent novel, <u>Kein Ort. Nirgends</u> (1979).25 Here, too, Kleist is clearly a paradigm for the suffering artist, including the contemporary writer who cannot reconcile the contradictions between his idealistic commitments and what Brecht called the "Mühe der Ebene," which turns out to be the desert of "real existierender Sozialismus." (Wolf uses the word "Wüste.") But however harsh the criticism, Christa Wolf is not suggesting abandoning these commitments. Kleist, who speaks of "das Unglück . . . von Bedingungen abzu-hängen, die mich ersticken, wenn ich sie dulde, und die mich zerreißen, wenn ich mich löse" (pp. 58-59), discovers in making a trip abroad "wie sich sein

13

Vaterland immer besser ausnahm, je weiter er sich von
ihm entfernte" (p. 95). The reader who suspects here
an allusion to the Biermann affair is probably not
mistaken, for an even more pointed reference occurs in
Wolf's recent afterword to her edition of Bettina von
Arnim's Die Günderode, where Bettina's reading of
Jakob Grimm's "Über meine Entlassung" brings to Wolf's
mind the "Göttingen Seven" who on November 18, 1837,
petitioned the king "in einer 'Untertänigsten Vorstellung'" to heed the constitution.[26] Grimm's essay
explains why so few had the courage to sign the petition and how others, who shared the sentiments of the
seven, held back, defending their cowardice with the
argument that by abandoning fundamental rights, they
were actually saving their institution (p. 294). If
one recalls Wolf's own tribulations as a signer of the
Biermann petition of November 17, 1976, the affinities
become obvious.

Whatever the extrinsic factors may be which have
led so many leading contemporary writers back to the
Romantics, their literary portrayals of these figures
are intrinsically a process of self-reflection rather
than representation. By abandoning the position of
the all-knowing narrator for one which does not exclude his or her own subjectivity and adopting a
narrative structure which tends to be complex and
many-layered, the writer simultaneously creates a
situation in which the subjectivity of the reader also
becomes engaged in critical encounter. The process of
communication becomes more important than the literary
product. Only slowly has the critical establishment
begun to realize the implications of this insistence
on subjectivity for its own enterprise and to acknowledge that writers may be justified in their dissatisfaction with criticism as it is currently practiced.
But until the self-examination of the critics, which
has barely begun, begins to yield perceptible results,
some writers--such as Christa Wolf, with her critical
essays on Bettina von Arnim and Karoline von Günder-
rode--are leaping in to fill the breach. The anger
and impatience which emerge in her introductory essay
to an edition of Günderrode's letters articulates
sentiments felt by most of the writers who have turned
to Romanticism:

> Die Literaturgeschichte der Deutschen,
> in den Händen von Studienräten und
> Professoren, orientiert an den retu-
> schierten Kolossalgemälden ihrer

Klassiker, hat sich leichtherzig und
leichtsinnig der als 'unvollendet'
abgestempelten Figuren entledigt, bis
in die jüngste Zeit, bis zu dem fol-
genreichen Verdikt, das Georg Lukács
gegen Kleist, gegen die Romantiker
aussprach. Der Dekadenz, zumindest
der Schwäche, der Lebensuntüchtigkeit
geziehen, sterben sie zum zweitenmal an
der Unfähigkeit der deutschen Öffent-
lichkeit, ein Geschichtsbewußtsein zu
entwickeln, sich dem Grundwiderspruch
der Geschichte zu stellen . . . Ein
zerrissenes, politisch unreifes und
schwer zu bewegendes, doch leicht
verführbares Volk, dem technischen
Fortschritt anhängend statt dem der
Humanität, leistet sich ein Massengrab
des Vergessens für jene früh zugrunde
Gegangenen, jene unerwünschten Zeugen
erwürgter Sehnsüchte und Ängste.[27]

Washington University

Notes

[1] These writers have been discussed in my essay,
"Die Wiederentdeckung der Romantik: Zur Funktion der
Dichterfiguren in der neueren DDR-Literatur," in Roman
in der Literaturgesellschaft, Vol. 11/12 of Amster-
damer Beiträge zur neueren Germanistik, ed. Jos Hooge-
veen and Gerd Labroisse (Amsterdam: Rodopi, 1981),
pp. 217-248.

[2] Johannes R. Becher coined this slogan in his
speech for the 200th birthday of Goethe in 1949, "Der
Befreier," in Von der Größe unsrer Literatur (Leipzig:
Reclam, 1971), p. 339.

[3] Anna Seghers, "Briefwechsel mit Georg Lukács"
(letter of June 28, 1938), in Die Tendenz in der
reinen Kunst, Vol. I of Über Kunstwerk und Wirklichkeit, ed. Sigrid Bock (E. Berlin: Akademie, 1975), p.
174.

[4] Papers in Krauss' honor were published in
Literaturgeschichte als geschichtlicher Auftrag, ed.

15

H. Scheel (E. Berlin: Akademie, 1978.)

[5] Hans Mayer, "Fragen der Romantikforschung," in his Zur deutschen Romantik (Pfullingen: Neske, 1963), p. 305.

[6] Winfried Schroeder, "Fragen der Wertung von Literatur und Kunst," Weimarer Beiträge, 26, No. 2 (1980), 128.

[7] Hans-Dietrich Dahnke et al., Geschichte der deutschen Literatur 1789 bis 1830, Vol. 7 of Geschichte der deutschen Literatur (E. Berlin: Volk und Wissen, 1978).

[8] Hans-Dietrich Dahnke, "Literarische Prozesse in der Periode von 1789 bis 1806," Weimarer Beiträge, 17, No. 11 (1971), 49.

[9] Hans-Dietrich Dahnke, "Zur Stellung und Leistung der Romantik," Weimarer Beiträge, 24, No. 4 (1978), 19.

[10] Claus Träger, "Geschichtlichkeit und Erbe der Romantik," in Arbeiten mit der Romantik heute, ed. H. Hess and P. Liebers (E. Berlin: Akademie der Künste der DDR, 1978), p. 27.

[11] Claus Träger, "Historische Dialektik der Romantik und Romantikforschung," Weimarer Beiträge, 24, No. 4 (1978), 56.

[12] Träger, "Historische Dialektik," p. 49.

[13] Margot Gerisch, "Zur künstlerischen Subjektivität im literarischen Schaffen," Weimarer Beiträge, 21, No. 7 (1975), 173.

[14] Kurt Hager, "Zu Fragen der Kulturpolitik der SED," speech given at the sixth session of the Central Committee of the SED, July 6-7, 1972, as quoted in Erwin Pracht, Einführung in den sozialistischen Realismus (E. Berlin: Dietz, 1975), p. 398.

[15] Horst Redeker, "Zur Systematik von Abbildung, Erkenntnis und Wahrheit in der Kunst," Weimarer Beiträge, 24, No. 1 (1978), 5.

[16] Dieter Schlenstedt, "Literatur der DDR im Spiegel ihrer Literaturgeschichte," Weimarer Beiträge,

26, No. 2 (1980), 36.

[17] Schlenstedt, "Literatur der DDR," pp. 35f.

[18] Cf. Dietrich Sommer, Dietrich Löffler et al., _Funktion und Wirkung. Soziologische Untersuchungen zur Literatur und Kunst_ (E. Berlin: Aufbau, 1978).

[19] Alexander Abusch, "Hölderlins poetischer Traum einer neuen Menschengemeinschaft," _Weimarer Beiträge,_ 16, No. 7 (1970), 26.

[20] Stephan Hermlin, _Scardanelli_ (W. Berlin: Wagenbach, 1970).

[21] Gerhard Wolf, _Der arme Hölderlin_ (E. Berlin: Union, 1972), p. 15.

[22] Günter de Bruyn, _Das Leben des Jean Paul Friedrich Richter_ (Halle/Saale: Mitteldeutscher Verlag, 1975), p. 226.

[23] Günter Kunert, "Pamphlet für K.," _Sinn und Form_, 27, No. 5 (1975), 1091-1097.

[24] Günter Kunert, _Ein anderer K._ (E. Berlin: Aufbau, 1977).

[25] Christa Wolf, _Kein Ort. Nirgends_ (E. Berlin: Aufbau, 1979).

[26] Christa Wolf, "Nun ja! Das nächste Leben geht aber heute an," _Sinn und Form_, 32, No. 2 (1980), 408.

[27] Christa Wolf, "Der Schatten eines Traumes," in _Fortgesetzter Versuch_ (Leipzig: Reclam, 1978), p. 294.

The Rediscovery of Romanticism in the GDR:
A Note on Anna Seghers' Role

Christiane Zehl Romero

Anna Seghers, who in 1980 celebrated her eighti-
eth birthday, is the German Democratic Republic's most
noted prose writer and thus, in terms of the country's
aesthetic self-interpretation, its foremost exponent
of socialist realism. In <u>Literatur der Deutschen Demokratischen Republik</u>--Volume Eleven of the ambitious
GDR project of writing a detailed Marxist history of
German literature--Anna Seghers figures prominently
and exemplarily at each stage of the way towards a
"sozialistische Nationalliteratur."[1]   Therefore, it
should be noted that the editor of this volume, Heinz
Neugebauer, in his 1978 monograph on Anna Seghers,
discusses her collection of stories <u>Sonderbare Begeg-
nungen</u> (1973) under the chapter heading "Möglichkeiten
des Phantastischen."[2] He and other GDR scholars and
critics have viewed these three stories (particularly
"Reisebegegnung") programmatically, that is, in the
light of Seghers' remarks at the Seventh Writers'
Congress in 1973:

> Der Schriftsteller soll seiner Phan-
> tasie nachgehen. Er wird gewiß sein
> Leben lang nicht nur Träume schildern,
> seine Leser nicht nur reizen mit phan-
> tastischen Stoffen. Manche Leser tei-
> len sein Bedürfnis, andere werden neu-
> gierig. Es erhöht ihre Lebensfreude.
> Auch umrankt von märchenhaft seltsamen
> Pflanzen, vergißt der Schriftsteller
> nicht, sich nach dem Kräutlein "Faktum"
> zu bücken, von dem Lichtenberg sprach.[3]

"Eine Reisebegegnung" is the account of an imaginary meeting in a Prague café between E.T.A. Hoffmann,

19

Nikolai Gogol, and Franz Kafka, three not exactly
contemporary poets. It is in fact "eine Literatur-
Geschichte," as Seghers herself called it in an interview, a fictionalized discussion on and plea for
fantasy, dreams, and play with historical time.[4]
Western critics in general misinterpreted the story
and ignored the context in which it was written and
received. "Anna Seghers kritisiert Kafka. Ein son-
derbarer Bestseller aus der DDR," was the title of a
West German critique by Marcel Reich-Ranicki. "Wer
hätte gedacht, daß ausgerechnet der Autor der Nacht-
stücke zum passionierten Sachwalter des Sozialistischen Realismus avancieren würde," he scoffed.[5] What
Reich-Ranicki forgot was that E.T.A. Hoffmann had been
the one Romantic acceptable to Marxist critics, e.g.,
Lukács, all along.

On the other hand, for GDR critics and readers,
including many fellow writers, Sonderbare Begegnungen,
and particularly "Reisebegegnung," signaled something
new: "Ein Beispiel für die kritische Aneignung und
produktive Weiterführung weltliterarischen Erbes."[6]
For the GDR, it showed "daß sich aus tief widersprüch-
lichen Traditionsbereichen Nutzbares für unsere sozialistische Gegenwartskunst gewinnen läßt."[7] Here is
the concluding statement from the review in Neues
Deutschland:

> Der Band Sonderbare Begegnungen wird
> nicht nur den vielen Freunden der
> Segherschen Dichtung willkommen sein.
> Er wird, so läßt sich erwarten, auch
> der gegenwärtigen Kunstdiskussion in
> unserer Republik Anregung geben, denn
> die von ihm aufgeworfenen Fragen der
> Erschließung neuer Möglichkeiten sozia-
> listisch-realistischer Gestaltung und
> der Traditionsbeziehungen sozialisti-
> scher Literatur stehen gerade jetzt im
> Mittelpunkt des Interesses.[8]

The discussion alluded to in Neues Deutschland concerns efforts by critics and writers to broaden the
important concept of "Erbe" beyond the narrowly defined traditions of Humanism-Classicism and Realism,
and, specifically, to reevaluate, albeit cautiously,
the Romantic heritage. These efforts were officially
sanctioned by the Plenum of the Central Committee in
1972, and Anna Seghers is being hailed as a legitimiz-
ing precursor and model to popularize the new develop-

ments. There is no doubt that the critics can justi-
fiably use her name and not only with reference to
Sonderbare Begegnungen or Seghers' remarks at the Seventh Writers' Congress.

Indeed, it is my contention that Anna Seghers'
understanding and practice of her art as a writer have
been informed from the beginning by a relationship to
the Romantic heritage that is much more positive than
the attitude of Marxist critics, which has traditionally been hostile to Romanticism, at least until very
recently.[9] In this respect, GDR critics have in fact
still not gone far enough. It is certainly not correct to say, as a GDR critic maintains in a recent
article, "daß die schon über Jahrzehnte reichende
Beschäftigung mit dem schwierigen romantischen Erbe
erst unter bestimmten gesellschaftlichen Bedingungen
in das eigene Schreiben eingeht."[10] The conditions
alluded to are supposedly those present in the GDR of
the later sixties and the seventies. But Anna Seghers
did not wait that long. On the contrary.

Her very first story, only recently discovered,
was a fantastic tale: "Die Toten auf der Insel Djal.
Eine Sage aus dem Holländischen - Nacherzählt von
Antje Seghers." (It appeared in the Christmas supplement of the Frankfurter Zeitung in 1924.) And she is
reported to have said that it was her ambition from
the beginning to find a way of combining her love of
fairy tales and her concern with contemporary reality:
"Erzählen, was mich heute erregt, und die Farbigkeit
von Märchen. Das hätte ich am liebsten vereint und
wußte nicht wie."[11] Throughout her career she tried
--successfully--to realize this goal by writing both
fantastic tales and factual chronicles, and above all
by giving her sober stories of poverty and struggle
legendary traits. She insisted that this, too, is a
part of reality: "Was ist Wirklichkeit? nicht nur was
man greifen und schmecken kann, auch Phantasie und
Träume gehören zur Wirklichkeit."[12] She attempted to
avoid the dichotomy of which her older contemporary
Döblin spoke in 1936: "Die aktiven, fortschreitenden
Schichten drängen heute nach der Berichtseite, die
nicht aktiven, beruhigten und gesättigten nach der
Märchenseite."[13] Anna Seghers could not and would not
accept this division between the fairy tale for the
reactionary right, and the report on contemporary
reality for the progressive left. During this period
she wrote both a reportage-like story, "Der letzte Weg
des Koloman Wallisch" (1934), and two legends, Die

schönsten Sagen vom Räuber Woynok (1936) and Sage von Artemis (1937).

Anna Seghers, unquestionably socialist and basically realist, has always maintained creative ties to some of the legacies, aspects, and figures of the Romantic period. When the Nazis were in the process of totally discrediting Romanticism and its preoccupation with fairy tale and myth, it was she who reminded her fellow exiles that Romantic writers still had a lot to say to them:

> Die Romantiker selbst, die angeblich
> Lieblinge des Nationalsozialismus sind,
> die wahrhaft Deutschen "aus deutschem
> Traum und Blut." Wenn sie es wirklich
> sind, dann lest sie doch unangefochten.
> Lest die Bettina Brentano, lest die
> Günderrode! Lest, was sie schreiben
> über Erziehung, Glaube, Judenfrage! [14]

Günderrode is again mentioned in connection with Kleist and others of their generation in Anna Seghers' contribution to the famous Expressionism/Realism debate with Georg Lukács in 1938/39. [15] This generation, she argues, lived in and reflected a period of transition, a "Krisenzeit," which had much more in common with her own time than the Classicism represented by the Olympian Goethe. Thus the methods and failures of Kleist and Günderrode's generation are more instructive than Goethe's successes. While Anna Seghers, in her two letters to Lukács, brings forth many arguments, names, and periods to define and to defend her modernist views against Lukács' orthodox concept of Realism, it seems that her love and understanding of some aspects of Romanticism played a significant role. Throughout her career as a writer and as a spokesman for writing, Anna Seghers managed to maintain some independence and resilience vis-à-vis cultural dogmatism. Although she joined the Communist Party in 1928 and has been a faithful member ever since, following and defending many of its cultural demands, she has nonetheless filtered them through a mind and an aesthetic sensibility which from the beginning had been open to the legacy of Romanticism, its emphasis on fantasy and intuition, its love of myth, its profound and, for the individual, often disastrous sensitivity to epochal changes.

In the seventies and now in the eighties, younger

writers have seized the opportunity and widened the
aperture of the door set ajar by Seghers in her essays
and stories. The Romantics Anna Seghers mentioned
most often--Heinrich von Kleist, Karoline von Günderrode, E.T.A. Hoffmann, Bettina von Brentano, and Arnim
--are all encountered in recent GDR writing: Kleist
and Günderrode in Christa Wolf's Kein Ort. Nirgends
(1979), Günderrode and Bettina von Brentano in essays
by Wolf,[16] Bettina in poems by Sarah Kirsch, E.T.A.
Hoffmann in Franz Fühmann's collection of essays Frl.
Veronika Paulmann aus der Pirnaer Vorstadt oder etwas
über das Schauerliche bei E.T.A. Hoffmann (1980).
Christa Wolf, younger friend and admirer of Anna
Seghers, writes in her 1979 essay on Günderrode:

> Ein Zufall kann es nicht sein, daß wir
> begonnen haben, den Abgeschriebenen
> nachzufragen, das Urteil, das über sie
> verhängt wurde, anzufechten, es zu
> bestreiten und aufzuheben--fasziniert
> durch Verwandtschaft und Nähe, wenn
> auch der Zeiten und Ereignisse einge-
> denk, die zwischen uns und denen lie-
> gen. [17]

Wolf needs to emphasize the distance in time, for a
little later in the essay she says of the late Romantic period to which she feels such affinity: "'Ein
pigmäisches Zeitalter, ein pigmäisches Geschlecht
spielt jetzt, recht gut nach seiner Art.'" [18] Implicitly at least, she suggests parallels with her own
time and country. Anna Seghers could not have seen
such parallels in the 1930s when antifascism was
indeed a heroic stance and "pigmy" was certainly not
the word to apply to her fellow communists. And she
would not have wanted to imply similarities with the
1970s. What becomes immediately obvious here is the
fact that Seghers' defense of the Romantics only
provided points of departure for younger GDR writers,
that they go far beyond her in the radicalism with
which they pursue the contemporary relevance of Romantic times and figures.

It should also be pointed out that subjectivity,
so central an issue to German Romanticism and so
important to its rediscoverers among GDR writers,
especially Christa Wolf, held no appeal for Anna
Seghers. On the contrary, in her own writing she
looked to a complementary side of Romanticism, its
rediscovery of fairy tale and myth. Well-educated and

bourgeois, Seghers wanted to escape the confines of her background and class and felt that these folk forms could provide her with a style and a structure in which she could speak of the common man to the common man. "Und die Zuschauer lauschten dem Märchen und hörten es raunen: Deine Sache wird hier erzählt," [19] writes Franz Fühmann in his fine ruminations on the subject in 22 Tage oder die Hälfte des Lebens, where he pays Seghers his highest compliment by calling her "eine Mythenerzählerin höchsten Ranges." [20] For Anna Seghers and Fühmann, myths, fairy tales, and fairy-tale elements contain great possibilities for socialist writing, because they are truly popular forms.

"Ich liebe Grimms Märchen. Aus ihrer Sprache lernte ich viel," Seghers has Kafka say in "Reisebegegnung." [21] She is also speaking of herself. At its best, her own unique tone, at once sober and poetic, has more affinity with Grimms' tales than with any of the styles current at the time she began to write. In the course of her long career she also experimented with many types of fantastic, fairy-tale, and legendary stories, and she incorporated many fairy-tale motifs and structures, not to mention figures, into her novels. Just to give one well-known example: Georg Heisler, in Das siebte Kreuz, so ordinary and lucky, can be seen as a typical fairy-tale hero; the story of his flight abounds with fairy-tale motifs, such as his encounter with the witch-like "Schublädchen," whose uncanny presence gives him protection for a short stretch of the way.

However, it is important to note that Anna Seghers did not simply equate the fairy tale and true popular literature. She was critical, by implication at least, of Goethe's "Märchen." In a short essay on Goethe's Unterhaltungen deutscher Ausgewanderten, which contains the famous "Märchen," she remarks in an aside: "Denn längst hat ein Märchen, wenn es in Europa zustandekommt, den engen Zusammenhang mit dem Sein und dem Leben der Menschen abgestreift, es wächst nicht mehr aus dem Alltag wie in Tausendundeine Nacht, als jeder Dämon noch im gewöhnlichen Leben verwurzelt war." [22] She is distinguishing between the popular form and the escapist, intellectualized fairy tale; she sides with the first, which she finds had faded from Europe by the time of Goethe's "Märchen" in 1795. Where she puts the early Romantics, who were just beginning to enter the literary scene at this point, she does not say, at least not directly.

Anna Seghers did, however, write two stories which take up early German Romanticism's central symbol, "die blaue Blume" from Heinrich von Ofterdingen, Novalis' great Romantic novel. Actually she only uses the color blue and each time associates it with something else, something less poetic taken from the everyday world. In "Crisanta" (1950), neither the reader nor the heroine knows at first what the association is.

> Sie war einmal in ihrer frühsten Jugend
> an einem Ort gewesen, der keinem an-
> deren auf Erden glich. Dort war's ihr
> so wohl zumute gewesen, wie nie mehr
> später. Als sei sie allein für sich
> von einem eigenen Himmel behütet. Wenn
> sie sich fragte, was es gewesen war,
> dann fiel ihr immer nur ein: Blau. Ein
> sanftes und starkes Blau, das es später
> nirgendwo gab. Die ganze Welt war vor-
> beigerauscht, doch nicht durch das Blau
> gedrungen. [23]

Crisanta's life is not a conscious search for that blue because she is too poor, too simple, too abused. Yet her memory of it never completely fades. She persists through desertion, abortion, prostitution, to give birth to a child and to take care of it. Then, at the end of the story, she discovers where the sustaining memory comes from. In the marketplace where Crisanta sells fruit, a sudden gust of wind makes her put her head into her reboso where she carries her baby. "Auf einmal fiel ihr der Ort wieder ein, an dem sie als Kind gewesen war. Das unbegreiflich tiefe und dunkle Blau. Das war der Rebozo, das Umschlagtuch der Frau Gonzales gewesen, und was dahinter strömte, ihr Volk" (p. 88). As a child, the orphan Crisanta had been taken in by Mrs. Gonzales, a poor Mexican like herself, who had held her then as she does her own child now. The color blue here symbolizes that Sehnsucht, which for Seghers is the most universal of human longings, that the evil spell of poverty and isolation cast over man be broken.

In the other story, "Das wirkliche Blau" (1967), the association of blue with something concrete is even closer. [24] Benito, again a Mexican, is a potter. All his life he has been using one particular kind of blue to decorate his pots. However, due to the war, import restrictions, and business machinations, he can no longer buy his blue. Half-hearted attempts to use another color fail. Benito tells his wife: "Ich habe mir etwas aufdrängen lassen. . . . Aus Angst vor Not. Anstatt immer weiter zu suchen, zu suchen nach dem Blau, an dem mein Herz hängt, das Blau, das mir allein und wahrhaftig zusteht. Weil ich mich nicht daran hielt, ist mir so was Schlechtes geschehn" (p. 110). After hearing from a wise aunt "mit uralten grüngelben Sternenaugen" of a possible domestic source for his blue, Benito sets out upon a difficult journey to find it and eventually succeeds. Again, as in "Crisanta," the color blue symbolizes that longing for and promise of happiness which motivate all human endeavor. The search and the story as a whole abound with parallels and contrasts to Novalis' Heinrich von Ofterdingen.[25] But, building on the color's complex ties to Novalis, Anna Seghers gives it a richer, more varied meaning. In a poetic dialogue with Novalis, she presents her own vision of the connection between "Poesie" and "Leben," between art and life, and shifts the emphasis towards "real" real life, real blue, a close connection with the everyday. Benito, the artist in the story, is an artisan, a potter. His work, through his special color and the design he creates with it, gives joy to others; at the same time, it is something people use to cook and eat with.

Clearly, Anna Seghers transforms Novalis' central motif into a more popular, less idealized, realm--the "real" world, so to speak. But she does not, as some GDR critics have claimed, assimilate it in order to overcome Romanticism. On the contrary, she was very sensitive to the suggestive power and poetic truth of the motif and tried to utilize it creatively. For her, that important "real world" would never do without a poetic dimension, "die Farbigkeit von Märchen," die "gar mühelos in die Herzen eindringt."[26] This to her was the function of art, and for realism to be art, it could never be narrowly defined. "Zum Realismus gehören auch Träume, auch Märchen, auch Phantasien," she never tired of insisting.[27] I do not believe it an overstatement to say that Anna Seghers has always felt that the Romantic heritage could only be rejected totally at the price of art itself.

In the seventies, GDR critics and writers began not only to see her blue light, but to speed through it. Besides the critical appraisals of Seghers' work

in that light, and reevaluations of the Romantics by
critics and, more importantly, by writers, there is,
above all, a blossoming of fantastic writing in the
widest sense, such as Irmtraud Morgner's Leben und
Abenteuer der Trobadora Beatriz nach Zeugnissen ihrer
Spielfrau Laura (1974), Klaus Möckel's "Das Märchen
vom Träumen" (in Die Gläserne Stadt, 1980), Erich
Köhler's Der Krott oder Das Ding unterm Hut (1980),
and the first almanac of fantastic literature Lichtjahr 1 (1980), to name but a few.

Tufts University

Notes

[1] Horst Haase et al., eds., Literatur der Deutschen Demokratischen Republik, Vol. XI of Geschichte
der deutschen Literatur (E. Berlin: Volk und Wissen,
1976).

[2] Heinz Neugebauer, Anna Seghers (E. Berlin: Volk
und Wissen, 1978), pp. 199-207.

[3] Anna Seghers, Aufsätze, Ansprachen, Essays
1954-1979, Vol. XIV of Gesammelte Werke in Einzelausgaben (E. Berlin and Weimar: Aufbau, 1980), p. 366.

[4] Interview with Werner Neubert in: Anna Seghers, Aufsätze, Ansprachen, Essays 1954-1979, p. 467.

[5] Marcel Reich-Ranicki, "Anna Seghers kritisiert
Kafka," Die Zeit, 12 October 1973, pp. 4f. Compare
also Fritz J. Raddatz, "Wenn alles banal wird," Frankfurter Allgemeine Zeitung, 27 November 1973.

[6] Friedrich Albrecht, "Neue Erzählungen von Anna
Seghers," Neues Deutschland, 25 July 1973, p. 4.

[7] Walter Kusche, "Die 'blaue Blume' und das
'wirkliche Blau.' Zur Romantik-Rezeption im Spätwerk
von Anna Seghers," Weimarer Beiträge, 20, No. 7
(1974), 58.

[8] Albrecht, "Neue Erzählungen von Anna Seghers."

[9] Cf. Klaus Peter, Romantikforschung seit 1945
(Königstein/Ts.: Athenäum, 1980), especially p. 29.

[10] Kusche, p. 77.

[11] This is reported first by Tamara Motylowa in Russian in Anna Zegers (Moscow: Gos. izd. chudožestvennoj literatury, 1953), p. 144. It is usually quoted in Christa Wolf's German rendition in "Glauben an Irdisches," Lesen und Schreiben (Darmstadt: Luchterhand, 1972), p. 84.

[12] Anna Seghers in an interview with Horst Simon, "Helfen, tiefer ins Leben einzudringen," Neues Deutschland, 22 September 1973.

[13] Cf. Kurt Batt, "Schriftsteller, Poetisches und Wirkliches Blau," in Anna Seghers. Ein Almanach, ed. Kurt Batt (E. Berlin and Weimar: Aufbau, 1975), pp. 299f.

[14] Anna Seghers, "Illegales legal," Aufsätze, Ansprachen, Essays 1927-1953, Vol. XIII of Gesammelte Werke in Einzelausgaben (E. Berlin and Weimar: Aufbau 1980), p. 70.

[15] Seghers, Aufsätze, Ansprachen, Essays 1927-1953, pp. 71-88.

[16] Christa Wolf, "Der Schatten eines Traumes: Karoline von Günderrode - ein Entwurf," introduction to Der Schatten eines Traumes: Gedichte, Prosa, Briefe, Zeugnisse von Zeitgenossen, by Karoline von Günderrode (Darmstadt: Luchterhand, 1979) and "Nun ja! Das nächste Leben geht aber heute an: Ein Brief über die Bettine," afterword to Die Günderode, by Bettina von Arnim (Leipzig: Insel Verlag, 1980).

[17] Wolf, "Der Schatten eines Traumes," p. 6.

[18] Wolf, "Der Schatten eines Traumes," p. 7.

[19] Franz Fühmann, 22 Tage oder Die Hälfte des Lebens (Rostock: Hinstorff, 1973), p. 203.

[20] Fühmann, p. 210.

[21] Anna Seghers, Sonderbare Begegnungen (Darmstadt and Neuwied: Luchterhand, 1973), p. 133.

[22] Seghers, Aufsätze, Ansprachen, Essays 1927--1953, p. 327.

[23] Anna Seghers, "Crisanta," in her Erzählungen, II (Darmstadt: Luchterhand, 1977), p. 72.

[24] Anna Seghers, "Das wirkliche Blau," in her Geschichten aus Mexiko (E. Berlin and Weimar: Aufbau, 1970), p. 110.

[25] Cf. Kusche, pp. 68-77.

[26] Seghers, "Motto der 'Schönsten Sagen vom Räuber Woynok,'" in Über Kunstwerk und Wirklichkeit, ed. S. Bock (E. Berlin: Akademie 1971), II, 16.

[27] Anna Seghers, Willkommen Zukunft (Munich: Damnitz Verlag, 1975), p. 41.

Christa Wolf and the Women Romantics

Sara Lennox

Marxism may derive its greatest appeal from its optimism, its confidence that it has history on its side, that a logic immanent in history ultimately assures the triumph of human reason. But in the past ten years at least (and perhaps since the 1920s) these assumptions have been increasingly called into question. The proletariat has obstinately refused to emerge as the subject-object of history to liberate humanity from its bondage to capitalism. In the West, political activism--what little of it remains--has shifted for the most part from the working class to marginal groups--women, ecologists, people of color, gay rights activists--who raise questions about the direction and dimension of social change which Marxism is ill-equipped to address and which sometimes pose challenges to Marxism's very central tenets--for instance, that the coming of socialism will clear the way for the solution of all human problems, including those of sexual hierarchy and personal life, and that the road to human happiness passes through the increasing human domination and control of nature. In Eastern Europe, as Rudolf Bahro has argued in Die Alternative, socialism, which promised to bring about human self-realization, has instead sunk below the nineteenth-century level of human achievement, and, as events in Poland most clearly demonstrate, those whom "socialism as it actually exists" rules over must struggle to achieve the most fundamental bourgeois civil rights: freedom of speech, of movement, of independent trade unions. Thus profound soul-searching has taken place among those who, clinging to the vision of human liberation which Marxism represented, still long to consider themselves Marxists, as they attempt to understand where Marxism went wrong and if it might be possible to mend Marxism's ways, its theory, and its practice. One form this has taken, of course, is a serious consideration by Marxists of other contemporary theories which impinge on and force a reassessment of Marxism: psychoanalysis, poststructuralism (with its roots in another tradition of German thought: Nietzsche, Freud, Heidegger), feminism. But another form which Marxist self-reflection has increasingly begun to take is a return to the roots of Marxism in the thought of the late eighteenth and early nineteenth centuries, when, for a brief moment, political revolution seemed about to clear away the obstacles to human happiness, and, as Wordsworth told us, "bliss was it in that dawn to be alive, but to be young was very heaven." [1]

Until the past decade, the reception of Romanticism within German Marxist thought was an extraordinarily hostile one, and for reasons which are not altogether unjustified. After a short period of interest in the revolutionary experiments of France, German thinkers and poets of the early nineteenth century in general closed ranks during the wars of liberation to assert the merits of Germanic values: see Hegel's defense of the Prussian state as the embodiment of the world spirit or the Heidelberg Romantics' anti-Semitic German-Christian Eating Society. After 1815 most German Romantics made their peace with the regimes of Metternich's Europe and, so it is argued, became ardent reactionaries themselves. [2] Even more importantly for the Marxist reception of Romanticism, at least since Lukács' Zerstörung der Vernunft (1954), orthodox Marxists have traced the origins of Nazi irrationalism to Romanticism, finding there many of the sources of the Nazi Blut-und-Boden ideology. As Klaus Peter has recently shown, however, a reconsideration of the Marxist condemnation of Romantic thought has taken place since the early seventies, particularly in the German Democratic Republic. There this new scholarly examination of Romanticism is very explicitly understood as a polemical opposition to an economistic and deterministic conception of Marxism which overemphasized technological progress and material well-being to the detriment of the human subject's self-realization and fulfillment, as Hans-Dietrich Dahnke argued at a conference in Frankfurt an der Oder in 1977:

> Die Polemik richtet sich gegen Erschei-
> nungen einer Disproportion zwischen
> Ökonomisch-Materiellem und Geistig-

Kulturellem, zwischen Sein und Bewußtsein, Äußerem und Innerem des Menschen,
gegen allzu einfache und durch die
Realität dann widerlegte Vorstellungen
von Modellierung und Lenkung des konkreten Menschen, gegen das Übergewicht
einer wissenschaftlich-theoretischen
Erklärung und Bestimmung von Mensch und
Welt, die die Lücken ihrer Kenntnis und
Durchdringung der Wirklichkeit nur allzu leicht durch normative Postulate zu
füllen geneigt ist.[3]

Marx, after all, asserted in his "Zur Kritik der
Hegelschen Rechtsphilosophie" that, during the period
of which we are speaking, Germans made their revolution in their heads, in their philosophy: "In politics, the Germans have thought what other nations have
done."

     Thus reexamination of Romanticism might reveal
human possibilities and modes of thought which, if
there has been a progressive degeneration of critical
thinking under capitalism, are today barely accessible, almost forgotten. It could also show how the
Romantics suffered under the weight of their social
conditions, protested against them, and longed for
some different way to live. Or, as Wolfgang Heise has
put it, "in der Kunst gewordenen Sehnsucht, in der
Kritik an dem, was Menschen niederzieht, quält, ein-
engt, verwundet, liegt die Größe der Romantik in
Deutschland, ihre Grenze, Banalität und Gefahr."[4]
Finally, GDR citizens, who, after a brief moment of
revolutionary hope that all could be completely different, saw the reestablishment of domination, may
return to Romanticism for assistance in understanding
their own self-alienation and the possibility of
enduring or even overcoming it.

     Christa Wolf's interest in Romanticism evidently
derives in part from this complex of concerns. In her
works Wolf has consistently pleaded for a conception
of socialism which understands its goal as human self-
realization, "dieses Zu-sich-selber-Kommen des Menschen," as the motto to Nachdenken über Christa T. had
it. Almost as consistently she has been attacked in
the East for her subjectivism, her alleged dreamy
inwardness which fails to give proper consideration to
the conditions of objective reality.[5] At least since
Christa T., her works can also generally be understood

as protests against the petrifaction of GDR society--
that very objective reality--which prevents the elaboration of human subjectivity, and as attempts to
articulate counter-models of human thought, feeling,
and action. Since 1973 in "Selbstversuch," she has
explicitly looked to women's experience for alternatives to the prevailing practice, and in her introduction to Maxie Wander's Guten Morgen, du Schöne she
posits "Berührung," in all its senses, as an epistemological model counterposed to the positivism which,
she would assert, the GDR also advocates. In her
quest for alternatives to the dominant order, Wolf has
been strongly influenced by the thought of Ernst
Bloch, under whom she studied at Leipzig, and more
particularly by his conception of "concrete utopia" as
those real moments of human experience when human
beings glimpse and articulate the possibility of some
other, better, and happier way to live.6 Since concrete utopias demonstrate that these sorts of transformations are not abstract pipe dreams but represent
real human potentialities, social theorists and activ-
ists can elaborate upon the hints and suggestions
which inhere in the concrete utopias to formulate more
precisely hopes for social change and the directions
in which it might proceed. Christa Wolf's recent
interest in the women Romantics can be located in the
conjuncture of an elaboration of women's experience,
the revived GDR interest in Romanticism, and the
search for concrete utopias.

     Since 1979 Wolf has published three explorations
of the lives and writing of the women Romantics, a
fictive account of an encounter between Kleist and
Karoline von Günderrode in 1804, an introduction to a
collection of Günderrode's writings, and an afterword
to a new GDR edition of Bettine von Arnim's epistolary
novel, Die Günderode. All three may be read as elabo-
rations on the ambiguity of the title to her Kleist-
Günderrode narrative, Kein Ort. Nirgends. In one of
its meanings, her title points to the utopian dimensions of these figures' experiences: "no place,
nowhere" is of course the literal meaning of the Greek
"ou" + "topos." For a small group of young people in
their twenties at the turn of the nineteenth century,
history, for a brief moment, seemed to offer unprecedented hopes for self-elaboration, and women, in part
because of the freedom their exclusion from the public
arena afforded them, became the particular bearers of
these new radical alternatives. "Frauen," Wolf
writes, "in diesen wenigen Jahren, einer Lücke zwi-

34

schen zwei Zeitaltern, plötzlich aus alten Schablonen
herausgefallen--auch aus den Schablonen, ihr Geschlecht betreffend--, schließen eine Art Bündnis,
[die Welt] gesund zu machen."7 Wolf comments upon the
remarkable similarity between Günderrode's developing
ideas and the "Systementwurf" produced a generation
earlier by Hegel, Schelling, and Hölderlin, students
together at the Tübinger Stift in the early 1790s.
Common to both is the dream of a reconciliation of
reason and sensuality, of philosophy and fantasy
within a harmonious community of equals in which
objective barriers to self-realization have been
abolished:

> Sie haben die Vision von einer "Mytho-
> logie der Vernunft", die "das Volk
> vernünftig" und "die Philosophen sinn-
> lich" machen soll, damit endlich "Auf-
> geklärte und Unaufgeklärte sich die
> Hand reichen" müssen und ein frommer
> Wunsch sich erfüllen kann: "Dann
> herrscht ewige Einheit unter uns.
> Nimmer der verachtende Blick, nimmer
> das blinde Zittern des Volks vor seinen
> Weisen und Priestern. Dann erst erwar-
> tet uns gleiche Ausbildung aller
> Kräfte, des Einzelnen sowohl als aller
> Individuen. Keine Kraft wird mehr
> unterdrückt werden, dann herrscht
> allgemeine Freiheit und Gleichheit der
> Geister."
>
> (ST, p. 20)

As a poet Günderrode possessed such a capacity to
reconcile apparent opposites 'and, in correspondence
with her friend Bettine Brentano, she began to explore
further the dimensions of human experience--sensu-
ality, eroticism, the unconscious--which rationalism
had wished to deny.

> Bettine nimmt die Gedanken der Freundin
> gierig auf, befeuert von diesem Rück-
> griff auf Kräfte, die dem "Mutterschoß"
> entspringen und nicht, wie Pallas
> Athene, dem Vaterkopf, nämlich dem
> Haupte des Zeus--eine Alternative zu
> den Quellen der Klassik, eine Hinwen-
> dung zu archaischen, teilweise matriar-
> chalischen Mustern. Der Mythos wird
> neu gelesen, und zu dem bisher allein-

> herrschenden Mythos der Griechen kommen
> die Vorgeschichte und die Lehren In-
> diens, Asiens, des Orients. Der Euro-
> zentrismus ist durchbrochen, mit ihm
> die Alleinherrschaft des Bewußtseins:
> Unbewußte Kräfte, die in Trieben,
> Wünschen, Träumen Ausdruck suchen,
> werden in diesen Briefen wahrgenommen,
> beschrieben, anerkannt. So weitet sich
> unendlich der Erlebniskreis und der
> Kreis dessen, was als Realität erfahren
> wird. (ST, p. 39)

Drawing on female experiences which remained distinct
from those of contemporary men, these women's passionate explorations of visions of human wholeness
may, Wolf suggests, be understood as unconscious
attempts to introduce female elements into a patri-
archally structured culture. In their adventure-
someness and range the women Romantics often surpass
the imaginations of their male associates.

Nor was, as the Romantics understood, their
struggle for new forms of human experience merely an
individual or an asocial one. In their voluminous
correspondence, collectively edited journals, and
salons and social groups--Romantic "Geselligkeit," as
Gisela Dischner terms it [8] --many Romantics expressed
their recognition that the human subject develops
through productive dialogue and interchange with
others. For women (though not only for them--one
thinks immediately of Novalis and Hölderlin), the
longing for self-creation through interaction with
others often took the form of romantic love. For
women like Günderrode and Bettine, love is a utopian
image of human connection, a kind of Hegelian reunion
with nature which passes through history, an encounter
which permits the lovers to recognize, explore, and
elaborate their deepest sensual, emotional, and intellectual needs. Within this utopian model, women would
no longer be compelled to choose between love and
work, the private and the public, for these would be
reconciled in the harmony of the lovers' relationship
with each other and with society. On the one hand,
this conception of love advances a vision of domi-
nance-free love between men and women which reality
has not fulfilled to this day: "Eine kühne Idee,
zwischen Mann und Frau könnten andre Beziehungen
walten als die von Herrschaft, Unterordnung, Eifer-
sucht, Besitz: gleichberechtigte, freundschaftliche,

hilfreiche. Schwester sein, Freund (die männliche
Form!)--unerhörte Angebote" (ST, p. 25). But more
surprisingly, Wolf also argues that this model of love
found its expression, and also a kind of fulfillment,
in love relationships between women which, though they
do not exclude relationships with men, offer women
possibilities for more unconstrained self-discovery
than is available with men. The aesthetic and human
model of such a relationship between two women who
loved each other physically and in every other way is,
Wolf maintains, preserved for us in the exchange of
letters between Bettine and Günderrode which Bettine,
true to her origins, published in 1834, at a time when
such hopes seemed almost extinguished:

> Liebe, Sehnsucht als Mittel der Er-
> kenntnis brauchen; denkend, erkennend
> nicht von sich selber absehn müssen;
> einander "die Schläfe brennen" machen
> von "heißem Eifer in die Zukunft".
> Einander Namen geben, Rollen spielen,
> die durch die Alltagswirklichkeit nicht
> gedeckt sind und sie doch aus sich
> heraustreten, über sich hinausgehn
> lassen. Mit der Sprache spielen, neue
> Wörter finden und einander zurufen:
> "Geistesauge", "Tagsnatur", "Kunstge-
> flecht", "Empfindnerven der Wirklich-
> keit". . . . Begreifen: Dieses Buch
> schildert ein Experiment, auf das zwei
> Frauen sich eingelassen haben, sich
> gegenseitig haltend, bestärkend, von-
> einander lernend.[9]

So much the worse, says Wolf, if this is a utopia the
present no longer dreams of realizing: "'Utopisch',
gewiß.   Es wurde nicht weitergeführt.   Aber wieso
haben wir das Wort 'Utopie' zum Schimpfwort verkommen
lassen?" (LS, p. 313).

Yet, given this "concrete utopia," it is nonetheless of central importance to recall the second,
and probably primary, meaning of the title of Wolf's
narrative Kein Ort. Nirgends.   For, Wolf argues,
exactly at the moment when such unprecedented possibilities of self-elaboration opened to human beings,
the historical development of bourgeois society, particularly in Germany, assured that their fulfillment
would be foreclosed.   In an interior monologue in
Wolf's narrative, from which she borrows her title,

Kleist recognizes that no place exists in this world
where these new needs can be met:

> Kleist zählt sich die Staaten auf, die
> er kennt, es ist ihm ein Zwang gewor-
> den. Daß ihre Verhältnisse seinen
> Bedürfnissen strikt entgegenstehen, hat
> er erfahren. Mit gutem Willen, angst-
> vollem Zutraun hat er sie geprüft,
> widerstrebend verworfen. Die Erleich-
> terung, als er die Hoffnung auf eine
> irdische Existenz, die ihm entsprechen
> würde, aufgab.
> Unlebbares Leben. Kein Ort, nirgends.[10]

The reality which counterposed itself to the fantastic
visions of this small group of young people--"Avant-
garde ohne Hinterland" (ST, p. 8), Wolf calls them--
was ruled over by the spirit of bourgeois commer-
cialism, coupled with a particularly German brand of
servility and authoritarianism:

> Die Borniertheit einer unentwickelten
> Klasse ohne Selbstgefühl, dafür voll
> Untertanenseligkeit, die sich vom
> bürgerlichen Katechismus nichts zu
> eigen gemacht hat als das Gebot: Be-
> reichert euch! und den hemmungslosen
> Gewinntrieb in Einklang zu bringen
> sucht mit den lutherisch-kalvinisti-
> schen Tugenden Fleiß, Sparsamkeit,
> Disziplin; dürftiger Lebensinhalt, der
> unempfindlich macht gegen die Forderun-
> gen der eignen Natur, aber empfindlich
> gegen jene, die sich selbst nicht kne-
> beln wollen oder können. (ST, p. 8)

While other European nations could put their Romantics
to political use, the German misère had no room for
these young people. Confronting irreconcilable contradictions, they were forced into grimaces, extrava-
gances, madness, and self-destruction. "Der Riß der
Zeit geht durch sie" (ST, p. 63), Wolf writes of
Günderrode; in her own words, Günderrode could at best
expect the "Schatten eines Traumes." Only, perhaps,
in art was there the possibility of a reconciliation
not attainable in life, as Günderrode wrote: "Gedichte sind Balsam auf Unstillbares im Leben" (KON,
pp. 93-94). Yet Romantic irony indicates how unten-
able even aesthetic solutions remained; or, as Günder-

rode tells Kleist in Wolf's narrative: "Für Unlös-
bares gibt es keine Form" (KON, p. 164).

    Moreover, Wolf argues, the women of the Romantic
period faced a still more dreadful fate, for men were
offered at least a minimal possibility of self-actu-
alization through some action in the world--a possibility closed to women--while at the same time the
adaptations required of men to the demands of bourgeois life made them increasingly less worthy partners
for these imaginative and creative women. Günderrode
tells Kleist: "Die Männer, die für uns in Frage
kämen, [sind] selbst in auswegloser Verstrickung. Ihr
werdet durch den Gang der Geschäfte, die euch oblie-
gen, in Stücke zerteilt, die kaum miteinander zusam-
menhängen. Wir sind auf den ganzen Menschen aus und
können ihn nicht finden" (KON, p. 137). What is left
for women? They become unrealistic, Wolf explains,
for what is realistic is determined by men: they
become childish, or vengeful furies, or beautiful
souls, or dutiful housewives. The single expression
for their longings becomes romantic love, which can
simultaneously become the vehicle for their own de-
struction. Such was the case for Günderrode, who
committed suicide because she could not be united with
the married man she loved. Precisely this so seemingly trivial cause of death, Wolf argues, reveals the
desperation of these young people:

        Die Utopie ist vollständig aufgezehrt,
        der Glaube verloren, jeglicher Rückhalt
        geschwunden. Sie kommen sich einsam
        vor in der Geschichte. Die Hoffnung,
        andre--ihr Volk!--könnten sich auf sie
        beziehn, ist verbraucht. . . . Weniges,
        so scheint es, genügt, sie in den
        Abgrund zu ziehn, an dessen Rand sie
        sehenden Auges gehn. Und es fragt sich
        noch, ob es weniges ist, was sie um-
        bringt. Ob nicht das, was sie schließ-
        lich tötet--eine unglückliche Liebe,
        mein Gott!--für sie nur das Zeichen
        ist, das ihr Schicksal, besiegelt
        ohnehin, ihnen gibt: verlassen, ver-
        kannt, verraten zu sein. Und ob sie
        diese Zeichen so gänzlich falsch ge-
        deutet haben. (ST, pp. 10-11)

    The contemporary relevance of these Romantics and
their fate for the GDR--and perhaps for the rest of

us—is evident: Wolf, not without bitterness, under-
lines the parallels between their time and our own.
"Ein Zufall kann es nicht sein, daß wir begonnen
haben, den Abgeschriebenen nachzufragen, das Urteil,
das über sie verhängt wurde, anzufechten, es zu be-
streiten und aufzuheben—fasziniert durch Verwandt-
schaft und Nähe, wenn auch der Zeiten und Ereignisse
eingedenk, die zwischen uns und denen liegen . . ."
(ST, p. 6). We find, she tells us, lines which speak
to us in the pages of their work: "'Ein pigmäisches
Zeitalter, ein pigmäisches Geschlecht spielt jetzt,
recht gut nach seiner Art'" (ST, p. 7). The fate of
Wolf's own Christa T. is similar enough to that of the
Romantics: initially embracing socialism as "der Weg
zu uns selber,"[11] Christa T., this remarkable and at
the same time very ordinary young woman, finds that
the GDR can provide no place after all for her to
explore her own uniqueness in creative service to her
fellows. The phrase which traces its way through
Wolf's Günderrode essay has its origin in Christa T.:
"man braucht sie nicht." Christa T., too, retreats,
faute de mieux, onto the only pathways open for female
fulfillment: home, a husband, children. "Sie nimmt
den Vorteil wahr, eine Frau zu sein" (CT, p. 155). Of
course this suffices no better, and, sapped of life,
she dies of leukemia. Like the women Romantics,
Christa T. makes claims on reality which reality
refuses to meet, dismissing her subjective needs as
"uferlose, gefährliche Phantasien" (CT, p. 197). No
one, her friend Kostja tells her, goes by Romantic
names like Bettine and Annette any more; she is out-
of-date.

Yet in neither her 1968 novel nor in her essays
about the women Romantics does Wolf conclude on a note
of despair. Neither the quest for Christa T. nor for
Günderrode and Bettine is a historicist one, to find
them, in Ranke's words, "wie sie eigentlich gewesen."
This is a dialectical use of history instead: to
learn from the victories and defeats of the past their
meaning for us in order to shape the future more
carefully. The narrator of Christa T. goes in search
of her dead friend, not for her sake, but for us who
outlive her: "Halten wir also fest, es ist unseret-
wegen, denn es scheint, wir brauchen sie" (CT, p. 9).
Moreover, in the person of Bettine Brentano von Arnim,
"die Verkörperung einer Utopie" (ST, p. 41), as Wolf
terms her, lies a more concrete example and hope for
the present. Confronted with the same historical
dilemmas as Günderrode, Bettine chose a route not too

unlike Christa T.'s: she married Achim von Arnim and, for twenty years in the depths of the European restoration after the Congress of Vienna, waited, bearing seven children, a devoted wife and mother. Then, after Arnim's death in 1831, Bettine, forty-seven years old, began to write, and her second book, an edited version of the letters exchanged between her and Günderrode, was dedicated to the rebellious students who might now realize the hopes of the past to which she had remained true--"wie sie nicht aufhören konnte," Wolf writes, "Vorschläge zu machen für eine andere, nicht tötende Art, auf der Welt zu sein" (LS, p. 318).

We know, of course, what happened to the German revolution of 1848, which Bettine's writing of this period helped to prepare. Wolf argues that Bettine, like many visionaries, was permitted to be radical at the cost of not being taken seriously: "Nicht ohne geheime Genugtuung sieht man ihr zu, wie sie den Vorteil zu nutzen weiß, der in dem Nachteil, Frau zu sein, in Männergesellschaften zeitweilig verborgen ist--falls die Betreffende und Betroffene es aushält, für leicht verrückt zu gelten" (LS, p. 294). We also know that Bettine was, in class, connection, and temperament, an extraordinarily privileged woman to whom we can scarcely compare ourselves; few of us now in the East or West can afford to be so indomitable. Nor can history be relied upon to make concessions to our human needs, as Wolf, with deep pessimism, reminds us in Kein Ort. Nirgends:

> Man wird uns für rasend halten. Unser
> unausrottbarer Glaube, der Mensch sei
> bestimmt, sich zu vervollkommen, der
> dem Geist aller Zeiten strikt zuwider-
> läuft. Die Welt tut, was ihr am leich-
> testen fällt: Sie schweigt. (KON, pp.
> 173-74)

Still the effort Wolf has made to revive the thought of those long gone for our consideration is evidence that she herself has not succumbed totally to historical pessimism, or at least that it is, in Gramsci's words, a "pessimism of the spirit, optimism of the will." For if human beings can formulate such "phantastische Einfälle" (ST, p. 25), does not the possibility also exist that they can be realized? In Kein Ort. Nirgends Kleist demands to know: "Wozu Ideen in die Welt gesetzt würden, wenn nicht zum Zwecke ihrer

41

Verwirklichung" (p. 68). In asserting the claims of the Romantics against the dismal reality of the present, there lies a hope of redeeming the past and transforming the future. Especially now, as Wolf reminds us in Kein Ort. Nirgends, despair is a very costly sentiment: "Wenn wir zu hoffen aufhören, kommt, was wir befürchten, bestimmt" (p. 171).

University of Massachusetts, Amherst

Notes

[1] Wordsworth, "The Prelude," Book XI.

[2] See, for example, Marx's passionate attack on Savigny in his "Critique of Hegel's Philosophy" in Karl Marx, Early Writings, ed. and trans. T. B. Bottomore (New York: McGraw Hill, 1964), p. 45.

[3] Hans-Dietrich Dahnke, "Zur Stellung und Leistung der deutschen romantischen Literatur: Ergebnisse und Probleme ihrer Erforschung," Weimarer Beiträge, 24, No. 4 (1978), 5, cited in Klaus Peter, "Einleitung," Romantikforschung seit 1945 (Königstein/Ts.: Verlagsgruppe Athenäum, Hain, Scriptor, Hanstein, 1980), p. 29.

[4] Wolfgang Heise, "Weltanschauliche Aspekte der Frühromantik," Weimarer Beiträge, 24, No. 4 (1978), 44.

[5] See, for instance, Annemarie Auer, "Gegenerinnerung," Sinn und Form, 29, No. 4 (July/August 1977), 847-878.

[6] For further discussion of Wolf's indebtedness to Bloch, see Andreas Huyssen, "Auf den Spuren Ernst Blochs: Nachdenken über Christa Wolf," Basis 5, ed. Reinhold Grimm and Jost Hermand (Frankfurt/M.: Suhrkamp, 1975), pp. 100-116.

[7] Christa Wolf, "Der Schatten eines Traumes: Karoline von Günderrode - ein Entwurf," introd. to Der Schatten eines Traumes: Gedichte, Prosa, Briefe, Zeugnisse von Zeitgenossen, by Karoline von Günderrode (Darmstadt: Luchterhand, 1979), p. 35. Wolf's introduction is hereafter cited in the text as ST.

42

[8] Gisela Dischner, _Bettina von Arnim: Eine weibliche Sozialbibliographie aus dem neunzehnten Jahrhundert_ (W. Berlin: Wagenbach, 1977), pp. 25-33.

[9] Christa Wolf, "Nun ja! Das nächste Leben geht aber heute an: Ein Brief über die Bettine," afterword to _Die Günderode,_ by Bettina von Arnim (Leipzig: Insel, 1980). Available in the West in Christa Wolf, _Lesen und Schreiben. Neue Sammlung_ (Darmstadt: Luchterhand, 1980), pp. 284-318. This citation is on p. 313 of _Lesen und Schreiben._ Hereafter cited in the text as LS.

[10] Christa Wolf, _Kein Ort. Nirgends_ (E. Berlin/ Weimar: Aufbau, 1979), p. 157. Hereafter cited in the text as KON.

[11] Christa Wolf, _Nachdenken über Christa T._ (Darmstadt: Luchterhand, 1968), p. 41. Hereafter cited in the text as CT.

The Plea for Artistic Freedom in Christa Wolf's
"Lesen und Schreiben" and Nachdenken über Christa T.:
Essay and Fiction as Mutually Supportive Genre Forms

Dieter Sevin

There were grave reservations on the part of the
GDR authorities when, in 1967, Christa Wolf submitted
her novel Nachdenken über Christa T. for publication.[1]
She had already stirred up considerable controversy
with her previous novel, Der geteilte Himmel (1963),
before finally being awarded the Heinrich Mann Prize.
The immediate result of this skepticism can be seen in
the reluctance of the GDR authorities to make Christa
T. available to the GDR public at large. Initially,
the novel appeared only in a very limited edition
(5,000 copies) and was distributed mainly to party
functionaries. There is evidence that a large portion
of this edition was sold to a West German publisher in
order to avoid distribution in the GDR.[2]

Undoubtedly, Christa Wolf, too, had qualms about
submitting her novel to the censorship of the "administrators of literature," as Stephan Heym labeled the
functionaries responsible for literature in the Ministry of Culture.[3] One need only think of some of the
mandates of socialist realism, such as the call for a
positive hero, the setting of an example (Vorbildlich-
keit), the demand for mass literature (Volkstümlich-
keit), simplicity (Verständlichkeit), and most of all
the strict adherence to the policy of the SED (Parteilichkeit). Hardly any of these criteria are easily
discernible in the novel. On the contrary, a case can
be made for their non-existence there.

It seems reasonable to assume that overcoming the
censorship problem was of foremost concern to Christa
Wolf while writing her essay "Lesen und Schreiben" in
1968, the same year the novel was published.[4] We

45

might even be justified in regarding the essay, at least in part, as a theoretical treatise in support of Nachdenken über Christa T.5 For any thorough analysis of the novel, it seems mandatory to consider the essay very carefully and, vice versa, to look to the novel for themes, ideas, sentiments, and theoretical comments expressed in the essay. The task of this study will be to analyze how Christa Wolf envisions and justifies her new prose in theory and in practice, i.e., in the essay and the novel, particularly vis-à-vis the literary functionaries of the GDR.

In "Lesen und Schreiben," Christa Wolf speaks of the strong need to write in a new way--as a consequence of living in a new world--and of the need to articulate the changes that occurred in the perception of the world. The desire to portray this vision of the new society is finally stronger than the temptation to ignore it, and the writer or would-be writer has three options to choose from in his attempt to cope with his longing for self-expression: 1) to reject the old ways as useless and to proclaim, tearfully or indifferently, the end of the prose genre, which, according to Christa Wolf, can only be seen as an attempt to cover up one's own failure; 2) to retreat into silence, honestly accepting the consequences of one's failure, and to admit to being rendered speechless ("daß es einem die Sprache verschlagen hat," p. 181), an attitude or non-attitude that would attract little attention; 3) to justify oneself through productivity, the only one option acceptable and open to Christa Wolf. This immediately raises the questions for whom one is to write and why. The reason why is very subjective, stemming, as Christa Wolf maintains in her essay, from a tremendous inner restlessness. It is the result of unsatisfied needs and entails the hope that expressing and describing might be important, if not essential, for the future, as the writer expects "daß seiner Hand, schreibend, eine Kurve gelingt, die intensiver, leuchtender, dem wahren, wirklichen Leben näher ist als die mancherlei Abweichungen ausgesetzte Lebenskurve" (p. 185). In short, the writer is compelled by the conviction that his articulation will provide him and his reader with depth and stimulus for growth, and "daß das nackte, bloße Leben nicht ohne weiteres mit sich selber fertig wird: unbeschrieben, unüberliefert, ungedeutet und unreflektiert" (p. 185).

Christa Wolf points out that the problem with

this basic conviction and motivating force is an underlying profound doubt as to the future of the genre itself in view of the increasing competition from modern communications technology. Newspapers, radio, film, and television are providing the public with instant entertainment and information. The sciences, too, are gaining ground at the expense of prose, fascinating the public by promising to influence the characteristics of our descendants through structural manipulation of our genes, to complete a technical model of the human brain, to increase our life span by an additional fifty years or to offer drugs that produce happiness or unhappiness. Indeed, the reality of this century is against prose writers, Christa Wolf maintains, because it is more fantastic than any product of the imagination: "Ihre Grausamkeit und ihre Wunderbarkeit sind durch Erfindung nicht zu übertreffen. Wer also 'die Wahrheit' lesen will, das heißt: wie es wirklich gewesen ist, der greift zu Tatsachenberichten, Biographien, Dokumentensammlungen, Tagebüchern, Memoiren" (p. 189). Or at least so it seems.

What then is left to the prose writer, Christa Wolf asks the reader of her essay and especially the functionaries who are evaluating <u>Nachdenken über Christa T</u>.? What does the prose writer have to say to his contemporaries who are engaged in constructing the streamlined man who can adjust himself to any and all demands of civilization, contemporaries, " [d]enen der Gedanke nicht fremd ist, daß nicht einmal die Identität des Individuums in der Zukunft gesichert sein wird, und die den Gattungstod der Menschheit in Erwägung ziehen . . . nicht durch Naturgewalten, sondern durch uns" (p. 189). Prose is, indeed, under increasing pressure, and all the more so the more firmly it rejects both "die esoterische Außenseiterposition als auch die banale Zeitvertreiberrolle" (p. 186). What is needed, if it is to be saved, is a prose that can do something, "was alle jene Mächte nicht können, die ihr zu Leibe rücken" (p. 190).

Christa Wolf strongly believes that her prose should be able to do just that, that the message of her new prose should be innovative and vitally important, especially for her society, and that this cannot be accomplished by clinging to conventional literary theories and themes, such as those dictated by socialist realism, or by dealing with topics such as those declared desirable during the Bitterfeld Conferences:

> Prosa, die wieder wirken wollte, mußte
> sich einer neuen Realität auf neue
> Weise bemächtigen, mußte, unter ande-
> rem, beginnen, sich von der zum Kli-
> schee erstarrten, aus Versatzstücken
> gefertigten 'Fabel' alter Provenienz zu
> trennen; mußte und muß ein mechanisches
> zugunsten eines dialektischen Weltver-
> hältnisses zu überwinden suchen.
> (p. 201)

The fiction writer in search of new ways, Christa Wolf
insists, has to abandon the old. That was true not
only for the <u>nouveau</u> <u>roman</u> of Robbe-Grillet, but also
for Büchner, Dostoyevsky, and Brecht, and is true, of
course, for herself also and her novel <u>Nachdenken</u> <u>über</u>
<u>Christa</u> <u>T</u>.

The idea of "epic prose" is introduced by Christa
Wolf to describe her efforts to encourage dialectical
thinking in prose fiction:

> Der Vorschlag, sich um eine 'epische
> Prosa' zu bemühen, scheint dagegen ein
> Unsinn zu sein. Und doch hat man eine
> Ahnung, daß es sie geben müßte: eine
> Gattung, die den Mut hat, sich selbst
> als Instrument zu verstehen--scharf,
> genau, zupackend, veränderlich--, und
> die sich als Mittel nimmt, nicht als
> Selbstzweck.   (p. 207)

Just as the reaction of and the effect on the spec-
tator was of primary importance for Brecht in his epic
drama, so the essential factor for Christa Wolf is the
reader of the new prose, the individual who withdraws
alone with a book:

> Die epische Prosa sollte eine Gattung
> sein, die es unternimmt, auf noch un-
> gebahnten Wegen in das Innere dieses
> Menschen da, des Prosalesers, einzu-
> dringen. In das innerste Innere, dort-
> hin, wo der Kern der Persönlichkeit
> sich bildet und festigt. . . . Diese
> Region kann die Stimme eines anderen
> Menschen, kann Prosa erreichen, kann
> durch die Sprache berührt und aufge-
> schlossen werden--nicht, um sich ihrer

zu bemächtigen, sondern um seelische
Kräfte freizusetzen, die an Gewalt mit
den im Atom gebundenen Energien zu
vergleichen sind. (pp. 207-208)

But how can these powerful forces be unleashed?
Christa Wolf quotes the famous atomic physicist Hei-
senberg, who said that not all processes in modern
physics can be described in traditional language.
Similarly, the prose writer cannot rely on traditional
language, but has to find new ways to articulate, in
order to penetrate and analyze the innermost spheres
of his characters and society. The analogy to the
atomic physicist is clear. The prose writer, if he
wants to be effective, has to be as searching as a
scientist, has to follow and examine premonitions to
unlock the innermost secrets of his characters and
society, if he wants to set free those potentially
powerful forces in his reader.

That is what Christa Wolf attempts with Nachdenken über Christa T. However, her novel is not to
be interpreted as a retreat into inwardness or private
life. On the contrary, she sees herself as a writer
who deliberately commits herself to tasks radically
different from simply modifying the content of the old
literary patterns. She considers probing into the
inner realms of man proper and essential:

Die absurde Meinung, die sozialistische
Literatur könne sich nicht mit den
feinen Nuancen des Gefühlslebens . . .
befassen; sie sei darauf angewiesen,
Typen zu schaffen, die sich in vorge-
gebenen soziologischen Bahnen bewegen .
. . wird niemand mehr vorbringen. Die
Jahre, da wir die realen Grundlagen für
die Selbstverwirklichung des Individuums legten, sozialistische Produktionsverhältnisse schafften, liegen
hinter uns. Unsere Gesellschaft wird
immer differenzierter. Differenzierter
werden auch die Fragen, die ihre Mit-
glieder ihr stellen--auch in Form der
Kunst. 6

Again and again, therefore, Christa Wolf pleads
for the new in her "epic prose" and for freedom from
"den jahrhundertealten und den brandneuen Zauberfor-
meln der Manipulierung" (p. 208). The "brand-new

49

magic formulae of manipulation" must be interpreted as a direct reference to the literary functionaries, whose insistence on antiquated criteria for evaluating literature might very well discourage the evolution of new, engaging, and timeless prose, a prose which can compete with the offerings of modern technology, a prose which can prevent its own extinction as a genre. She concludes the first section of "Lesen und Schreiben" by asking rhetorically: "ob wir ihr [der Prosa] Mut machen, zu wollen, was sie kann" (p. 190). The unmistakable implication is that this might not always have been the case in the GDR, in spite of all the official encouragement, such as Ulbricht's call "Kumpel, greif zur Feder!" during the first Bitterfeld Conference. Such general encouragement is fine, but will not suffice for the prose envisioned by Christa Wolf. What is necessary is absolute artistic freedom, freedom to experiment unencumbered by fear. The engaged writer needs to work unhindered by any manipulation of his own experience, which would force the author, "Gespenster auszustoßen, Mißgeburten, die mit verdrehten Augen und falschen Zungen reden" (p. 216).

Christa Wolf's plea for artistic freedom as well as for conditions conducive to innovative new prose is clearly the general thrust of the essay. As I hope to show, it is also an important, though not generally recognized theme in Nachdenken über Christa T.[7] Supporting an interpretation which assumes that the problem of the writer in the GDR is one of the primary themes of the novel is its autobiographical dimension, as Christa Wolf explains in her essay "Selbstinterview":

> Frage: So schreiben Sie also eine Art von posthumen Lebenslauf . . .
> Antwort: Das dachte ich zuerst. Später merkte ich, daß das Objekt meiner Erzählung gar nicht so eindeutig sie, Christa T., war oder blieb. Ich stand auf einmal mir selbst gegenüber, das hatte ich nicht vorhergesehen.[8]

Into the two main invented characters, Christa T. and the narrator, the author has injected herself, her experiences gained through an extensive preoccupation with the development of her society. Indeed, in "Lesen und Schreiben" she asserts that there can be no question that art needs the artist, "der mit seinem

50

Lebensschicksal und seinem Lebenskonflikt zwischen der 'Realität' und der leeren Seite steht und keine andere Wahl hat, diese Seite zu füllen, als die Auseinandersetzung zwischen der Welt und sich selbst darauf zu projizieren" (p. 203).

The reality projected into her novel is of course the reality of the GDR, as delimited by the time frame of the story, but with obvious implications for the present and future. The development of her society and the individual in it is a major concern of the novel, as indicated in its motto borrowed from Johannes R. Becher: "Was ist das: Dieses Zu-sich-selber-Kommen des Menschen?" Both of the two main figures--at different levels--are seeking to find themselves and, significantly, both are trying to accomplish this, at least in part, by writing. Hesitantly and not at all omnisciently, the narrator is trying to write about a deceased friend, who was neither a strong, positive, exemplary nor unusual person. The non-conformist subject matter fills the narrator with self-doubt and skepticism about her attempts to write. After all, who will read what she writes, and what good will it do? Furthermore, will she ever be able to understand and portray the secret, the vision, of this Christa T.? The self-doubt of the narrator corresponds to the insecurity of Christa T. and her half-hearted efforts to write. While the narrator, however, manages to continue being creative, Christa T. herself never settles down to write seriously; still, there can be no doubt that that is what she really hoped to do.

Why don't you write? This leitmotival question is repeated throughout the novel, but Christa T. fails to give a convincing response to others and herself. Why didn't she write? The answer must be sought in her skepticism about her own ability and about language as a proper vehicle for articulation, and, perhaps most importantly, in a serious doubt that her kind of subjective, sensitive, and personal concerns, such as those expressed in the short story about her own childhood, "Kind am Abend," could possibly be of interest. In fact, she knows that her kind of writing would not be welcome during this phase of GDR development dominated by pragmatic, up-and-doing people, "Hopp-Hopp-Menschen" (p. 52), as Christa T. calls them, whose primary mission is to catch up with the productive capacity of the West. Comparing herself with the goals and heroes of those days instills a

51

deep feeling of inferiority in Christa T., because she believes in the new society. She agrees with the necessity to build up industry, but she realizes that she can contribute little to this effort. She looks for faults within herself, and it is significant that the narrator includes herself in the interpretation of what took place by changing her narrative perspective from "ich" to "wir":

> So daß nicht mehr sie uns mißtrauten,
> sie und die schrecklich strahlenden
> Helden der Zeitungen, Filme und Bücher,
> sondern wir uns selber: Wir hatten den
> Maßstab angenommen und . . . begonnen,
> uns mit jenen zu vergleichen. Es war
> dafür gesorgt, daß der Vergleich zu
> unseren Ungunsten ausfiel. So entstand
> um uns herum, oder auch in uns . . .
> ein hermetischer Raum, der seine Ge-
> setze aus sich selber zog, dessen
> Sterne und Sonnen scheinbar mühelos um
> eine Mitte kreisten, die keinen Ge-
> setzen und keiner Veränderung und am
> wenigsten dem Zweifel unterworfen war.
> . . . man erfreute sich an der absolu-
> ten Perfektion und Zweckmäßigkeit des
> Apparates, den reibungslos in Gang zu
> halten kein Opfer zu groß schien--
> selbst nicht das: sich auslöschen.
> (p. 57)

This surprisingly open analysis of the times indicates how immense the pressures for conformity were, especially on intellectuals. There was no room for intimate personal writings. Christa T., who desperately wants to contribute to the new society, writes to her sister: "Ich will arbeiten, Du weißt es--mit anderen, für andere. Aber meine Wirkungsmög-lichkeiten sind . . . schriftlicher, mittelbarer Natur. Ich muß mich mit den Dingen in Stille, be-trachtend, auseinandersetzen können" (p. 71). And, the narrator insists, she has precisely the kind of imagination needed for a real understanding of the world: "Christa T., sehr früh, wenn man es heute bedenkt, fing an, sich zu fragen, was denn das heißt: Veränderung. Die neuen Worte? Das neue Haus? Ma-schinen, größere Felder? Der neue Mensch, hörte sie sagen und begann, in sich hineinzublicken" (pp. 56-57). She turns inward for answers--an obvious paral-lel to Christa Wolf's analogy of the atomic scientist's cautious gropings--but what she finds makes her fall silent. She sees absolutely no hope for her kind of prose writing. How could her childhood story be of any possible significance in view of the perfect machinery of industry and the state? She finds no encouragement whatsoever for her calling, for her unending passion to write, because she cannot convince herself that her contribution, that she herself, might be necessary for the world's perfection. The narrator's comment that nothing less could have given validity to her life bears witness to Christa T.'s dangerously high standard, a standard which corresponds to Christa Wolf's own and the demands she places on her new prose.

Christa T.'s conviction about what she considers necessary, even essential, for the survival of mankind, namely conscience (i.e., absolute truthfulness) and imagination, contrasts sharply with the idea of a figure like Blasing, who sees the exploitation of all the earth's energy resources as indispensable for man's survival. Indeed, in Blasing Christa Wolf has created a figure that might well be viewed as the exact opposite of Christa T., an author and opportunist who adjusts to what is expected of him. He gets a divorce, moves to Berlin, and makes a name for himself. For him literature is a product to be concocted without any scruples; it only has to be printable and saleable. The criticism of that kind of conforming authorship and literature is unmistakable, and a figure like Blasing stands in sharp contrast to the task of a socialist author as Christa Wolf interprets it:

> Diese Aufgabe würde ich für sozialistische Autoren sehen, nicht als eine unter anderen, sondern als ihren Beitrag zu den Grundbedingungen, die nötig sind, damit die Menschheit sich nicht selber in die Luft sprengt oder auf andere Weise zerstört. Der Autor müßte also ohne Rücksicht auf augenblickliche Schwierigkeiten, die ihm dabei entgegentreten mögen, diese Bedingungen untersuchen und seine Figuren, die er gefunden hat oder erfindet, in solche Bedingungen bringen und mit ihnen experimentieren. Was er da sieht oder findet, müßte er ohne Scheu sagen, aufschreiben und nicht fürchten müssen,

daß das der Gesellschaft, in der er
lebt, schadet, sondern davon ausgehen,
daß alles, was wahrheitsgemäß gesagt
ist, ihr nutzt. . . . [9]

In the final analysis, Christa T. sees only two
options for herself: to say all or nothing. Her
opting for the latter leads to the self-accusing conclusion that she has sacrificed originality out of
cowardice (p. 139), which in turn precipitates her
increasing deep tiredness. She is unable to realize
the vision she has of her life, and that destroys her:

> All ihre Versuche, den toten Kreis zu
> verlassen, der sich um sie gebildet
> hatte, kamen in schrecklichem Gleichmut
> nur immer wieder zu ihr zurück. Sie
> spürte, wie ihr unaufhaltsam das Ge-
> heimnis verlorenging, das sie lebens-
> fähig machte . . . Sie sah sich in eine
> unendliche Menge von tödlichen banalen
> Handlungen und Phrasen aufgelöst.
> (p. 153)

That she cannot break the banal cycle of her existence destroys her spiritually as well as physically.
At the very end, when realizing that her potential,
her vision will be lost forever, she rebels against
death, only to conclude that she has lived too early.
She now knows: "Nicht mehr lange wird an dieser Krankheit gestorben werden" (p. 177). The narrator and, I
think we are justified to say, the author let the
story end on the optimistic note that in time society
will not be indifferent to aspiring writers like
Christa T. But there is also a sad note: "Wenn ich
sie erfinden müßte--verändern würde ich sie nicht.
Ich würde sie leben lassen . . . Würde sie an dem
Schreibpult sitzen lassen . . . die Erfahrungen auf-
zeichnend, die die Tatsachen des wirklichen Lebens in
ihr hinterlassen haben" (p. 170).

And that, of course, is exactly what Christa Wolf
herself has done in her novel: articulate in an
artistically intense and complex prose her own doubts,
conflicts, visions, and also the dangers she perceives
as a prose writer in GDR society. She did not choose
the first two options open to prose writers. She has
not proclaimed the end of the prose genre or fallen
silent. Instead, she has tried to justify herself
through productivity, in spite of all the forces

amassed against her. In so doing, she has gone through all the trials, conflicts, and tribulations reflected so intensely in her novel.

Christa Wolf, who in 1980, perhaps more deservingly than most, received the Federal Republic's most prestigious literary award, the Georg Büchner Prize, has emphasized her affinity to this 19th century German author and especially his novella _Lenz_, which she considers her "literarisches Urerlebnis." [10] In her essay "Lesen und Schreiben" she again holds up Büchner as an example of an author who was rejected in his own days, but whose novella _Lenz_ stands "hoch über dem trüben Strom konventioneller Prosa, die seitdem in deutscher Sprache produziert wurde" (p. 204). Just as Büchner rebelled against the fate of the author Lenz, who was driven to madness by unbearable pressures, Christa Wolf rebelled against the pressures that lead to the death of Christa T. Indeed, Christa Wolf's comments about Büchner in "Lesen und Schreiben" apply also to herself, because, like Büchner, she paid the full price by projecting her own life-threatening conflicts into the novel:

> "Mit wenigen Mitteln" hat er sich
> selbst dazugetan, seinen unlösbaren
> Lebenskonflikt, die eigene Gefährdung,
> die ihm wohl bewußt ist. Ein Konflikt,
> in dem sich die tausendfache Bedrohung
> lebendiger, entwicklungshungriger und
> wahrheitssüchtiger Menschen in Restau-
> rationszeiten gesteigert spiegelt: der
> Dichter, vor die Wahl gestellt, sich an
> unerträgliche Zustände anzupassen und
> sein Talent zu ruinieren oder physisch
> zugrunde zu gehen.   (p. 204)

By including himself, the author adds a dimension to his prose which alone will provide the intensity, depth, and involvement necessary to arouse the reader's genuine concern with what, Christa Wolf insists, is a matter of the survival of mankind (p. 217). We might react with reservation to such claims; however, Christa Wolf means what she says. She is convinced that the danger of non-survival lies ultimately in the loss of the individual and subjective elements in a social order where everything depends on science and technology, where personality is an outmoded idea and streamlined man the ideal (p. 218). To counteract the tendency in modern industrialized societies toward consuming stereotypes, existing in the midst of artificial stimuli, there is a need for precisely the kind of intensely subjective element which the functionaries made an issue of in regard to Christa Wolf's novel. Only such subjective prose, containing very personal motifs, can maintain man's contact with his roots and consolidate his self-confidence, which, as Christa Wolf points out, has become so shaky, "daß in hoch technisierten Ländern viele Menschen in den Selbstmord oder in die Sackgasse der Neurosen flüchten" (p. 219). That complicated narrative techniques and structures are used in this prose has nothing to do with arbitrariness. Rather, such prose is necessary: "Sie baut tödliche Vereinfachungen ab, indem sie die Möglichkeiten vorführt, auf menschliche Weise zu existieren. . . . Sie kann Zeit raffen und Zeit sparen, indem sie die Experimente, vor denen die Menschheit steht, auf dem Papier durchspielt . . ." (p. 219). As formulated in her Büchner Prize speech, literature in our endangered world must be research for peace: "Die Literatur muß heute Friedensforschung sein."[11] This is what Christa Wolf tries to explain and justify in her essay, and what she does so successfully in her novel.

Vanderbilt University

Notes

[1] Christa Wolf, Nachdenken über Christa T. (Neuwied: Luchterhand, 1971). All quotes are taken from this edition; references will appear parenthetically in the text. English edition: The Quest for Christa T., trans. Christopher Middleton (New York: Farrar, Straus & Giroux, 1979).

[2] See Heinrich Mohr, "Produktive Sehnsucht: Struktur, Thematik und politische Relevanz von Christa Wolfs Nachdenken über Christa T.," in Basis, 2, ed. Reinhold Grimm and Jost Hermand (Frankfurt: Athenäum, 1971), pp. 216-17.

[3] Stefan Heym used this term during a lecture, entitled "Problems of the Writer under Socialism," delivered at Vanderbilt University in the fall of 1978.

[4] Christa Wolf, Lesen und Schreiben. Aufsätze und Prosastücke (Neuwied: Luchterhand, 1972), pp. 181-220. Subsequent references will appear parenthetically in the text. English edition: The Reader and the Writer. Essays, Sketches, Memories, trans. Joan Becker (New York: International Publishers, 1977).

[5] In a 1974 interview with Hans Kaufmann, Christa Wolf stated: "Als ich den Aufsatz Lesen und Schreiben verfaßte--es war 1968, Nachdenken über Christa T. war seit einem Jahr beendet, aber noch nicht erschienen (aus ersten kritischen Äußerungen dazu konnte ich mir die Richtung der öffentlichen Kritik an diesem Buch vorstellen)--damals also beunruhigte mich nicht etwas so Hochtrabendes und Allgemeines wie 'das Schicksal des Romans'. . . . Aber ich hatte das Bedürfnis, die Erfahrung aufzuarbeiten, die ich beim Schreiben dieses Buches gemacht hatte, indem ich sie zu artikulieren suchte. . . . Prosa und Essay sind unterschiedliche Instrumente, um unterschiedlichem Material beizukommen, zu verschiedenen, doch nicht einander entgegengesetzten oder einander ausschließenden Zwecken." Hans Kaufmann, "Gespräch mit Christa Wolf," Weimarer Beiträge, 20, Nr. 6 (1974), 90-91.

[6] Christa Wolf, "Selbstinterview," in Lesen und Schreiben, p. 79.

[7] In his rather general interpretation of the novel, Manfred Durzak does recognize Christa T. as being "potentiell eine Dichterin," whose vision of herself can be understood "zum Teil zumindest . . . als Vorstellung von ihrer künstlerischen Aufgabe" ("Ein exemplarisches Gegenbeispiel. Die Romane von Christa Wolf," in Der deutsche Roman der Gegenwart, ed. Manfred Durzak [Stuttgart: Kohlhammer, 1971], p. 287). Heinrich Mohr, on the other hand, admits that interpreting Christa T. as a writer is a problem for the reader ("Produktive Sehnsucht. Struktur, Thematik und politische Relevanz von Christa Wolfs Nachdenken über Christa T.," p. 214). Alexander Stephan, in his very useful introduction to Christa Wolf, sees Christa T.'s attempts to write primarily as a "Möglichkeit zur Bewältigung der Wirklichkeit" and as a "Schutzwall gegen das Unverständnis der prosaischen Ansprüche der Gesellschaft" (Christa Wolf [Munich: Beck, 1976], p. 74). Christa Thomassen interprets similarly in her very thorough book, where she sees Christa T.'s attempts to write as essentially "Therapie" and "Versuche der Identitätsfindung" (Der lange Weg zu uns

selbst. Christa Wolfs Roman 'Nachdenken über Christa T.' als Erfahrungs- und Handlungsmuster [Kronberg/Ts.: Scriptor, 1977], pp. 138-44). None of these interpretations recognizes Christa T.'s attempts to write as a primary theme of the novel.

[8] "Selbstinterview," p. 76.

[9] Christa Wolf, "Unruhe und Betroffenheit," in Fortgesetzter Versuch. Aufsätze, Gespräche, Essays, ed. Joachim Walther (Leipzig: Reclam, 1979), p. 71.

[10] "Mein Urerlebnis in der deutschen Literatur," in Meinetwegen Schmetterlinge. Gespräche mit Schriftstellern, ed. Joachim Walther (E. Berlin: Buchverlag Der Morgen, 1973), p. 121.

[11] Christa Wolf, Büchner-Preis-Rede. Sonderdruck für die Freunde des Luchterhand Verlages (Neuwied: Luchterhand, 1980), p. 13.

Christa Wolf's Use of Image and Vision
in the Narrative Structuring of Experience

Marilyn Sibley Fries

Of her great model, Anna Seghers, Christa Wolf
writes: "Sie sagt keinen Satz, den sie nicht erfahren
hat." 1   In appreciation of the Swiss writer Max
Frisch, with whom she also has much in common, Wolf
again stresses the importance of personal experience:
"'Große Stoffe' verbieten sich ihm in der Prosa, die
sein intimstes Ausdrucksmittel ist, aus Aufrichtigkeit: Er hat sie nicht erfahren." 2   Wolf considers
"Erfahrung," personal experience, to be the necessary
point of departure for the creation of an honest
literary work.   However intangible "truth" might be,
however much "reality" is colored by the subjectivity
of the writer, Christa Wolf's writings testify to her
commitment to these criteria for a work of art. 3
Throughout her critical writings, Wolf demands that
art deal honestly with "truth" and "reality." 4   While
she insists on experience as the primary point of
reference, she implies through her dialectical structure a utopian vision resulting from the integration
of the narrated subjective experience into the objective experience of reading.   Her own reading of
Seghers, Frisch, and others illustrates the manner in
which she would wish to be read: the reading is
fundamentally synthetic and open-ended.

Wolf's fictional writings can be seen as attempts
to reconcile her notions of "Erfahrung," "truth," and
"reality" with certain exigencies of literary form
which would seem anathema to her particular fluid,
dialectical understanding of these terms.   Especially
the image, which tends to impose artificial temporal
and spatial boundaries on that which it describes,
would appear to undermine the progressive motion Wolf
would create in her narratives.   She wants to evoke

59

the continuum of a life or an historical span of time,
but eschews linear presentation and imagistic stasis.
In the essay "Lesen und Schreiben," the section entitled "Medaillons" hints at the dangers of the reduc-
tive tendencies of imagistic presentation. Wolf describes "Medaillons" as "ehemals aktive, jetzt aber
durch Einkapselung stillgelegte Lebensflecken."[5] She
continues: "'Erinnerung' aber pflegen wir es zu nennen, wenn wir diese recht hübsch gemachten Kunstgewer-
bestücke als echt unter die Leute bringen . . ." (p.
24). The "miniatures" are necessary to "memory," but
must be recognized as artificial relics of times past.
Their relation to the present is essentially dishonest; to allow them falsely to represent "reality"
is to relegate that "reality" to a moribund historical
state in which it has no honest continuing significance for the present. Wolf's uneasiness about images
and image-making and the destructiveness of their in-
flexibility leads, at the end of "Medaillons," to her
demand that "Prosa sollte danach streben, unverfilmbar
zu sein."[6] Reacting (in <u>Nachdenken</u> über <u>Christa</u> <u>T.</u>)
to the "filmability" of Christa T.'s life, to <u>its</u>
<u>apparent</u> imagistic accessibility, the narrator ven-
tures her "unfilmable" narrative concerning her.[7]

The "nachdenkende Erzählerin" of this report on
Christa T., like Christa T. herself, is supremely
aware of the fallibility of language, of its tendency
to create lies, and associates this creation with the
production of verbal images. It is therefore somewhat
puzzling that one of her stated reasons for her compulsion to tell Christa T.'s story appears to contradict the very essence of her friend's existence: the
narrator wants to present Christa T., "[d]aß man sie
sehen kann" (p. 156). Such a project contradicts
itself in several ways. First, it suggests the possibility of a finalized imagistic (spatial) perception
of Christa T., a character who, in her interactions
with others and herself, defied the very habit of
fixing an individual (or societal) existence through
the static image. A second contradiction involves the
writer's attempt to bring about a visual perception
through the use of words. This is image-making on a
different level; it is the imagery of literary art.

The act with which Christa T. impresses herself
upon the consciousness of the narrator contains both
the insoluble paradox of her being and the questions
of the narrative itself, which are unanswerable,
because they are always newly formulated. While

walking along the street with some of her classmates,
Christa T., newcomer and aloof stranger in city and
classroom, suddenly "hielt sich . . . eine zusammen-
gedrehte Zeitung vor den Mund und stieß ihren Ruf aus:
Hoohaahoo, so ungefähr" (p. 14). The impulsive action immediately defines her in the eyes of the narrator, establishes her as someone who knows unknown
things, who has achieved a sense of selfhood still
foreign to her peers, someone about and from whom one
must learn. What is ultimately learned, however, is
that the kind of selfhood her friend reads out of this
gesture is and will always be impossible for Christa
T.; her being must be defined in the act of writing
about it, and the static image occasioned by the
trumpet-blowing scene (and others), while containing a
statement of being, comprises merely an element there-
of. To permit her character to be thus statically
defined is to restrict it to an almost photographic
visual image which conveys nothing beyond its own
frame. It is just such definition which Christa T.
abhors and fears, which forces her to rebel against
externally imposed patterns or titles and to refuse to
proclaim what she intends to be or do with her life.[8]
The narrator's perception of this reluctance to be
defined and her attempt to explain it without doing an
injustice to her dead friend comprise the lesson of
Christa T. and the narrative concerning her. The
insight into her complex and ultimately undefinable
character dictates the form and content of the narrative.

The narrator demonstrates the problem of the
finality of language, and suggests the association of
form and content, when she constructs an etymological
game with "dichten" to mean "dicht machen" (p. 23):
"dicht machen" implies an enclosure which provides
security, but this security prevents freedom of movement and development. This particular paradox may
well explain the fragmentary nature of most of Christa
T.'s writings. Christa T. seeks to secure herself
against those elements of "das Dunkle" which continually threaten to throw her existence off balance,
especially because they stand in such contradiction to
the "new world" in which she lives. "Das Dunkle" is
represented throughout the narrative by a series of
recurring visual reminders: "Da knallt der schwarze
Kater noch einmal an die Stallwand. Da zerschellen
noch einmal die Elsterneier am Stein. Da wird noch
einmal der Schnee von einem steifen kleinen Gesicht
gewischt. Noch einmal schnappen die Zähne zu. Das

61

hört nicht auf" (pp. 137-38). These images represent
the visual leitmotifs which accompany Christa T.
throughout her life and maintain her awareness both of
death and of the ignoble in man against which she
wishes to fight and which she wants to see eliminated
from her society. The repetition of these images
provides, with an odd kind of certainty, a dialectical
counterbalance to the uncertainties of the present in
which Christa T. lives and the future towards which
she and her society are working. Her hyperawareness
of the omnipresence of such images, her need both to
accept them and to protect herself against that which
they represent, give dimension and dynamism to her
character and her story.

The narrator creates for herself a similar set of
visual leitmotifs in regard to Christa T. The process
she ascribes to Christa T. of "dicht machen," of
surrounding a subject with words, is fundamental to
the process at work in her "Nachdenken"; but the
narrator is reluctant to make the verbal fence too
impenetrable, for fear of imprisoning Christa T. in
the lie of an image. She frames her images in the
language of uncertainty. She asks:

> Wäre es nicht möglich, das Netz, das
> für sie geknüpft und ausgelegt wurde,
> erwiese sich am Ende als untauglich,
> sie zu fangen? Sätze, die sie ge-
> schrieben hat--ja. Auch Wege . . . ein
> Zimmer . . . eine Landschaft . . . ein
> Haus, ein Gefühl sogar--nur nicht sie.
> Denn sie ist schwer zu fangen. Selbst
> wenn ich es schaffen könnte, alles
> getreulich wiederzugeben, was ich von
> ihr noch weiß oder in Erfahrung ge-
> bracht habe, selbst dann wäre denkbar,
> daß derjenige, dem ich alles erzähle,
> den ich brauche und jetzt um Beistand
> angehe, daß er am Ende nichts von ihr
> wüßte. (pp. 147-48)

Here the narrator is implying the impossibility of
"catching" an individual in a verbal net and the
inability of language to weave that net and, at the
same time, she is consciously asserting that the
reality of a life cannot be summed up in any number of
words. She undertakes to insert miniatures or images
into her narrative of re-collection in such a way as
to revitalize them and give them a present meaning and

active function. Moments, yes. Snap-shots are per-
missible, even necessary. Moments must be captured,
both by Christa T. in her fragmentary writing, and by
her narrator, in order to establish something perma-
nent on which to build, to move on the path to herself. But they must always be viewed as Augenblicke,
just as--and herein lies the paradox in the juxtaposition of image and vision, of schon and noch
nicht,--"der Augenblick, sie zu sehen, nach [dem] Ende
[dieses Berichts] eintreten wird" (p. 112).

The narrator's task in remembering Christa T., in
engaging in dialogue with her dead friend, is ultimately to say the most important thing about her, as
she tells us in the continuation of the long quotation
given above: "So gut wie nichts. Wenn es mir nicht
gelingt, das Wichtigste über sie zu sagen: sie,
Christa T., hat eine Vision von sich selbst gehabt"
(p. 148). The narrator knew about that vision, we are
informed, the moment she saw Christa T. "blowing her
trumpet." With this reference the narrator combines
the two fundamental elements of visual perception at
work in this narrative: the momentary, literary-
verbal image, on the one hand, and, on the other, the
ultimately inexpressible vision, which contains her
message (here the most important thing she could say
about Christa T.), a perception which lies beyond the
boundaries of the text, for it involves the dialectical participation of the reader. The narrator's use
of the impersonal pronoun "man" when citing her
reasons for writing about Christa T. suggests that
"Sehen" is not the task of the narrator alone. Rather
the process which should lead to the reader's ultimate
perception of Christa T. involves conception as well,
in a dialectical interplay of several levels, the most
basic of which juxtaposes first and third person,
subject and object, in one individual. In her use of
images, Wolf faces the challenge of simultaneously
making visible and withholding closure. The image
which succeeds in fulfilling this contradictory aim
contains past, present, and future; it contains being
and becoming, stasis and development. The image
functions not only as a literary device but constitutes a statement and illustration of the dialectical
narrative method Christa Wolf employs as well.

The presence of schon and noch nicht, of sein and
werden in one entity emerges as one of Christa Wolf's
major themes in her narrative about Christa T. and
remains crucial throughout her later works. My con-

cern here is the manner in which this theme is realized in the narrative structure of the works. I have selected three passages from three different works which may serve to demonstrate how she uses images in the juxtaposition of subject and object both to structure her narrative and to seek to represent truthfully her understanding of herself in its broadest context. I have chosen to look at Christa T., Kindheitsmuster, and Kein Ort. Nirgends, although the selection is difficult--the conceptual web which connects all of Wolf's mature writings tempts to continual reference to a great variety of works.

In Christa T., Christa Wolf employs images frequently. She uses them to create the motif of the "dunkle Welt" into which Christa T. has had too many disturbing glimpses, and against which she tries to protect herself through writing. They are used as well, in contrapuntal juxtaposition to these dark visions, to present Christa T. in a positive light. In the narrator's memory there remain these moments: Christa T. blowing the trumpet or chasing the red and white ball on the beach; and they are held in reserve as a kind of proof of Christa T.'s vision of herself. But there is another dominant image which does not come from the apparently "present" perspective of one or the other of the characters, but belongs rather to the historical perspective of the narrator and presents the two girls together in a confusing moment in past time. This image is remarkable; it demonstrates the manner in which Wolf's presentation moves from the static picture into one of the most complicated narrative moments in the book. I refer to the following passage:

> Dünner, kalter Schnee begann zu fallen.
> Wir blieben länger da stehen, als wir
> etwas zu sagen wußten, und wenn ich
> malen könnte, würde ich jene lange
> Mauer hierhersetzen und uns beide, sehr
> klein, an sie gelehnt. . . . Das kalte
> Licht würde ich nicht beschreiben
> müssen, und die Beklemmung, die ich
> spürte, würde ohne weiteres von dem
> Bild ausgehen. . . . Auch würde man
> ahnen, daß man sich schnell verlieren
> kann unter solchem Himmel, in diesem
> Licht. Und daß uns kurz bevorstand,
> uns verlorenzugehen: einander und jeder
> sich selbst. So daß man ungerührt

"ich" sagt zu einem Fremden, die Unbe-
fangenheit bewahrt, bis zu einem Augenblick, da dieses fremde Ich zu mir
zurückkehren und wieder in mich einge-
hen wird. Mit einem Schlag wird man
befangen sein, das läßt sich voraus-
sagen. Vielleicht ist man darauf aus
und darauf angewiesen, diesen Augenblick zu wiederholen. Vielleicht hat
es Sinn, daß sie, Christa T., Krischan,
noch einmal dabei ist. (p. 20)

The moment of losing oneself--this moment which
must be repeated if the self is to be rediscovered and
redefined in truthful understanding--gives sense to
the renewed "presence" of Christa T., for the losing
and the finding again of "einander und jeder sich
selbst" are intricately bound up with the return of
"dieses fremde Ich." This particular moment occurs
towards the end of the war--a time which will bring
utter chaos into the lives of Christa T. and the
narrator. It is that historical moment which is
defined here as the moment of losing oneself, of the
disjunction of the "Ich" into an alien object and a
familiar subject. The historical consciousness of
self required to understand honestly one's own "Weg zu
sich selbst" confronts, in Christa T., an historical
moment of reality beyond which, it seems, it was not
possible for Wolf to penetrate at the time of writing
that book. The image of the two girls leaning against
the school wall establishes a "beginning" of a dialectical process which extends into the continuing narrative and beyond. But that image denies a past; in
setting the moment of self-alienation here, it assumes
a wholeness of self up to that historical moment, and
asks no questions of the time preceding it.

If we may assume the fundamentally autobiographical nature of Christa Wolf's work, we can trace the
development of her historical consciousness in direct
relationship to the backward reach of her works. What
a temporal leap exists between the moment of self-
alienation in 1944 and the implicit claim to identity
with those figures of 1804 (in Kein Ort. Nirgends),
who were so thoroughly alienated from themselves and
the others! The future-oriented dialectical process
of "Zu-sich-selber-Kommen" requires a past-oriented
exploration of the elements of that self--through
memory, documentation, imagination, understanding,
association--to comprehend "[w]ie . . . wir so ge-

worden, wie wir heute sind."[9]

There is a step along Christa Wolf's "Weg zu sich selbst" which I consider the significant moment in her self-exploration; it permits that honesty which is only implicitly present in <u>Christa T.</u> (where the narrator transfers the same experience to Christa T.).[10] I am referring to that experience in <u>Kindheitsmuster</u> which describes the self-alienation of the three-year-old child Nelly. The creator of the image presents and then dialectically engages it in the narrator's perceptual process. The narrator seeks and locates the image of the child, but then proceeds to describe the complexity and unreliability of memory, the dialectical splitting of one individual, and the impossibility of gaining <u>honest</u> access to that child:

> Da hättest du es also. Es bewegt sich, geht, liegt, sitzt, ißt, schläft, trinkt. Es kann lachen und weinen . . . sich fürchten, glücklich sein . . . lieben und hassen und zum lieben Gott beten. Und das alles täuschend echt. Bis ihm ein falscher Zungenschlag unterliefe, eine altkluge Bemerkung, weniger noch: ein Gedanke, eine Geste, und die Nachahmung entlarvt wäre, auf die du dich beinahe eingelassen hättest.
> Weil es schwerfällt, zuzugeben, daß jenes Kind da--dreijährig, schutzlos, allein--dir unerreichbar ist. . . . Das Kind ist . . . von dir verlassen worden. . . . von dem Erwachsenen, der aus ihm ausschlüpfte . . . Jetzt, obwohl es unmöglich ist, will er es kennenlernen.
> . . . . Die Hauptmerkmale der verschiedenen Lebensalter sind dir geläufig. Ein dreijähriges normal entwikkeltes Kind trennt sich von der dritten Person, für die es sich bis jetzt gehalten hat. Woher aber dieser Stoß, den das erste bewußt gedachte ICH ihm versetzt? . . . Warum sind Schreck und Triumph, Lust und Angst für dieses Kind so innig miteinander verbunden, daß keine Macht der Welt, kein chemisches Labor und gewiß auch keine Seelenanalyse sie je wieder voneinander trennen werden?[11]

It is here that the author Christa Wolf confronts her greatest dilemma. She can visualize the child. She can present the believable image of the three-year-old who has been left behind and forgotten by the adult. But such a presentation, fixing that three-year-old in an inflexible frame and thus denying its development, is dishonest, both to the child and to the adult she has become. It is necessary for the adult to reach back and "enliven" the child, as it were, just as she "enlivens" Christa T. and the others, for only in this way can adult and child engage in that dialogue which the narrator of this work describes as "[e]in Spiel in und mit der zweiten und dritten Person, zum Zwecke ihrer Vereinigung" (p. 209). Only the dialogue, the dialectic "game," will permit the honest statement sought by the narrator. And only the prolonged and agonizing self-engagement of Kindheitsmuster, which moves beyond that temporal barrier of 1944 noted in Christa T., to include the entire disturbing history of the narrator, can free the author to delve into an even more distant fictional past in search of her "Vorgänger," to suggest an even earlier historical point for the beginning of the process of self-recognition.

Wolf's most recent novel, Kein Ort. Nirgends, seems initially not to have any relation to her other works. How did she move from her contemporary Christa T., through her autobiographical character Nelly to the world of Karoline von Günderrode, Heinrich von Kleist, Bettina, Clemens von Brentano, and their circle? Leaving Kulturerbe and the renewed GDR interest in the Romantics aside, disregarding even the importance for Anna Seghers of the particular group of German writers of which Günderrode and Kleist are representative[12]--how does the narrator of Kein Ort. Nirgends come to refer to the subjects of this narrative as "Vorgänger"? "Vorgänger ihr, Blut im Schuh,"[13]--whose "Vorgänger," whom did they precede, in what historical line are they perceived, why are they important here, now? Christa Wolf's motivations for the presentation of certain figures in her works to date establish all these figures as essentially significant to an Ich or a narrator, and we must thus assume that these figures are as important to us as is Christa T., whom, as her narrator reminds us, we need--and who has much in common with Kleist and Günderrode, being "not of her own time."

67

In one of the interior monologues (actually, interior dialogues) of Kein Ort. Nirgends, Kleist is observing the party to which he has been invited, and the particular "idea" he has here serves well as a literary illustration of our theme as well as of Christa Wolf's method. Here we have the image and the vision, the co-existence in one image of being and becoming, a representation of the dialectical process:

> Zugegeben, ihm sind Frauen lieber, die
> im Rahmen bleiben, wie diese Gunda,
> diese Lisette, Savignys und Esenbecks
> Frauen, die sich auf die Couchette
> unter das große Ölgemälde gesetzt ha-
> ben, das durch sorgfältigste Behandlung
> aller Schattierungen von Grün einer
> einfachen Landschaft unglaubliche Glie-
> derung, Tiefe und Heiterkeit zu geben
> weiß. Putzige Idee: Ein zweiter
> Maler, falls er anwesend wäre, könnte
> sich hinstellen und aus diesem neuen
> Motiv--dem Bild des ersten, der Cou-
> chette und den sehr verschiedenen jun-
> gen Frauen darauf--ein weiteres Gemälde
> anfertigen, geeignet, über der sanft
> geschwungenen Kommode an der jenseiti-
> gen Schmalseite des Raumes zu hängen
> und wieder eine Gruppe zu bilden, die
> ihrerseits ein malenswertes Sujet her-
> gäbe. Dies ginge so weiter, und es
> brächte doch auch einen gewissen Fort-
> schritt in die Malerei. (p. 18)

"Putzige Idee," indeed! What Kleist's pre-Marxist dialectical concept does here, besides setting the observed static image in motion, that is, bringing "a certain progress to painting," is to suggest a future and progressive development resulting from the continual juxtaposition of the existing with the new. That which exists and is counterposed to the new, only to integrate that new element into itself as part of its being, contains all of the previous components of the initial painting. The dialectical process need not be further elucidated here; I wanted to offer this quotation as a primary example of the method Wolf employs to create movement in that which she makes visible. The significant point here is how Wolf integrates her dialectical point of view into the narrative by permitting this observation to be made through the eyes of a fictional character. The series

68

of perceptions of perceptions creates movement in the narrative; in turn, those perceptions and their dialectical progression become models for the reader's perception.

This quotation also serves to illustrate Wolf's method as a writer, and suggests an answer to our question of how she arrived at Kleist and Günderrode. In that fictional account of a meeting of two historical figures in the year 1804, she is combining future reference (well illustrated by the quotation above, and by many others as well) and historical perspective (a look back from her present moment to the time of the fictional encounter), in which her own present and an assumed future figure constantly as temporal points of reference. This practice is not new to Christa Wolf, of course--there is a complex temporal structure in all her works, beginning with the frame constructed for Rita's recuperative recollection in Der geteilte Himmel, through the far more oblique time levels of Christa T. and "Unter den Linden," to the contemplative remembrances of Kindheitsmuster. In all of these works, the momentary reality of a visible or invisible first-person narrator provides the fulcrum for visions of the past and future.

What brings Christa Wolf to the narrative concerning Günderrode and Kleist is, I submit, ultimately the honesty of her own "Weg zu sich selbst"--the fictive imagination admits to a certain identity with these characters who are to be counted among Wolf's own "Vorgänger." The narrative is not merely a tribute to those writers who could not or did not belong to their times; it is not just a recognition of the vulnerability of the extremely individual in confrontation with an unbending society. It is a testimony to the integration of these doomed poets into the present (and future) existence of the writer. Just as she does with Christa T., Wolf brings these figures to life once more, first to attest to their present significance for her and then to deliver them, in a new interpretation, to the reader of her fiction. What Wolf presents to the reader involves a synthesis of their existence and her understanding of and identification with that existence.

The levels of dialectical function in this work are too many to be delineated here (the two "sehr verschiedenen jungen Frauen" of our quotation provide the least significant example, and the variations on

the theme of opposition and synthesis underlie the
entire structure of the narrative). The chief reason
for my concern with this work in this context involves
its relationship to the subject of its author. For
what Wolf does here--and what she always does--is to
suggest the integration of an historical object into
the subject, the process with which she concerns
herself so pointedly in Christa T. and Kindheitsmuster
in order to answer her two most important questions:
"Was ist das: Dieses Zu-sich-selber-Kommen des
Menschen?" and "Wie sind wir so geworden, wie wir
heute sind?" [14] The difficult steps along the route
toward an answer to these questions involve honesty in
remembering and the presentation of continually tem-
pered and relativized images. The relativized verbal
image, presented to avoid the dishonesty of fixedness,
functions much in the way Kleist's "putzige Idee"
would suggest.

The honest reworking of personal experience as
the basis for fictional reality leads to an increasing
complexity of narrative structure in Wolf's more
recent works. Her skepticism regarding the validity
of the traditional linear narrative, recounted by an
omniscient narrator, is markedly evident already in
Nachdenken über Christa T. The structural devices she
employs in her writings are developed with sophisti-
cated subtlety in such works as "Unter den Linden,"
Kindheitsmuster, and Kein Ort. Nirgends. These works
are indicative of Wolf's artistic development as well
as examples of her repeated attempts to understand her
individual self in the larger context of her past,
present, and future environment. The complexity of
Wolf's texts is characterized by an inconsistency in
the narrator's perspective and a non-linear representation of time. The narrative voice, which is
apparently unwilling to maintain one identity, fluc-
tuates continually from first to second or third
person singular; the historical experience which
informs the fictional creation has ultimately no
finite chronological boundaries; future becomes present and then past, depending on the temporal situation of the narrator. Personal (historical) experience invokes much more than just the biography of the
author or narrator; it becomes more a matter of identity and identification than of physical presence at a
given time and place. In focusing on an individual
character, real or fictional, Wolf enters as subject
into dialogue with that character and illustrates
through the process of writing the process by which an

object is integrated into and thus contributes to the ever-progressing subject.

For Christa Wolf, as for her character Christa T., writing is a way of "overcoming things." Both understand what they confront by analyzing the impact of the world on their particular existence. If what is confronted cannot be thus internalized or subjectified, if the raw experience provides no basis for reflection transmitted through the verbal art, then it becomes insignificant. This factor, more than any other, contributes to the subjectivity of her writings and causes her considerable difficulties, for she seeks not only to understand herself in the process of artistic creation, but also to transmit that creation --and a record of its process--as object to the reader. The reader should, ideally, continue the dialogue of her text beyond the text by following her subjective experience as outlined in narrative form and engaging in turn in a subject-object exchange, where the reader becomes the subject.

The passage toward self-recognition may be replete with imagistic references, but the combination of the images should not permit an artificial sense of wholeness. The Ich which functions as reference point for all of Wolf's narratives determines the essentially dialectical structure of her works, for this Ich (or some manifestation of it) is, in its progression toward itself, continually involved in dialogue, in interchange, in synthesis, and in movement.

That self-recognition is not presented cannot surprise us, for the dialectical engagement continues, of course, beyond all texts and can only be implied with the utopian concept of a vision. What we are presented with in the texts is a deftly constructed literary example of one solution to the fundamental conundrum of the committed artist, namely the dishonest position of that artist vis-à-vis the life observed and described. Christa Wolf refers to this dilemma (in Kindheitsmuster) as: "die Unmoral dieses Berufes: Daß man nicht leben kann, während man Leben beschreibt. Daß man Leben nicht beschreiben kann, ohne zu leben" (p. 397). She attempts in her dialectical narrative structure, which demands the subjectification of the object and vice versa, not only to understand herself and her own individual process of becoming better, but also to maintain that self continually as part of the narrative world which she

71

creates and thus to give an open-ended honesty to her works. This open-endedness is fully in keeping with the concept of vision, equally applicable to the individual artist, to her created world, and to the world in which both she and her creation exist.

Yale University

Notes

¹ Christa Wolf, "Glauben an Irdisches," in her Lesen und Schreiben. Neue Sammlung (Darmstadt/Neuwied: Luchterhand, 1980), p. 119.

² "Max Frisch, beim Wiederlesen oder: Vom Schreiben in Ich-Form," in Lesen und Schreiben. Neue Sammlung, p. 202.

³ Wolf delineates this commitment most explicitly in the seminal essay, "Lesen und Schreiben." In that essay she establishes the foundations of the poetic principle which she will come to call "subjektive Authentizität." See Hans Kaufmann, "Gespräch mit Christa Wolf," first published in Weimarer Beiträge, 20, Nr. 6 (1974), 90-112; republished as "Die Dimension des Autors. Gespräch mit Hans Kaufmann," in C. Wolf, Lesen und Schreiben. Neue Sammlung, pp. 68-99; also published as "Subjektive Authentizität und gesellschaftliche Wahrheit. Interview mit Christa Wolf," in Auskünfte. Werkstattgespräche mit DDR-Autoren, ed. A. Löffler (Berlin/Weimar: Aufbau, 1976), pp. 485-517; and in C. Wolf, Fortgesetzter Versuch. Aufsätze, Gespräche, Essays (Leipzig: Reclam, 1979), pp. 77-104. Her insistence on being faithful to the spirit of this "inner authenticity" reduces the concepts of "truth" and "reality" from a universal to the particularly individual realm of the writer. But internally realized truths must be made accessible to the external reader through art. For critical discussions of this principle, see especially Alexander Stephan, "Die 'subjective Authentizität' des Autors. Zur ästhetischen Position von Christa Wolf," in Christa Wolf, text + kritik, No. 46 (Munich: edition text + kritik, 1975), pp. 33-41. See also A. Stephan, Christa Wolf, 2nd ed. (Munich: Beck, 1979), pp. 7-22, and Karin McPherson, "In Search of the New Prose: Christa Wolf's Reflections on Writing and the Writer

in the 1960s and 1970s," <u>New</u> <u>German</u> <u>Studies</u>, 9, Nr. 1 (Spring 1981), 1-13.

[4] I refer here chiefly to Wolf's most recent critical essays, in which she exhibits a rather personal sense of identification with both thought and method of her subjects. The best of these essays are collected in <u>Lesen</u> <u>und</u> <u>Schreiben</u>. <u>Neue</u> <u>Sammlung</u> and include discussions of Ingeborg Bachmann, Maxie Wander, Vera Inber, Fred Wander, Thomas Mann, Bettina von Arnim, Karoline von Günderrode, among others.

[5] <u>Lesen</u> <u>und</u> <u>Schreiben</u>. <u>Neue</u> <u>Sammlung</u>, p. 24.

[6] <u>Lesen</u> <u>und</u> <u>Schreiben</u>. <u>Neue</u> <u>Sammlung</u>, p. 27.

[7] Her concerns are expressed in the introductory passage to the narrative, and suggest the paradox of the two kinds of "seeing" with which we are dealing here: "Ich aber sehe sie noch. Schlimmer: Ich verfüge über sie. Ganz leicht kann ich sie herbeizitieren wie kaum einen Lebenden. Sie bewegt sich, wenn ich will. . . . Beschwörend, meinen Verdacht betäubend, nenne ich sogar ihren Namen und bin ihrer nun ganz sicher. Weiß aber die ganze Zeit: Ein Schattenfilm spult ab, einst durch das wirkliche Licht der Städte, Landschaften, Wohnräume belichtet," <u>Nachdenken</u> <u>über</u> <u>Christa</u> <u>T.</u>, 4th ed. (Neuwied/Berlin: Luchterhand, 1970), pp. 7-8. All subsequent quotations from this work are from this edition and will be indicated in parentheses in the text.

[8] It is this resistance to labels, among other things, which puts Christa T. out of step with her contemporaries. When asked: "[w]as willst du werden, Krischan?" she rejects all possible titles and responds: "Ein Mensch" (pp. 45-46). And when she finally does assume a title by marrying, she refers to herself in this capacity, "ironisch natürlich", as "Tierarztfrau in mecklenburgischer Kleinstadt" (p. 173).

[9] For the full quotations and their sources, see Note 14 below.

[10] See the discussion of Christa T.'s "Kind am Abend," p. 30.

[11] Christa Wolf, <u>Kindheitsmuster</u> (Berlin and Weimar: Aufbau, 1976), pp. 14-15. All subsequent quotations from this work are from this edition; the

page references will appear parenthetically in the text.

[12] Seghers refers to Kleist and Günderrode, among others, as follows: "Diese deutschen Dichter schrieben Hymnen auf ihr Land, an dessen gesellschaftlicher Mauer sie ihre Stirnen wund rieben." Quoted by Wolf in "Glauben an Irdisches," in Lesen und Schreiben. Neue Sammlung, p. 120.

[13] Christa Wolf, Kein Ort. Nirgends (Darmstadt/ Neuwied: Luchterhand, 1981), p. 5. All subsequent quotations from this work are from this edition and will be indicated in parentheses in the text.

[14] The first of these quotations (from Johannes R. Becher) serves as motto to Christa T., the second is given in the "Inhalt" as the title to Chapter 9 and recurs as a refrain throughout Kindheitsmuster (Berlin and Weimar: Aufbau, 1976), p. 276. All subsequent quotations from this work are from this edition and will be indicated in parentheses in the text.

Use of the Fantastic in Recent GDR Prose

Sibylle Ehrlich

In 1970 Anna Seghers wrote the short story "Sage vom Unirdischen," and in 1980 the first almanac of fantastic literature printed in the GDR, Lichtjahr 1, appeared. The intervening decade offers such a proliferation of titles and topics dealing with the supernatural and with fantasy that this new form of GDR literature deserves further examination.[1]

Fantastic writing has, of course, existed as long as man has fabulated. It flourished in German Romanticism, has a strong tradition in Russia and Poland, and has recently achieved new popularity in English and American literature. It was not until 1970, however, that the first international symposium on science fiction took place. This symposium in Japan was followed in 1971 by a congress in Budapest, at which authors and proponents of fantastic literature from socialist countries met. At this latter conference it was resolved that science fiction should "promote friendship among nations, peace, and social progress."[2]

Although it is not the intent of this study to limit or to define fantastic literature--no one definition exists, nor would one suffice--some clarification is needed. Science fiction is the term which first comes to mind, and it was foremost in the minds of those writers who assembled in Japan and Budapest; but science fiction comprises obviously only one offshoot of a much broader field of literature. Generally a fantastic or supernatural situation occurs when the author distorts or ignores one or more laws of the natural order. This may manifest itself as a tinkering with chronology, as in Anna Seghers' "Reisebegegnung," a short story in which the non-contemporaries E.T.A. Hoffmann, Gogol, and Kafka meet in a Prague café.[3] Our normal concept of time is aufgehoben, and the author determines its limits. Futuristic or utopian writers often combine the dissolution of time with that of space, as Seghers did in the "Sage vom Unirdischen."[4] Here non-earthlings descend from outer space into the Germany of the late Middle Ages.

Another encroachment upon the rules of nature consists in reassigning the sex of one or more characters. Not elaborate hospital operations but mysterious science-fiction or fairy-tale devices bring about these transformations. The anthology Blitz aus heiterm Himmel contains perhaps the best-known GDR treatments of this theme, which has won new appeal with the current search for identity, more specifically, women's identity.[5]

The ancient, medieval, and romantic tellers of myths, fables, and fairy tales often endowed animals with human characteristics. Christa Wolf followed this tradition in her short story "Neue Lebensansichten eines Katers."[6] In modern science fiction, however, machines rather than animals usually replace man and man's mind, thus giving rise to futuristic, utopian, or, more correctly, anti-utopian literature. Many science-fiction stories could serve as examples here, outstanding among them not only Christa Wolf's "Neue Lebensansichten eines Katers," but also the charming parable by Günter and Johanna Braun, Der Irrtum des Großen Zauberers.[7]

In addition to the control of time, space, and sex and the use of technology, we find emphasis placed upon the depth and expanse of the human mind. The realm of dreams and daydreams can be mixed with or superimposed onto reality. Franz Fühmann's well-known introductory chapter to Das Judenauto,[8] which appeared already in 1962, and the more recent "Unter den Linden" by Christa Wolf, in her collection of stories by the same name,[9] both explore the mind's aberrations.

Fantastic literature appears to be inconsistent with socialist realism, which has been the official aesthetic theory in the GDR for many years. Fantasy, after all, does not reflect the processes of production, nor does it realistically portray the problems of the young republic. Acknowledging this apparent incongruity, various writers have discussed their use of the fantastic in their literary works.

To clarify her own concern about reality and fantasy, Anna Seghers orchestrated the imaginary encounter of Gogol, E.T.A. Hoffmann, and Kafka in "Reisebegegnung." Sufficient concrete details are provided so that the reader understands that the story takes place when Masaryk is in power and Kafka is aware of his impending death--which means it must take place between 1919 and 1924. In the story, Hoffmann arrives at the café where he is supposed to meet Gogol and notices a slim young man sitting by himself and writing feverishly. Kafka seems not in the least surprised when Hoffmann introduces himself; he expresses relief to learn at last what the initials E.T.A. stand for. Hoffmann engages Gogol and Kafka in a discussion about fantasy and reality. "Was die Leute für pure Phantasie halten, kann manchmal auch ein Stück handfeste Wirklichkeit enthalten," he exclaims (p. 122). Kafka, less outspoken, muses: "Sobald die Wirklichkeit in Geträumtes übergeht, und Träume gehören zweifellos zur Wirklichkeit--wozu sollten sie denn gehören?--, verstehen die Leser nicht viel" (p. 123). In a discussion about the necessity of retaining chronological order, Gogol chastises Hoffmann twice for treating time too frivolously. Hoffmann responds most convincingly when he points out: "Wir drei, wir säßen hier doch nicht beisammen an diesem Tisch, wenn wir ernstlich die Zeit einhalten würden. War ich nicht lange vor Ihnen, Gogol, geboren? Und Sie, Gogol, fast hundert Jahre vor Kafka?" (p. 127). Hoffmann summarizes the discussions about dreams and fantasies thus: "Symbolische oder phantastische Darstellungen, Märchen und Sagen wurzeln doch irgendwie in der Wirklichkeit. Genausogut wie greifbare Dinge. Ein richtiger Wald gehört zur Wirklichkeit, doch auch ein Traum von einem Wald" (p. 147). The story concludes with Gogol's return home to a good Russian meal consisting of bread, sausage, pickles, cold fish, and piroshki, and then a prosaic ride in a horse-drawn buggy back into the previous century.

In a somewhat lighter vein, Günter and Johanna Braun also engage the reader in a dispute about literary theory in the introductory piece of their pioneer project, Lichtjahr 1, the first GDR almanac of fantastic literature. 10 Their contribution, an ingenious fictional correspondence entitled "Briefe, die allerneuste Literatur betreffend," gives credit to H.G. Wells' time machine, which permits a correspondence between Herr Aristodemos, a Greek citizen of classical times, and the fictitious twentieth century gentleman Klaus Meier. The latter familiarizes his 2400-year-old pen pal with the term "utopian literature." Aristodemos becomes enraged that a term which means "no land" should be used to define a literature which creates other worlds and other ways of thinking.[11] Aristodemos finally and reluctantly accepts the term, misnomer though it may be, as applying to the Gegenwelt which Aristophanes created in his Birds. Klaus Meier cites Aristophanes' Women's Congress as another example of a Gegenwelt which suggests a reorganization of society--one in which all goods will be held in common. In it there will be neither rich nor poor, and neither slaves nor servants will be kept; ". . . Frauen werden für alle dasein und mit dem schlafen, mit dem sie es wünschen, und von dem ein Kind empfangen" (p. 26). In short, tantalizing possibilities are explored. Klaus Meier, presumably with the approval of the authors Braun, concludes the correspondence with the remark that mankind is still concerned with the very problems Aristophanes once considered: "die gerechte Verteilung des von Menschen Geschaffenen, die Gleichberechtigung für die Frau, die Abschaffung des Krieges, aber auch die Kunst, bislang unheilbar Kranke wieder gesund zu machen. Fliegen indes können wir bereits" (p. 28). This last laconic remark refers to Aristodemos' criticism of Aristophanes' sensational bestseller Peace, a work which the former considers "albern," simply because one of its human characters is endowed with the ability to fly.

The use of alienation to achieve a new perspective and thereby a critical stance vis-à-vis contemporary society and its problems is by no means a recent innovation. Narrators of myths and fairy tales have used alienation for centuries; Brecht did not invent it, nor did he corner the market. It is therefore not surprising that GDR writers of fantastic literature are turning their chronoscopes and telescopes on social problems and absurdities in the contemporary scene. Most science-fiction, utopian, and futuristic literature wishes to achieve precisely this focus. Three works, one well-known, "Neue Lebensansichten eines Katers" by Christa Wolf, the other two more whimsical and lesser known, Der Irrtum des Großen Zauberers by Günter and Johanna Braun and the more recent "Das Märchen vom Träumen" by Klaus Möckel,[12] will serve as examples.

"Neue Lebensansichten eines Katers" is the middle story in the volume Unter den Linden, published in 1974, and subtitled "Drei unwahrscheinliche Geschichten." A quotation from Hoffmann's Kater Murr precedes the satire, thus removing any doubt about the model for Max, the cat. While Hoffmann's tom cat discovers bourgeois vanity, Wolf's gives a terrifying account of the research of a three-man team made up of the psychologist Barzel, the sociologist Hinz, and the nutritionist and physiotherapist Dr. Fettback. The cat fulfills the threefold function of reporting the efforts of the team--this provides the framework of the story, participating personally in their research, and sabotaging their endeavors. The three scientists want to control certain aspects of human existence in order to achieve the utopian TOMEGL--Totales Menschenglück. According to them, TOMEGL will occur only when man is liberated from all weaknesses and impractical emotions such as selflessness, the spirit of adventure, and the love of fantasy. Max the cat enjoys surreptitiously rearranging the files in which human qualities are carefully catalogued, and delights in the confusion which results. In contrast to Max, who observes from his impish and critical feline point of view, Heinrich, the computer, encourages the three scientists to relentlessly purge humans of all but those qualities which Heinrich considers essential. When Dr. Hinz jokingly proposes to amputate creative thinking, Heinrich responds with "Bravo!" (p. 115). Imagination is struck; the appreciation of beauty, out; reason, out--it's only a hypothesis, after all. Sex? This decision becomes critical. Man must become a Reflexwesen if TOMEGL, Totales Menschenglück, is to come about. Finally, even the computer is saddened by the truncated possibilities, and Max, the faithful scribe, is unable to complete the manuscript. He dies of a cat's disease.

Just which form of society, the socialist or the capitalist, is taken to be the target of Christa Wolf's chastisement, depends on the bias of the reader. Horst Simon writes in the SED newspaper Neues Deutschland that socio-psychological research studies such as TOMEGL belong in "jene andere Welt."[13] Alexander Stephan, in his Autorenbuch Christa Wolf, seems to feel that the satire is directed against Wolf's own socialist country with its technological obsessions and planned structure.[14] That the overly

technological society, the society that can be cate-
gorized, computerized, and thereby manipulated, is to
be feared on both sides of the iron curtain is beyond
question. The year 1984 is almost upon us, and
Christa Wolf's appeal to mankind to remain human and
humane is surely a universal one.

A lighter and more optimistic counterpart to the
"Neue Lebensansichten eines Katers" is the parable by
Günter and Johanna Braun, Der Irrtum des Großen Zauberers. Subtitled "Ein phantastischer Roman," it is
indeed just that. In the land of Plikato, ruled by
the dictator Multiplikato, all citizens, young and
old, must eat daily rations of extraordinary pears,
which act as a pleasant, but mind-controlling nar-
cotic. Only the inquisitive and adventurous schoolboy
Oliver Input refuses his pear allotment. As the sole
pupil who still has the ability to reason and think
independently, Oliver is sent to the electronic academy, where he is taught, nourished, reprimanded when
necessary, but also praised when he deserves it, by a
computer. Eventually Oliver Input becomes the sorcer-
er-dictator's heir and finally outwits his ruler by
persuading him to partake of the mind-dulling pears
himself. In this fairy tale, the human qualities of
desire for adventure and independence, and the capacity to love, which the computer Heinrich and the three
scientists in Christa Wolf's story had insisted on
discarding, are the very traits which save not only
our hero, Oliver Input, but also eventually the people
of Plikato.

"Das Märchen vom Träumen," a short story in Klaus
Möckel's collection of fantastic tales, Die Gläserne
Stadt, singles out the ability to dream as one of
man's unique qualities. While pears render minds
obtuse in Der Irrtum des Großen Zauberers, a special
anti-dream pill keeps the inhabitants of the land of
Praktika on the straight path of useful reality. The
plot of the story is insignificant; the message is
clear. "Das große Gesetz, nach dem sich alles bewegt,
hieß: zweckmäßig. . . . Klar, daß im Land Praktika
kein Platz für Phantasterei blieb. . . . Die Technik
war dagegen allgemein geachtet und sehr weit entwik-
kelt" (pp. 65-66). The desire to fly, the dream of
the ancients, has been usefully fulfilled by technology, but now the impractical desire to dream needs
to be obliterated. All the authors, Christa Wolf, the
Brauns, and Klaus Möckel perceive man's dreams, "Phantasterei," as the quality which most distinguishes man

from the machine.

Man's ability to have visions need not be directed only towards the universe around him, but may reach
into the depth of his being. The search for identity,
a topic which has had great appeal in the GDR
literature of the last decade, has branched out to
include, on the one hand, the attempt of women to
define themselves within the strictures of socialist
society, and the attempt of male authors to formulate
their own sentiments about womanhood, on the other.
The use of the fantastic, the grotesque, and the
supernatural has been a safe and appropriate mode of
expression for these concerns.

The unique anthology _Blitz aus heiterm Himmel_,
resulting from Edith Anderson's invitation to GDR
authors to submit stories dealing with biological sex
change, pays due homage to the new awareness of the
role of women. The topic, of course, is not new.
Aristophanes wrote about such beings, and in the
literature of our own century Brecht's Shen-Te finds
it necessary to change into Shui-Ta whenever social
and economic pressures overwhelm her.

Sarah Kirsch's contribution to the anthology, the
title story "Blitz aus heiterm Himmel," though seemingly exuberant and carefree and ending happily,
includes a devastating indictment of her society.
(The story was written while Kirsch was still residing
in the GDR.) Katharina, the protagonist, alleviates
the monotony of housework by discovering patterns in
the colors and shapes of pieces of laundry she hangs
on the clothesline. Katharina enjoys provoking
people. Her boyfriend Albert's clothes are hung in
full view of the neighbors' inquisitive eyes. Traces
of Albert are everywhere in the small apartment; his
dirty dishes, the unconnected electric plug of the TV,
which he has not replaced after shaving, stones
brought back from his trips as a truckdriver. After
finishing her chores, Katharina falls asleep. In a
magic way she sleeps for three days. Awakening, she
realizes that she has all the physical characteristics
of a man. She readily accepts her new bodily features
and starts adjusting to her new life and therefore to
her new role also. The feminine clothes and no longer
appropriate furnishings are put away. Just as Katharina accepts her change without fuss, so does Albert
when he returns. Together they shovel coal, work on
the truck, and share the household tasks. "Jetzt, wo

81

ich selbern Kerl bin, jetz kriekich die Ehmannzipatz-
jon, dachte Max [Katharina]" (p. 21). And so, if Karl
Marx is correct in stating that social progress can be
measured by the status of the fair sex, society still
needs to change, for true partnership seems possible
only among equals--men.

One of the most outspoken and daring feminist
novels of the 1970s is Irmtraud Morgner's Leben und
Abenteuer der Trobadora Beatriz nach Zeugnissen ihrer
Spielfrau Laura.15 Morgner skillfully weaves a mam-
moth montage utilizing all the usual techniques of
fantastic literature. The passage of time is askew;
Beatriz, born in the Provence in 1130, awakens after a
sleep of 800 years. Her sister-in-law, the beautiful
Melusine, not only instructs her in the language and
customs of the 20th century but at times also provides
transportation on her dragon-like back. After reading
Marx and participating in the Paris revolution of
1968, Beatriz decides to seek the promised land, that
is, the German Democratic Republic. Dreams, fantasies, fairy tales, poems, magic formulas, a sphinx-
like dragon, and sex changes are liberally inter-
spersed in this collage. Later, when the troubadoura
sets out from Berlin to seek the renowned unicorn, she
leaves her work as Spielfrau in the able hands of her
friend, Laura Salman. Morgner's work ends on an
optimistic note in regard to her own country: "Denn
natürlich war das Land ein Ort des Wunderbaren" (p.
688). Morgner's message is clear; the style is innovative and manifold; the story, however, is unfortunately obfuscated by its complexity. Morgner, no
novice in the sort of writing that confronts realism
with forms of fantasy, explores all possibilities to
create utopia as she sees it. She affirms what her
heroine Beatriz reads on her way to Paris in 1968:
"Seid Realisten, verlangt das Unmögliche!" (p. 70) and
"Der Traum ist die Wirklichkeit!" (p. 70). Or the
words the Spielfrau Laura reads on the occasion of the
troubadoura's funeral: "die Menschen glauben große
Wahrheiten eher in unwahrscheinlichen Gewändern" (p.
683).

The unlikely, the unreal, the fantastic are
perhaps the only alternatives to utter confusion in
attempts to depict in literary form the innermost
subterfuges of the human mind. Two authors, both
steeped in German Romanticism, typify the "geheim-
nisvolle Weg nach Innen": Christa Wolf, once again,
especially as exemplified by her short story "Unter

den Linden," a dream-like tale reminiscent of Kafka, and Franz Fühmann, many of whose works, though rooted in reality, reveal the vagaries of the human mind by means of the supernatural. The work chosen here, however, is Erich Köhler's Der Krott, which plastically describes the mysterious side of man.[16]

Köhler, a miner as well as a writer, and deeply rooted in the productive process of his time and society, analyzes in his novel the creative force of both the material and the spiritual and the drawbacks of excessive sensitivity. The novel begins with a description of Paul Jordan's dream of a Garden of Eden, where nature is still in perfect balance and harmony. Later, in relating Paul's banal life in the workaday world, Köhler employs an inordinate number of passive grammatical constructions, as if to give evidence of the lack of initiative which prevents man from creating a new paradise. As Jordan then swims in a pond distantly reminiscent of the spring in which Novalis' Heinrich von Ofterdingen swam and which led to the Blaue Blume, the Krott attaches itself to Jordan's head. This parasytic animal always instills in its unwilling host such skepticism and acute sensitivity that the individual is no longer capable of performing his functions as before. While the other miners have their names written on their hard hats, Jordan carries his "Aufgabe," namely the Krott, under his hat. Hence the subtitle: "Das Ding unterm Hut." Jordan is finally miraculously liberated from the Krott by a sharp blow on the head rendered by a fellow worker and as he convalesces his creativity is restored to him.

Köhler, the author-theorist, may have limited skill in propounding fine points in discussion, but Köhler, the author-worker, does successfully metaphorically juxtapose the problems of production and the motives of man. If the invention of the Krott is intended to show workers the dangers of an exaggerated sensitivity, it has probably failed. Its reading public is confined largely to the educated; it is, for instance, unlikely that the chapter on the Kantian imperative as a means of changing the world will have wide appeal. Nevertheless, Köhler is not an amateur writer, and some of the passages in Der Krott, be they reportage or fantasy, are imaginative and moving.

Surveying GDR fantasy prose of the last decade, one can assert that it does offer relief from the

83

straightforward style of socialist realism. Both the
writers themselves and the literary critics agree that
forms of fantasy are in no way contradictory to
reality; on the contrary, fantasy can serve as an
expansion of realist possibilities. Karelski states
in his article on Anna Seghers' "Wiederbegegnung in
diesem Jahr" that her allegories and fantastic writings are "keine Abkehr von der Wirklichkeit, sondern
eine neuerliche Erweiterung ihres poetischen Blick-
felds."[17] As GDR literature has moved from describing
and promoting class struggle to portraying the individual in his new society, one notices the steady trend
towards the inconspicuous hero, who may be less heroic
than the earlier one, but whose inner struggles are
far more challenging than were the overtly social
problems of the GDR heroes of the 1950s and 1960s.

It remains debatable whether or not fantastic
literature serves "friendship among nations, peace,
and social progress," as was resolved at the Budapest
conference. It does make accessible, however, to a
wide reading public and in a variety of ways, the
hopes and fears for the future of our world, the
problems of our society, the role of the individual
within it and his self-awareness, as well as his own
fears and hopes. That the fantastic can articulate
all of these very tellingly has been demonstrated.
And if, as psychiatrists wish to convince us, insight
can free the individual to be more creative and productive, to be a liberated member of society, then the
Budapest resolution no longer seems so naively
visionary, and we may indeed be led to agree with
Christa Wolf, who, in her speech accepting the Büchner
Prize, declared: "Die Literatur muß heute Friedensforschung sein."[18]

Goucher College

                          Notes

    [1] See Heinz Entner's article "Mauserung einer
Gattung," Neue Deutsche Literatur, 24, No. 12 (1976),
137-153. Also an update of this article: "Gut ge-
meint--gut gedacht?" NDL, 28, No. 7 (1979), 153-158.

    [2] Jürgen Kagarlizki, Was ist Phantastik? (E.
Berlin: Das Neue Berlin, 1977), p. 14.

³ Anna Seghers, "Reisebegegnung," in her Sonderbare Begegnungen (Darmstadt and Neuwied: Luchterhand,
1973). Subsequent parenthetical references in the
text are to this edition.

⁴ Anna Seghers, "Sage vom Unirdischen," in her
Sonderbare Begegnungen.

⁵ Blitz aus heiterm Himmel, ed. Edith Anderson
(Rostock: Hinstorff, 1975). A shortened version
appeared in the FRG in 1980 under the title Geschlechtertausch (Darmstadt and Neuwied: Luchterhand, 1980).
This volume includes only "Blitz aus heiterm Himmel"
by Sarah Kirsch, "Selbstversuch" by Christa Wolf, and
"Die gute Botschaft der Valeska" by Irmtraud Morgner,
from her novel Leben und Abenteuer der Trobadora
Beatriz nach Zeugnissen ihrer Spielfrau Laura. This
last selection was not included in the GDR version.
The FRG version was used in this study and page references in the text refer to this edition.

⁶ Christa Wolf, "Neue Lebensansichten eines
Katers," in her Unter den Linden (Darmstadt: Luchterhand, 1974). Parenthetical page notations appearing
below in the text refer to this edition.

⁷ Günter and Johanna Braun, Der Irrtum des Großen
Zauberers (E. Berlin: Das Neue Berlin, 1972).

⁸ Franz Fühmann, Das Judenauto (E. Berlin and
Weimar: Aufbau, 1962).

⁹ Christa Wolf, "Unter den Linden," in her Unter
den Linden.

¹⁰ Lichtjahr 1: ein Phantastik Almanach (E.
Berlin: Das Neue Berlin, 1980). Subsequent references
will appear parenthetically in the text.

¹¹ Note that the title of Christa Wolf's novel
Kein Ort. Nirgends is a literal translation of
"utopia."

¹² Klaus Möckel, "Das Märchen vom Träumen," in
his Die Gläserne Stadt (E. Berlin: Das Neue Berlin,
1980). References appearing in the text below are to
this edition.

¹³ Horst Simon, "Zur Erfindung dessen, den man

lieben kann," Neues Deutschland, October 1974, as cited by Alexander Stephan in his Christa Wolf (Munich: Beck, 1976), p. 113.

[14] Alexander Stephan, Christa Wolf, p. 112.

[15] Irmtraud Morgner, Leben und Abenteuer der Trobadora Beatriz nach Zeugnissen ihrer Spielfrau Laura (E. Berlin and Weimar: Aufbau, 1974). Subsequent references will appear parenthetically in the text.

[16] Erich Köhler, Der Krott oder das Ding unterm Hut (Rostock: Hinstorff, 1980). References appearing in the text are to this edition.

[17] A. Karelski, "Wiederbegegnung in diesem Jahr," NDL, 28, No. 11 (1980), 148.

[18] Wolf, "Den Bestand des Irdischen sichern helfen," Neue Zürcher Zeitung, 18/19 Oct. 1980, pp. 65-66.

Von "italienischen Amseln" und "provenzalischen Eulen": Sarah Kirschs westliche Dichtungen Drachensteigen und La Pagerie

Christine Cosentino

Als Betrachter von deutsch-deutscher Literatur kann man kaum umhin, Vermutungen über die künstlerische Zukunft jener exilierten Künstler anzustellen, die den Wechsel von der DDR in die BRD vollzogen haben. Man denkt u.a. an Wolf Biermann, Sarah Kirsch, Reiner Kunze, Thomas Brasch, Jürgen Fuchs, Hans-Joachim Schädlich und Jurek Becker--Künstler also, die politisch in Mißkredit geraten sind und die als Republikverbannte, freiwillig Ausgebürgerte oder (wie im Falle Jurek Beckers) als Empfänger eines langjährigen Dauervisums Einzug in die Bundesrepublik hielten. Die Tatsache, daß es sich hier um in der DDR großgewordene, ehemalige prominente Parteimitglieder handelt, die das Kulturbild der DDR mitbestimmten, führt zu der spekulativen Frage, wie sich diese Künstler in den bundesdeutschen Kulturbetrieb eingliedern lassen. Bleiben diese Schriftsteller in ihrer Themenwahl der DDR auch weiterhin verhaftet, so müßte man von "DDR-Künstlern im Exil" sprechen; gelingt es ihnen jedoch, den Polit- und Kulturschock zu überwinden und sich anzupassen, so würde man sie als "bundesdeutsche Autoren" ansehen müssen; und sollten sie den Weg politischer Mitte oder völlig unpolitischer Mitte einschlagen, so bestände die fragliche Möglichkeit, ein gesamtdeutsches Publikum anzusprechen. Neben diesen, auf künstlerisches Weiterwirken ausgerichteten Spekulationen, gibt es jedoch noch eine vierte, nämlich die des künstlerischen Ruhestandes, des Verstummens.

Blicken wir auf den Fall Sarah Kirsch, die als eine der bedeutendsten zeitgenössischen deutschen Lyrikerinnen gilt. Sie war Parteimitglied, Mitglied

des Schriftstellerverbandes und gelangte zu Ruhm und
Ehren hauptsächlich als Autorin von drei Lyriksammlungen: Landaufenthalt (1967),[1] Zaubersprüche (1973)[2]
und Rückenwind (1976).[3] Ihre Gedichte waren vorwiegend Natur- und Liebesgedichte, die sich vordergründig
von plakativen Politaussagen freihielten, hinter-
gründig jedoch durch komplizierte, interpunktionsarme
Satzverschränkungen und zwielichtige Metapherntechnik
politische Signale ausstrahlten. Ihre zweideutigen,
sich bedeutungsmäßig überlagernden Gedichte bezeich-
nete Kirsch selbst in einem Gespräch mit Schülern in
Westberlin als Gedichte offenen Spielraums, in denen
der Leser nicht festgelegt wird.[4] Als sich Kirsch im
November 1976 für den zwangsausgebürgerten Politsänger
Wolf Biermann einsetzte, wurde sie von der Liste der
Partei gestrichen und fühlte sich Schikanen ausgesetzt. Im August 1977 übersiedelte die Künstlerin
nach Westberlin. Seit diesem Ortswechsel sind zwei
neue literarische Werke erschienen: 1979 der schmale
Band Drachensteigen[5] und 1980 das noch schmalere
Bändchen La Pagerie.[6] Es ergibt sich hier die Frage,
inwieweit sich der politisch-kulturelle Klimawechsel
auf Kirschs Künstlertum ausgewirkt hat, ob er sich in
ihrer Themenwahl und Sprachstruktur niederschlägt.
Blicken wir zunächst auf Kirschs eigene Aussagen, die
sie in einigen Interviews im Westen über ihre Rolle
als Künstlerin in der BRD machte und prüfen wir dann,
ob das offiziell Gesagte mit den im Westen entstandenen literarischen Werken in Einklang steht.

1978, in dem erwähnten "Gespräch mit Schülern"
des Französischen Gymnasiums in Westberlin, ist sich
Sarah Kirsch über ihre erfolgreiche Integration in den
westlichen Kulturbetrieb sicher: "ich glaube nicht,"
sagt sie, "daß sich die Art, wie ich schreibe . . .
beeinflussen läßt oder daß ich hier alles völlig
anders mache, weil ich denke: im Westen schreibt man
anders. . . ."[7] Diese Überzeugung bestätigt sie in
einem zweiten Interview, das am 3. Mai 1979 von Hans
Ester und Dick von Stekelenburg in Amsterdam geführt
wurde. Kirsch bekennt sich durchaus zu ihrer mit der
DDR verbundenen Vergangenheit, der sie viel verdankt,
ihrem Kontakt mit Menschen der DDR und ihrer Zusammen-
arbeit mit dortigen Dichtern und Kollegen. Sie räumt
allerdings ein, daß "andererseits . . . andere Lebens-
verhältnisse sich auf das Resultat letzten Endes nicht
so unterschiedlich ausgewirkt hätten."[8] Damit stellt
sie die Auffassung in Frage, daß ihre Dichtung nicht
anders denkbar sei, als unter den besonderen sozialistischen Bedingungen der DDR.[9] Kirsch lehnt es ab, als

"DDR-Autorin" oder "DDR-Autorin im Exil" etikettisiert zu werden:

> Nein, ich bin überhaupt nicht im Exil.
> . . . Es ist dieselbe Sprache. Ich habe keine großen Schwierigkeiten, mich in eine andere Mentalität einleben zu müssen. Ich empfinde mich als einen deutschsprachigen Schriftsteller, weiter nichts. Es ist nicht so, daß ich mich nun mein Leben lang als DDR-Dichter fühle. . . . Ich habe manchmal -- ein bißchen übertreibend--gesagt, ich bin nur umgezogen.[10]

Kirsch scheint also auf eine deutsch-deutsche Leserschaft zu zielen. Auf die Frage, ob sich mit ihrem Umzug ihr Ausdrucksgestus ändern werde--das komplizierte Spannungsverhältnis zu Staat, Gesellschaft und Publikum--und ob damit ein wesentlicher Impetus zum So-und-nicht-anders-Schreiben wegfalle, antwortet Kirsch:

> Nein, ich glaube nicht daran, ein solches Spannungsverhältnis kann sich woanders auch einstellen; der Schriftsteller reibt sich immer an einer gesellschaftlichen Umwelt--das ist universell. Es nimmt ein wenig Zeit, bis man sich in einem anderen gesellschaftlichen System zurechtgefunden hat, bis man dort, wie man es in der DDR war, in positivem wie in negativem Sinne zuhause ist.[11]

Zusammenfassend läßt sich also sagen, daß Kirsch sich als deutsch-deutsche Dichterin empfindet; daß sie glaubt, bei der Anpassung an die bundesdeutsche Mentalität keine großen Schwierigkeiten zu haben; daß das Spannungsverhältnis zur Gesellschaft auch weiterhin, unter neuen Bedingungen, bestehen bleibe, d.h., daß sich der ihr typische Ausdrucksgestus nicht ändern werde. Zugegeben wird allerdings, daß der Integrationsprozeß ein wenig Zeit in Anspruch nehmen wird. Kirsch lebt jetzt seit ungefähr dreieinhalb Jahren auf westlichem Boden, und man fragt sich, ob ihr künstlerisches Schaffen ihre Aussagen bestätigt.

Blickt man auf die in der Bundesrepublik veröffentlichten Werke Drachensteigen (1979) und La Pagerie

(1980), so kann man sich des Eindrucks nicht erwehren,
daß sich Kirsch mit ihrer Annahme über eine relativ
reibungslose Anpassung an eine andere Mentalität etwas
übernommen hat. Es scheint, daß sie die Zeitspanne
für das Sich-Einleben in ein anderes gesellschaft-
liches System unterschätzt hat. Das, was in nur "ein
wenig Zeit" geschehen sollte, scheint sich nun doch in
einem langwierigeren Prozeß abzuwickeln. Das auffällige Fehlen bundesdeutscher Problematik, also des
gesellschaftlichen Spannungsverhältnisses unter neuen
Bedingungen, weist darauf hin, daß die Künstlerin
immer noch verunsichert und in der BRD noch nicht
völlig "zuhause" ist. Das faszinierend Zweideutige
des offenen Spielraums, das ihren DDR-Gedichten inne-
wohnte, erscheint in ihren beiden neuen Werken ge-
dämpft oder tritt völlig in den Hintergrund, vermutlich, weil sich die Dichterin immer noch im Eindeu-
tigen bundesdeutscher Wirklichkeit zurechtzufinden
versucht.

Der 1979 erschienene Lyrikband Drachensteigen ist
ein schmaler Band im Vergleich zu den Lyriksammlungen,
die in der DDR entstanden sind. Im Landaufenthalt
befanden sich 56 Gedichte, in den Zaubersprüchen 63
und im Rückenwind 62. Der neue Band Drachensteigen
enthält 40 Gedichte, von denen die ersten neun noch in
Ostberlin entstanden sind. Das zehnte Gedicht, "Der
Rest des Fadens," spiegelt den Schnitt zwischen Ost
und West, denn es ist der erste Text aus Westberlin.
Kirsch weist in einem Nachwort selbst darauf hin.
Fünf weitere Gedichte folgen, ebenfalls in Westberlin
geschrieben, und dann macht die Dichterin einen weiteren Schnitt. Nach den erwähnten 15, in Ost- und
Westberlin geschriebenen Gedichten, die unter dem
vielsagenden Titel "Allerleirauh" zusammengefaßt sind,
folgt ein zweiter Teil von 25, ausschließlich in
Italien entstandenen Gedichten, genannt "Italienische
Amseln." Aus der Anordnung der Gedichte erhält der
Leser folglich biographische Informationen. Die
ersten neun, noch in Ostberlin geschriebenen Gedichte,
fallen in die Zeit nach der Biermannaffaire im November 1976. Sie spiegeln ein lyrisches Ich, das sich
nach dem in Westberlin lebenden Geliebten sehnt, das
sich verlassen und politischen Schikanen ausgesetzt
fühlt: "Ich war Komparse in einem fortlaufenden Film,
dessen Handlung mir niemand erklärte," heißt es in dem
Gedicht "V." (S. 11); oder wir hören: "Nachts führe
ich Telefongespräche und eile in der Stadt umher. Das
ist ungefährlich, vor den wichtigen Gebäuden treten
höchstens Posten aus dem Nebel und wieder hinein"

90

("Nebel," S. 10). In dem Gedicht "Der Rest des Fadens," das die politische Nahtstelle darstellt, wird der Bruch vollzogen: der Geduldsfaden ist gerissen, symbolisch der Faden, der einen Drachen hält; der Stern aus Papier ist unhaltbar geworden; er entfernt sich ins Weite. Am Ende dieses doppelbödigen Gedichts vom Typ des offenen Spielraums wird die Bilanz gezogen: "Uns gehört der Rest des Fadens, und daß wir dich kannten" (S. 16). Die folgenden, ebenfalls in Westberlin geschriebenen Gedichte stehen immer noch unter dem Eindruck des Bruchs, des räumlich-politischen Ortswechsels. Von der Mauer, "dem furchtbaren Ort" ist die Rede ("The Last of November," S. 17) und von einer in die Brüche gegangenen Liebe, vom "Dichter M. im Grunewald," der das "Gedächtnis verloren" hat (S. 18).

Der zweite Teil des Drachensteigens, der eine auffällige Hinwendung zur Prosa zeigt, steht unter dem Zeichen einer neuen, erfüllenden Liebe und neuen Eindrücken in einem anderen Land, Italien. Kirsch hielt sich seit Mai 1978 als Stipendiatin der BRD in der römischen Villa Massimo auf, wo sie den notwendigen politischen Abstand nahm. Bei diesem Abstand scheint es jedoch geblieben zu sein, denn in diesem zweiten Teil des Drachensteigens, den "Italienischen Amseln," sowohl wie in dem 1980 folgenden Band La Pagerie, fehlt--hintergründig und vordergründig--das Thema politischer und gesellschaftlicher Reibung in der BRD. Kirsch hält sich von Reflexionen über die BRD völlig fern, und die wenigen gesellschaftspolitischen Aussagen, die sie macht, beziehen sich ausschließlich auf die DDR. Die Dichterin nimmt Distanz von Deutschland, indem sie sich auf dem politisch neutralen Boden des Auslands bewegt. Ihre Themen in den beiden neuen Bänden sind Urlaub, Reisen, Natur und Liebe. Das ist nichts Neues. Das waren auch vorher bevorzugte Themen. Was fehlt, ist der gesellschafts-politische Hintergrund, an dem sich das lyrische Ich reibt, das Spannungsverhältnis, das Kirschs früheren Gedichten den irritierend zweideutigen Ausdrucksgestus gab, den "Sarah-Sound," wie ihn Peter Hacks einmal bewundernd nannte.[12] Hat sich Kirsch--für den Augenblick jedenfalls--in eine Art Elfenbeinturm des Persönlichen, der Liebe und politisch unverbindlicher Natur- und Reisedichtung zurückgezogen? Blicken wir auf die beiden Auslandsdichtungen, "Italienische Amseln" aus dem Drachensteigen und La Pagerie, etwas näher, denn auch hier lassen sich Unterschiede feststellen, die zu vorsichtigen Vermutungen über neue Richtungen, neue

Trends im künstlerischen Schaffen Kirschs Anlaß geben.

Kirschs Italiengedichte in den "Italienischen Amseln" sind dem Gefühl des Glücks in einer neuen Liebe und in einem neuen Landschaftserlebnis entsprungen. Immer wieder wird dem Leser das Gelöstsein des lyrischen Ichs versichert: "Ich bin glücklich in Italien," heißt es ("Brief," S. 47) und: "Die Wiese durchwächst mich in sieben Stunden. Ich stehe mit jedem Fuß in einem anderen Brunnen und schlage mir das Glück aus dem Kopf" ("Die Wiese," S. 25). Sie macht die schlichte Feststellung: "Ich gewöhn mich ins Glück" ("Kiesel," S. 44). Kirsch gestaltet eine Landschaft, die mit allen Sinnen erlebt wird. Sinnliches ist Natürliches: "Das ist ein schöner Tag. Ich setze mich in ihn hinein, die Eukalyptusblätter fliegen ab und auf, sehr lange auf, und seh ich den Baumleib nackt und weiß weiß ich was das ist ein schöner Tag" ("Dankbillett," S. 26). Ihre Gedichte sind Liebes- und Naturgedichte, denn Liebe wird als Natur erlebt: "Wir . . . reden / Natürlich; einer in der Haut des anderen" ("Licht," S. 41).

Auch Kirschs frühere Liebesgedichte waren von starker Intensität und ungehemmter Erotik. Was in diesen neuen Gedichten fehlt, ist der spannungsreiche Spielraum der verschiedensten Gefühle, der etwa in den Zaubersprüchen vorhanden war: wildes Verlangen, Ungeduld, Ärger, Hingabe, Wut und oft brutal anmutender Besitzanspruch auf den Mann. Die Italiengedichte sind gelöst und beinahe märchenhaft: "Jeder Baum am richtigen Fleck. Man könnte sagen Felder gibts die mein Herz sind: blauer Weizen und Mohnblumen reingeworfen. . . . Tage später träume ich den Platz. Drauf stehen, die ich liebe, nun zwei" ("Die Toscana," S. 30). Die Welt ist in Ordnung, zumindest die privat-erotische. Kirsch kann es nicht häufig genug versichern: "Die Landschaft ist groß und voller Bewegung. . . . Er legt mir die Hand in den Schoß" ("Das schöne Tal," S. 42); "In Olevano / Fangen die Berge / Im Schlafzimmer an" ("Rot," S. 43); "Das Bett hat sich / Weit von der Wand entfernt, die Bewegung / Ist groß" ("Verloren," S. 46). Es ist eine Liebe mit dem Reiz der Neuheit, in einer neuen Landschaft, im Urlaub, in einer "Extra-Welt" ("Viele Farben," S. 49), entfernt von deutsch-deutschen Problemen: "Ich lebe in Saus und Braus, du spazierst / In meinem Kopf den ganzen / Verrückten Sommer" ("Jetzt," S. 45). Nur gelegentlich melden sich Erinnerungen an die DDR. In einem "Dankbillett" reflektiert die Dichterin: "Die ganz scharfen Carabi-

nieri--warum fällt mir das Militär immer noch ein--
halten Wache mit Federhüten und rauchen; alles anders
als in Preußen . . . ach wie danke ich meinem vorletz-
ten Staat, daß er mich hierher katapultierte" (S. 26);
oder sie kommt zu dem Schluß: "Die Zeit heilt Wunden .
. . italienische Amseln sind besser als ihre Verwand-
ten aus Deutschland" ("Italienische Amseln," S. 27).

Bemerkte man bereits im Drachensteigen eine
größere Hinwendung zur Prosa, so ist der nun folgende,
1980 erschienene Band La Pagerie völlig in Prosa geschrieben. Wiederum handelt es sich um eine Art
Reise-, Auslands- oder Urlaubsliteratur, aber die
poetische Transformation der Welt in Bilder und Asso-
ziationen tritt in den Hintergrund zugunsten von
nüchterneren, sachlicheren Beobachtungen in zumeist
lapidarem Grundton. In 55 Prosaminiaturen schildert
Kirsch die Landschaft der Provence, wo sie mit ihrem
Freund einen Urlaub verbrachte. Es handelt sich um
eine Mischung von tagebuchartigen Reflexionen, Notizen
und photographisch anmutenden Momentaufnahmen der
südfranzösischen Landschaft. In dieser Landschaft--
das überrascht nicht--wird die Handlung von den beiden
Liebenden vorangetrieben. Aber auch dieses Thema wird
prosaischer gestaltet. Es ist immer noch derselbe
Mann aus den "Italienischen Amseln," und es scheint,
als mokiere sich Kirsch über sich selbst, über ihre
frühere Unbeständigkeit und Zerrissenheit in Liebes-
verhältnissen.

In der Nähe des Ortes Fontaine-de-Vaucluse an der
Sorgue begegnet sie Petrarca und Laura, denen sie
Jahre zuvor schon einmal, mit einem anderen Geliebten
--so wissen wir es aus dem Band Rückenwind--in den Weg
gelaufen war. Die beiden sind älter geworden, und
Petrarca beklagt sich bitter über die Menschheit, die
in den "Banden der Gewohnheit fest gebunden" ist (S.
26). Damit nicht genug. Der berühmte Verfasser der
Liebessonette an Laura "zeigte auf die Toiletten der
Gasthäuser, die sehr direkt über der Sorgue hingen und
keinen Hehl daraus machten, wie einfach sie hier seit
Jahrhunderten Kanalisationsprobleme lösen" (S. 27).

Die Ironie ist evident. Kirsch bleibt in diesem
schmalen Urlaubs- und Reisebüchlein auf dem Boden der
Realität. Sie wartet mit Berichten auf, die beides,
scharf beobachtet und lyrisch untermalt, aber kaum
doppelbödig oder zwielichtig sind. Anklänge an ihren
früheren metaphernschweren, satzzeichenarmen Ausdrucksgestus findet man in lyrischen Betrachtungen wie

den folgenden: "Mittags kommen die Falter. Buntes
Seidenpapier, zarte Drachen in Rosa Rot Gelb" (S. 13);
oder: "Das Glück springt mich an" (S. 11); oder in der
zweiten Miniatur, in der sie ihr Urlaubsdomizil
beschreibt:

> Im Garten von La Pagerie, einem Schlöß-
> chen an der Stelle, wo die Camargue in
> die Provence überläuft, sitzt eine rote
> gebrannte Dame und liest in einem Buch
> seit hundert Jahren die gleiche Seite.
> Derart versunken hat der Efeu sie über-
> wachsen. Der Wind bewegt ein einzelnes
> Blatt auf ihrem Finger. Der endlose
> Himmel die verwirbelten Wölkchen darin,
> der uralte Mann auf dem Trecker von
> 1902—verwunschenes Lachen.   (S. 6)

Trotz romantischer Requisiten wird die Welt von
La Pagerie jedoch nicht verwunschen und märchenhaft
gestaltet. Verblichene Rokokomöbel, Tapetentüren, ur-
alte Gemälde und Galerien ohne Treppen, in denen Eulen
leben, deuten auf Verfall und Verarmung, auf die fi-
nanziellen Probleme des Patrons, der gezwungen ist,
Zimmer zu vermieten und der sich hilflos wehrt, das
Schlößchen vor der Vermarktung für den Tourismus zu
retten. Kirsch reflektiert darüber:

> Wie haben Sie das Haus hier gefunden,
> Monsieur . . . ? Und wenn Sie vorüber-
> gefahren wären an dem Tag, als Sie
> Kopfschmerzen hatten, und nicht mit dem
> Stein angeklopft hätten - wie wäre Ihre
> Biographie verlaufen? Und wenn kein
> Geld dagewesen wäre für den Ausbau -
> und ist jetzt etwas da? Mit uns ver-
> dienen Sie nichts, das ist klar.
>   (S. 8)

Oder sie notiert sachlich:

> Das ist kein Hotel. Hier gibt es nur
> unsern Patron und Thibalde, den Hund.
> Monsieur holt mit dem Auto Croissants
> Milch und Butter, deckt den Frühstücks-
> tisch wenn wir noch schlafen. Er be-
> sorgt das Haus allein. . . . Hat Wein
> für uns. Trinkt selber keinen. Wir
> haben die schöneren Zimmer. (S. 9)

94

Kirsch macht Notizen über Waldbrände, Raketen-
stellungen, den Mistral, amerikanische Touristen in
einem weißen Cadillac, die La Pagerie kaufen wollen,
und sie wandelt auf den Spuren künstlerischer Vorgänger: im Kloster von St. Remy etwa, wo sie etwas "über
Vincent erfahren will" (S. 28), in der Mühle Daudets
und am Denkmal Petrarcas. Der Leser folgt ihr durch
die Landschaft der Provence, durch Bergdörfer, in die
Täler und ans Meer. Die meisten der Miniaturen sind
kurz; die kürzesten bestehen aus nur einem Satz oder
zweien, wie etwa die folgenden: "Ein riesiges
Schlauchboot segelt quer durch die Luft" (S. 42);
oder: "Es gibt Warnschilder an der Straße mit einem
bockigen Schaf. Es hat zu lange und dünne Beine und
ist immer dasselbe" (S. 44). Auch an geschichtlichen
und sozialen Reflexionen fehlt es nicht. Die Prote-
stantenverfolgungen in Frankreich werden erwähnt: "Im
18. Jahrhundert stach man in diesem Landstrich, wenn
sie verraten worden waren, den Protestanten die Augen
aus" (S. 46). Ein Lied aus dem Jahre 1940 kommt ihr
beim Autofahren in den Sinn, das Soldatenlied vom
Polenmädchen: "Wer weiß wie weiß die Knöchlein nun
sind" (S. 52); und in einem Bergdorf sieht sie ara-
bische Arbeiter, die keine französischen Freundinnen
haben, denn "welcher Vater würde das seiner Tochter
erlauben, bis gestern besaß man Kolonien" (S. 53).

Sechsmal wird direkt oder indirekt die DDR erwähnt. Das Thema bedrückenden Eingeschlossenseins,
strenger Reisebeschränkungen und politischer Schikanen
beim Ausländergrenzübertritt wird berührt: "Abends
reden wir über die Welt. Beratschlagen, wieviel Kar-
ten mit verführerischen Bildern wir unseren Freunden
ins kleine Land schicken können. Daß sie nicht trau-
rig werden oder unsere Grüße als Nötigung ansehn" (S.
16). Oder, sich an eine frühere Frankreichreise erin-
nernd, auf der sie sich "aus dem Lande mogeln mußte,"
konstatiert sie: "Jetzt besitze ich einen fröhlicheren
Paß, ein rechtes Sesam-öffne-dich-Blättchen ohne die
Angst das seh ich nicht wieder" (S. 23); und von Mon-
sieur, dem Besitzer des Schlößchens La Pagerie, wird
berichtet, auch er sei einmal in Ostberlin gewesen:
"Da hatte er Schwierigkeiten mit seinem gültigen Paß
wegen eines Barts auf dem Foto den er nicht trug, und
lieber würde er sich erschießen, als dort zu leben"
(S. 50). An die Ursache des Übels, an die Mauer, wird
in einer kurzen Notiz erinnert: "Montag, der 13.
August"--ein Datum, an dem selbst die sonst so sanften
provenzalischen Eulen, die nächtlichen Gesprächspart-
ner der beiden Liebenden, aufsässig werden und "mes-

95

singne Glöckchen an den Füßen [tragen]. Da stieben
sie über die Dächer" (S. 18). Der einzige indirekte
Bezug auf die BRD liegt in der Erwähnung des neuen
Passes, daß sie also Bürgerin eines Staates ist, der
ihr unbegrenzte Bewegungsfreiheit gewährt.

Rückblickend und zusammenfassend läßt sich fol-
gendes feststellen: die beiden im Westen entstandenen
Werke Drachensteigen und La Pagerie sind quantitativ
reduzierter als die in der DDR erschienenen Werke.
Vom ersten Teil des Drachensteigens, dem "Allerleirauh," abgesehen, handelt es sich um Auslands-,
Reise-, Natur- und Liebesdichtung, vorwiegend in Prosa
geschrieben. Die Bundesrepublik wird nicht erwähnt.
Da somit das Thema des gesellschaftlichen Spannungsverhältnisses von Individuum und Staat noch nicht
berührt ist, vermißt man den für Kirsch sonst so
typischen, faszinierend zweideutigen Ausdrucksgestus
des offenen Spielraums, der ihren DDR-Gedichten eigen
war. Zwielichtig schillernde Bildverschlingungen und
komplizierte Satzverschränkung treten in den Hintergrund, besonders im Band La Pagerie. Kirschs Stil
zeigt hier eine Wendung vom Zweideutigen zum Eindeu-
tigen. Trotz lyrischer Grundhaltung bemerkt man ein
Betonen des Objektiven, also den Stil eines nüchterneren, sachlicheren, vereinfachteren Registrierens.

Damit sei kein Werturteil verbunden. Kirschs
westliche Auslandsdichtung hat ihren eigenen Reiz und
sagt etwas Wesentliches über die Künstlerin aus. Das
Umschalten auf ein anderes politisches System nimmt
Zeit in Anspruch und kann entweder zum temporären
Verstummen führen oder zur Wahl von neutral unverbind-
lichem Territorium, wie das Ausland. Kirsch scheint
sich ihrer augenblicklichen Position der Unverbind-
lichkeit bewußt zu sein, denn in dem erwähnten Interview in Amsterdam spricht sie einerseits von Ent-
deckerfreude und der unbegrenzten Eroberung neuer
Landschaften, die ihr vor 1977 untersagt war--was
überzeugt. Andererseits reflektiert sie zweifelnd
(und daraus könnte man Unbehagen der Künstlerin ent-
nehmen): "Ich hoffe, daß meine Reisebilder trotzdem
keine Tourismus-Gedichte geworden sind. . . . Natürlich kann da jeder sagen: Das ist alles so leicht und
unverbindlich; wo bleiben die gesellschaftlichen
Probleme?"[13] Politik hatte sie zwar auch in ihren
DDR-Gedichten nie plakativ betrieben, und doch war ihr
Verwurzeltsein in der DDR trotz Zweifels und unter-
kühlter Reflexionen überall spürbar. Dichtung der
Zukunft, die das lyrische Ich in irgendeinem Reibungs-

verhältnis mit der BRD zeigen würde, wäre der erste
Hinweis, daß diese begabte, phantasiereiche, DDR-
geprägte Dichterin nicht nur "umgezogen" ist--wie sie
einmal sagte--sondern wirklich eingezogen und "zuhause" ist.

Rutgers University-Camden

Anmerkungen

[1] Sarah Kirsch, Landaufenthalt (Ebenhausen: Langewiesche-Brandt, 1969).

[2] Kirsch, Zaubersprüche (Ebenhausen: Langewiesche-Brandt, 1973).

[3] Kirsch, Rückenwind (Ebenhausen: Langewiesche-
Brandt, 1976).

[4] Kirsch, "Ein Gespräch mit Schülern," Erklärung
einiger Dinge (Ebenhausen: Langewiesche-Brandt, 1978),
S. 13. Eine erweiterte Ausgabe von Erklärung einiger
Dinge ist 1981 bei Rowohlt erschienen.

[5] Kirsch, Drachensteigen (Ebenhausen: Langewiesche-Brandt, 1979). Die Seitenzahlen für die aus
diesem Band zitierten Gedichte befinden sich im Text
der Arbeit.

[6] Kirsch, La Pagerie (Stuttgart: Deutsche Ver-
lags-Anstalt, 1980). Seitenzahlen für Zitate aus
diesem Band befinden sich im Text der Arbeit.

[7] Kirsch, "Ein Gespräch mit Schülern," S. 25.

[8] Hans Ester und Dick von Stekelenburg, "Gespräch
mit Sarah Kirsch," Deutsche Bücher, 9, No. 2 (1979),
S. 107. Nachdruck des Gesprächs in: Sarah Kirsch,
Erklärung einiger Dinge. Dokumente und Bilder (Reinbek bei Hamburg: Rowohlt, 1981), S. 66-81.

[9] "Gespräch mit Sarah Kirsch," S. 107.

[10] "Gespräch mit Sarah Kirsch," S. 107.

[11] "Gespräch mit Sarah Kirsch," S. 108.

[12] Peter Hacks, "Der Sarah-Sound," in seinen
Maßgaben der Kunst. Gesammelte Aufsätze (Düsseldorf:
Claassen, 1977), S. 268.

[13] "Gespräch mit Sarah Kirsch," S. 108-109.

Traditionelle und moderne Idyllen: Überlegungen zu Uwe Greßmanns Der Vogel Frühling

Wolfgang Ertl

Uwe Greßmanns Biographie erinnert, wie Axel Schulze schreibt, an Romane von Dickens. Der 1933 in Berlin geborene Dichter wurde in Waisenhäusern und Kinderheimen aufgezogen, begann 1949 eine Lehre als Elektroinstallateur, verbrachte fünf Jahre im Krankenhaus mit schwerer Tuberkulose, war dann tätig als Montierer, Bote und Postabfertiger, ein "physisch gebrochener Mann, der im Alter von sechsunddreißig Jahren in einem immer beharrlicher geführten Kampf der Krankheit unterliegt." [1] Seinen Vater hat Greßmann nie gesehen, und die Mutter verließ ihn nach etwa drei Wochen. "Sonst lebte ich unter Fremden," schrieb Greßmann in einer autobiographischen Aufzeichnung. [2] Durch autodidaktisches Studium fand er den Weg zur Literatur und veröffentlichte 1961 zum ersten Mal in der Zeitschrift Neue Deutsche Literatur Gedichte.

"Greßmann . . . gibt uns Rätsel auf," sagt Adolf Endler in seinem Vorwort zu dem 1966 erschienenen ersten Lyrikband des Dichters, dessen allegorisierender Titel Der Vogel Frühling allein schon befremden mag. [3] Es sei schwer, "sich der Magie Greßmanns zu entziehen," heißt es weiter. Die "Visionen des Lyrikers," so vermutet Endler, "werden wahrscheinlich gespeist von der Spannung zwischen einem 'naiven' Weltbild und der Beunruhigung des Dichters durch die Mitteilungen der modernen Naturwissenschaften." Das mache die "bedrängende Aktualität dieser Gedichte aus" (S. 6). Genauer zu untersuchen ist aber, worin diese magische Anziehungskraft und das Visionäre dieser Gedichte bestehen und welcher Art diese Naivität ist.

So scheut sich Greßmann zum Beispiel nicht vor einer kindlich-naiven Anrede an Arkadien, als trauere er einem pastoralen Leben in glückseliger Isolation nach, was eine gehörige Portion Weltfremdheit vermuten ließe. Aber schon in den ersten beiden Strophen des Gedichtes "An Arkadia" wird weder ein bukolisches Paradies beschworen noch eine utopische Vision entfaltet:

Die Straßen sind des Stadtbaumes Äste,
Wie Blätter wogen die Lichter daran,
Vom Lärm zittert der Wald,
Der Mund eines Kindes, das Auto spielt.

Mitten in der Spielstube
Umarmen sich zwei wie in einer Haustür,
Als ob sie es schon ernst meinten;
Auch richtige Schaufenster gibt es da,
An denen wir Kinder vorbeigehen
Oder stehenbleiben.
Aber niemand sieht das Glück. (S. 98)

Es ist nicht surrealistische Versponnenheit, die den Dichter zur Genitivmetapher "des Stadtbaumes Äste" und zum Wie-Vergleich greifen läßt, sondern einfach eine besondere Art der Beobachtung von einem "erhöhten" Standpunkt, von dem aus sich die Verzweigungen der Straßen und ihre Lichter mit einem Baum mit seinen Ästen und Blättern vergleichen lassen. Greßmann hat in seinem Aufsatz "Wie entsteht ein Gedicht?" diesen Vorgang selbst erklärt.[4] Er beschränkt die Frage "auf die Welt um meinen Kopf her im Verhältnis zu den Vorgängen der Welt in meinem Kopf bezogen. Die Vorgänge in meinem Kopf sind daher die Gegenstände, von denen ich die Entstehungsursache eines Gedichtes ableiten kann" (S. 5). Von entscheidender Wichtigkeit für Greßmanns Aufnahme der ihn umgebenden Wirklichkeit ist die Distanz, die er zu seinem Gegenstand einnimmt. Je größer der Abstand, desto poetischer wird das Ergebnis: "Liegen die Bauklötzer vor mir in der Ferne wie eine Stadt zum Spielen über den Gärten ausgebreitet, so ist der Eindruck, den ich nun von den Häusern gewinne, ein poetischer: die Feier" (S. 5). Mittlere Entfernung regt den Dichter eher zur Reflexion an, zum "Grübeln," wie Greßmann sagt, "über das Kommen und Gehen der Menschen, über das Bleibende, das Vergängliche" (S. 5). Die Langeweile des grauen Alltags schließlich entsteht durch völligen Mangel an Abstand: "Stehe ich dicht vor einem Haus, so daß ich bloß Mörtel, Risse . . . der Wände anstiere, so ist der Eindruck, den ich von der Welt gewinne, langweilig" (S. 5).

100

Die nächste Strophe des Gedichtes "An Arkadia"
macht vollends klar, daß es mit diesem Arkadien eine
besondere Bewandtnis hat:

Und die Kinder räumen das Gebirge weg
Und die Bäume und Wiesen, die künstlich sind,
Und holen den Baukasten,
In dem die Stadt von morgen eingepackt ist,
Und machen es den Erwachsenen nach
Und bauen tatsächlich eine Zivilisation auf.
(S. 98)

Zwischen dem kindlichen Spiel mit Bausteinen aus der
ländlichen Natur und der städtischen Zivilisation
besteht im Grunde kein Unterschied. Greßmann spielt
keineswegs das eine gegen das andere aus. Beide
Bereiche sind heute zweifellos "künstlich." In der
traditionellen Auffassung ist Arkadien "überall, wo
sich des Alltags Last und Mühe, Not und Häßlichkeit
der Welt vergessen, deren Ursachen verschleiern lassen, und statt dessen die Natur in ihrer unendlichen
Güte die Armen wie die Reichen ihrer angeborenen
Ungleichheit gemäß mütterlich umsorgt."[5] Greßmanns
Arkadien dagegen erfaßt sowohl das Phänomen der vom
Menschen veränderten Natur als auch die urbane Welt
zivilisierter Gesellschaft und ist mitten im Alltag
anzutreffen.

In der letzten Strophe kommt jetzt das "Spiel" zu
einem bedauerten Ende:

Und da es Zeit ist, schlafen zu gehen,
Knattert der Erzieher wie ein Moped,
Das eine Straße fährt: Dein Spiel ist zu Ende,
Arkadia; wie schade um dich. (S. 99)

Greßmann bleibt also im Bild der Kinderwelt, ohne
seine distanzierte Haltung aufzugeben. Mit dem Vers
"Arkadia; wie schade um dich" trauert der Dichter
nicht etwa einer verlorengegangenen Harmonie nach, er
markiert vielmehr den Abschluß dessen, was er in
seinem Aufsatz über die Entstehung eines Gedichtes als
"Feier im Alltag" bezeichnet (S. 6, 7). Hinter den
kindlicher Sprechweise angeglichenen syndetischen Rei-
hungen der dritten Strophe stehen ernsthafte, aber
unaufdringliche Überlegungen des Erwachsenen über eine
durchaus zeitgemäße Problematik. Die traditionelle
Vorstellung von Arkadien wird gleichermaßen problema-
tisiert und in einem neuen Sinne akzeptiert. Greßmann

versucht, die unvereinbar scheinenden Bereiche menschlicher Existenz, die sich zwischen naturhaftem Zustand
und künstlicher Zivilisation bewegt, zu versöhnen.

Kehren wir zurück zur Ausgangsfrage nach dem
magischen und visionären Charakter dieser Gedichte.
Wenn wir Greßmann beim Wort nehmen--und das sollte man
wohl auch tun--so tritt der Dichter ein in die Natur,
das Weltall, und spricht mit Sonne, Mond und Sternen
mit märchenhafter Selbstverständlichkeit. Diese
versponnenen Beziehungen zwischen den personifizierten
Dingen lassen sich sicher als eine Art poetischer
Visionen kennzeichnen. Es ist eine überaus lebendige
Welt, in die der Leser dem Dichter folgt, schmunzelnd,
auch zögernd, besonders wenn er auf Passagen philoso-
phischer Spekulation stößt, die sich gelegentlich in
ein leicht prätentiöses Gewand allegorisierender
Bildlichkeit kleidet. Mit seinen oft überraschenden,
unerwarteten Wendungen gewinnt Greßmann dabei aber den
Leser meist wieder und macht ihm den Aufenthalt in
seiner poetischen Welt vergnüglich. Die Kennzeichnung
"Magie" ist nur bedingt brauchbar, denn Greßmann
beschwört oder verdunkelt nichts durch verführerische
Klangmalerei und Endreim.

Adolf Endler berichtet, wie Greßmann ihm einmal
nahegelegt habe, "daß es sich bei seinen Gedichten um
Idyllen handle" und er seine Gedichte in zwei Gruppen
einteile: "Die ältere Gruppe ist den natürlichen Idyllen, der märkischen Landschaft, die jüngere den künstlichen Idyllen, der Großstadt Berlin gewidmet" (S. 6).
Endler geht dieser Selbstdeutung nicht weiter nach.
Die Interpretation des Gedichtes "An Arkadia" legt
jedoch nahe, der Frage auf den Grund zu gehen, inwieweit der traditionsbefrachtete Begriff der Idylle zu
einem Verständnis der eigenwilligen Poesie Greßmanns
beiträgt.

Für Schiller war die Idylle eine "Spezies der
sentimentalischen Dichtung," das heißt unter anderem,
daß es sich dabei um eine "Empfindungsweise" handelt,
der gemäß Natur und Ideal der Kunst und Wirklichkeit
entgegengesetzt werden. Wogegen der naive Dichter,
besonders des klassischen Altertums, sich im Zusammenhang mit der Natur sieht, reflektiert der sentimenta-
lische Dichter über die Natur. 6 Wenn wir an die
Geschichte der Dichtungsart Idylle denken, an die
Beispielreihe Theokrit, Vergil, Geßner, Voß etwa, so

läßt sich leicht feststellen, daß die Formen der
Schäferidylle in der deutschen Tradition leicht in
Stagnation oder Regression münden, denn "sie können
nur dem kranken Gemüte Heilung, dem gesunden keine
Nahrung geben; sie können nicht beleben, nur besänfti-
gen."7 Schillers dichtungsphilosophische Kategorie
der Idylle dokumentiert dagegen den idealistischen
Versuch des Dichters, einen Weg der Zukunft zu projizieren. Seine Forderung an den modernen Dichter
lautet daher: "Er mache sich die Aufgabe einer
Idylle, welche jene Hirtenunschuld auch in Subjekten
der Kultur und unter allen Bedingungen des rüstigsten,
feurigsten Lebens, des ausgebreitetsten Denkens, der
raffiniertesten Kunst, der höchsten gesellschaftlichen
Verfeinerung ausführt, welche, mit einem Wort, den
Menschen, der nun einmal nicht mehr nach Arkadien
zurück kann, bis nach Elysium führt."8

Es geht Greßmann natürlich nicht um den Versuch,
eine "Hirtenunschuld" in seinem neuen Subjekt, nämlich
der von ihm in der DDR erlebten Realität, auszuführen
und irgendein Ideal zu proklamieren. Wohl aber versucht er, die Trennung der Bereiche Natur und Gesellschaft zu überwinden, und zwar auf eine höchst "bele-
bende," sinnliche Weise.

Unter dem Titel "Schöpfung" finden sich im Lyrikband Der Vogel Frühling viele Gedichte, die nun tatsächlich in kindlich-naivem Ton Naturphänomene besin-
gen. Der "Vorbericht" gibt dabei den kosmischen Rah-
men:

> Ich, Mensch, ein kleiner Kosmos, wie Philosophen
>   sagten,
> Trug die Erde am Schuh und in mir die Idee der
>   Schöpfung;
> Da ging ich auf der Straße des Himmels bummeln.
>   (S. 9)

Daß es dabei aber nicht um eine weltfremde Pose geht,
zeigt schon das zweite Gedicht "Einladung," das den
Leser einerseits auf das kommende Thema Natur vorbe-
reitet, die Behandlung dieses Themas andererseits aber
in den Kontext gesellschaftlicher Gepflogenheiten
rückt:

> Da gehen Einladungen hinaus;
> In ansprechender Weise
> Öffnen sie den Mund
> Und sagen,

Auf der Tagesordnung steht das

Thema:
Luft, Licht, Erde, Himmel, Sonne . . .
Ihr Wandel in den Räumen des Kosmos,
Dem unendlichen Haus, wie man meint.
Und: wer da sonst noch tagt,
Lasse seine Birne über dem Tisch
    leuchten;
Und: höre.   (S. 10)

Die poetischen Mittel der oft überraschende Wirkungen
auslösenden Personifizierungen und der geradezu hymnischen Anrede charakterisieren viele der folgenden
Gedichte.   Dazu kommt aber auch hier schon die Neigung, das ernsthafte Gehabe seiner Mitmenschen humori-
stisch zu verfremden.   Das Gedicht "Einladung" kündigt
weiterhin die hymnische Feier der Natur an, ruft dabei
aber gleichzeitig zu kritischer Reflexion über ihre
Gefährdung auf:

Es spricht:
Im hymnischen Ton nämlich
Und feiert die Natur,
Die dort Geist und Welt und Wille ist
Und doch den Sinn verlöre,
Sähe man das bloß so an,
Ohne sich dabei etwas zu denken,
Daß das ein Baum, ein Pferd,
Und: das ein Grashalm sein soll;
Ja, daß es so was überhaupt noch gibt
Trotz der Schlote,
Die man in der Stadt qualmt.   (S. 11)

In der letzten Strophe steht dann die Frage, die als
Motto über all denjenigen Gedichten stehen kann, die
im Sinne von "natürlichen Idyllen" die am stärksten
bewahrende Tendenz Greßmanns aufzeigen, sowohl was den
Inhalt, als auch was die poetischen Mittel anbelangt:
"Kennst du die Natur, / Die eine Fremde unter vielen
ist?" (S. 11).

Daß Bilder aus dem Bereich der Natur dazu herhal-
ten, alle möglichen inneren Empfindungen und äußeren
Zustände zu verdeutlichen, ist nichts Neues in der
Geschichte der Lyrik.   Greßmann ist aber mit vielen
seiner Gedichte in einem strengeren Sinne Naturly-
riker, weil die Natur selbst, "die Fremde," zum Gegenstand wird.   Da sind die schon erwähnten Personifika-
tionen: Die Sonne ist zum Beispiel einmal Steuermann

104

("Deine Mütze ist ja blutrot, Steuermann," S. 23), ein
andermal der Hahn im Stall ("Den Horizont rötet / Dein
dämmernder Kamm," S. 24), der Mond ein Pfeifenraucher
("Und redest du und nickst, / Bläst der Sturm und
hüllt dich / In qualmende Wolken auch," S. 36). Die
Zeit ist eine "moderne Seherin," die ans Mikrophon
tritt und Nachrichten aus aller Welt ansagt oder eine
Zeitungsverkäuferin, die unter dem "Pressebaum" Blätter verkauft:

> Die Prawda, die Times, le Monde, die Morgenpost,
> Trud, das ND . . . liest man da;
> Und da, an dem Nagel noch aufgespießt, hängt
> Der zerbrochene Spiegel. (S. 57)

Erstaunlich ist, daß es Greßmann meist gelingt, diesem
abgenutzten Stilmittel humoristische Wirkungen abzuge-
winnen.

Eine wichtige Eigenart von Greßmanns Poesie ist
auch die Wahl von Vorstellungen und Bildern aus dem
Bereich gesellschaftlicher und künstlicher Produkte
mit dem Ziel, die Natur nahezubringen. So führt er in
dem Gedicht "Kosmos" zum Beispiel die Weite und Un-
durchdringlichkeit des Kosmos vor Augen, indem er ihn
als riesige bürokratische Behörde darstellt, in der
man umherirrt, ohne die zuständige Stelle zu finden.
In "Feierabend" lesen wir:

> Die Ofentür geht zu.
> Da dunkelt der Himmel.
> Es schalten sich Sterne
> Und Mond an im Raume. (S. 31)

Die "natürlichen" oder traditionellen Idyllen in dem
Buch Der Vogel Frühling lassen sich durchaus als
leicht modernisierte Stimmungsbilder kennzeichnen, die
aber der Gefahr, in sentimentale Schwärmerei und
weltfremde Verinnerlichung abzugleiten, entgehen, und
deren Berechtigung nicht zuletzt darin besteht, daß
sie zu sinnlichem Genießen und damit auch zur ruhigen
Besinnung auf den poetischen Reiz alltäglicher Situa-
tionen auffordern.

Im zweiten Teil seines Lyrikbuches finden wir
besonders die "künstlichen" oder modernen Idyllen, mit
denen der Dichter meist auf humoristische Weise die
städtische Landschaft erfaßt, und zwar nicht als
Kontrast zur natürlichen, sondern als selbstverständ-
liche Ergänzung. In dem Gedicht "Moderne Landschaft"

zum Beispiel poetisiert Greßmann das Stadtbild mit
Bildern aus dem Bereich der Natur, kehrt also sein in
den "natürlichen" Idyllen verwendetes Verfahren um:

> Stahlbäume wachsen auf den Bürgersteigen;
> Und es zweigen die Drähte
> Von Baum zu Baum.
> Darunter brüllen
> Die elektrischen Tiere
> Mit Menschen im Herzen vorüber
> Und so mancher gehet vorbei dort
> Und findet nichts weiter dabei;
> Denn die steinerne Landschaft
> Ist ja auch seine Mutter. (S. 100)

Das Gedicht "Das moderne Idyll" ist insofern von
Bedeutung, als es zeigt, daß Greßmann sich der Problematik des Versuchs idyllischer Dichtung bewußt ist.
Eine Rückkehr zu einer vorindustriellen Natursicht ist
offensichtlich nicht möglich. Die Natur der traditionellen Idylle gibt es nicht mehr:

> Doch sucht ihr das Idyll
> Mit den Augen eines Schafkopfs;
> Und weil kein Hirte mehr da sei,
> Die Herde wie einst dort zu hüten,
> Meint ihr: Die Zeit ist eben vorbei.
> Sicherlich, sage ich dann,
> Du stehst nicht mehr am Baum,
> Der Weide, die kleinen Freuden zu grasen,
> Die Natur. (S. 103)

"Nein, jetzt bist du ein Mensch" heißt es in der
zweiten Strophe, die dann aber trotzdem noch einmal
eine exotische Urwaldlandschaft beschwört und von der
Möglichkeit spricht, "daß die Landschaft Erdes auch
ihre guten Launen hat" (S. 103). Das Bedürfnis nach
der Geborgenheit in der Natur ist sicher vorhanden,
hinzu kommt aber die Gewißheit, dieses Bedürfnis auch
in der städtischen Landschaft befriedigen zu können.
Die "Landschaft Erdes," wie Greßmann mit seiner eigen-
tümlichen Vorliebe für personifizierende Neubildungen
sagt, umfaßt die traditionell getrennten Bereiche:

> Und wo sie immer auch wohne,
> Sei es in den schleierhaften Bergen der Ferne;
> Oder: in den Häusern der Stadt . . .
> Da wandeln der Kommenden viele
> Ihr Gesicht über den Füßen lang,
> Und sei es auch nur die Seitenstraße,

Wo Mondampeln in Fensterhimmeln brennen;
Und: dahinter stürzt ein Rollo,
Dem Grundstück stehen Gärten bei.

Und du, bist du kein Schafskopf mehr,
Der weiden will, ja Weiden,
Und siehst ein funkelndes Prisma vorbeifahren,
Eine Straßenbahn, die davor klingelt, du
Kannst dann doch Dunkel sein, das keiner sieht
Im Winkel der Geborgenheit: ein geometrisches
Idyll. (S. 104)

Konrad Franke nennt Greßmann einen Naturdichter, "der
noch einmal von vorn beginnt, so, als könnte er dieses
Genre begründen, als ließe sich die Welt noch einmal
in seine Gedichtwelt eingemeinden, wo Liebe eine
'große Wolke' ist und Hochspannungsmasten als 'Fisch-
grätenbäume' gesehen werden."9 Daß es sich bei einem
solchen Unterfangen um eine selten anzutreffende
Täuschung handeln muß, ist Greßmann selbst klar. Das
"moderne Idyll" entspricht keiner Realität, es gibt es
nur in seinem Gedicht. Bemerkenswert ist aber Greßmanns Überzeugung von seiner Notwendigkeit in unserer
Welt. In seinem Essay "Wie entsteht ein Gedicht?"
findet er hierfür die schlichte Erklärung:

Denn ein Geigenspiel in den Kurven der
Straßenbahn, wer hat das schon gesehen?
So etwas gibt es doch gar nicht. Gewiß.
Doch in der akustischen Täuschung, die ich
im Verhältnis zur Straßenbahn in einem be-
stimmten Abstand wahrnehme, höre ich die
Geige in den Kurven spielen. Nur eine
Täuschung, sicher; aber sie ist die Poesie des
Sinnenlebens, ohne die der Mensch wohl kaum
Poesie erleben könnte . . .10

Von den an dem antiken Modell herausgearbeiteten
Merkmalen der Idylle, etwa dem Vorherrschen des Räum-
lich-Zuständlichen, der Landschaftsbeschreibung, dem
locus amoenus, der statischen Weltauffassung, ist bei
Greßmann streng genommen wenig übriggeblieben. Der
Raum ist bei ihm, wie wir gesehen haben, nicht be-
schränkt auf häusliche Szenen oder ein abgeschirmtes
Stück Natur. Es gibt in diesem Sinne daher auch nicht
die Flucht in einen solchen Bereich der Geborgenheit.
Ebenso wenig plausibel wäre der Versuch, in Greßmanns
Gedichten kritisch-utopische Gegenbilder zur Realität
sehen zu wollen. Dafür sind sie nämlich bei aller
Naivität zu realistisch, indem sie von tatsächlich

beobachtbaren Erscheinungen ausgehen und diese dann poetisieren. Die Wirklichkeit wird nicht am Ideal gemessen. Daher läßt sich auch Schillers Idyllendefinition auf Greßmann nicht mehr anwenden. Wie Axel Schulze schreibt, "die bekannte Trennlinie zwischen naiver und sentimentalischer Dichtung, zwischen direkter und spekulativer Sicht auf die Dinge, erwies sich, wie für einen gegenwärtigen Dichter kaum anders zu erwarten, als verwischt." [11] Am ehesten entspricht Greßmanns Werk Schillers Vorstellung darin, daß er nicht zurückgeht, sondern von der Möglichkeit Gebrauch macht, unter den Bedingungen des gegenwärtigen Lebens das Künstliche der Natur und das Natürliche im Künstlichen in einer poetisch-phantastischen Synthese vor Augen zu führen. Das Erstaunliche liegt darin, daß er dabei doch oft zur Harmonisierung neigt. Der Interpret steht daher vor derselben schwierigen Aufgabe, mit der sich die Forschung der Idyllik des 18. und 19. Jahrhunderts beschäftigt. Mit dem verstärkten soziologischen Interesse innerhalb der Germanistik hat die traditionelle Idylle eine Aufwertung erfahren, indem ihr emanzipatorische Potenz und utopischer Entwurf zugebilligt werden. [12] Die bisher ausgewählten Gedichtbeispiele legen dagegen eher nahe, von einem poetischen Refugium in die Imagination des Dichters zu sprechen. Biographisch-psychologische Gründe ließen sich als Erklärung für diese, wenn man so will, Neigung zu poetisch-versöhnlicher Neuschöpfung anführen.

In den Gedichten "Klassengesellschaft" und "Klassenlose Gesellschaft" finden sich gesellschaftskritische Ansätze, die aber allzu vage bleiben und meist doch mehr dem humoristischen poetischen Einfall frönen. "Klassengesellschaft" bleibt im Sinne der "natürlichen Idylle" zunächst ganz im Bild der Natur, genauer des Waldes: "Grün ist die Gesellschaft / Und unter Bäumen von Kerlen / Und dicht gedrängt" (S. 122). Das Adjektiv "grün" impliziert aber gleichzeitig einen unreifen Zustand. Die zweite Strophe beschreibt das Naturwidrige der Klassengesellschaft:

> Und auf dem Waldweg stiefeln viele
> Zu unterdrücken
> Mit den Sohlen;
> Denn klein und für sich wächst man da auf:
> Jeder ein Grashalm. (S. 122)

In der letzten Strophe nimmt Greßmann allerdings eine

utopische Position ein, von der aus er "noch" die
Spuren der alten Gesellschaftsordnung wahrnimmt:
"Aber die Fußspur deutet noch an: / So muß der Mensch
dort gewesen sein / Auf der Erde" (S. 122). In dem
hierauf folgenden Gedicht "Klassenlose Gesellschaft"
stößt Greßmann zu sozialkritischer Satire vor, indem
er die alphabetische Anordnung des Fernsprechbuchs, wo
"Staat und Gesellschaft / In allen Seiten gedruckt"
sind, als Beweis der klassenlosen Gesellschaft an-
führt: "Und so durchblättert ihr sie selber: / Die
klassenlose Gesellschaft" (S. 123).

Eckart Krumbholz liest in Greßmanns Gedichten
"das totale Sich-nicht-abfinden-Können mit der vorge-
fundenen Welt" und erfaßt damit möglicherweise über-
zeugender als Adolf Endler, was Greßmann so beunru-
higt.[13] Diese Haltung erklärt die Neigung zur Idylle.
"Der Mensch darf nicht in solcher idyllischen Geistes-
armuth hinleben, sondern er muß arbeiten," lesen wir
beim strengen Hegel.[14] Bleibt also nach wie vor die
Frage, welche Funktion idyllische Züge in der Literatur eines sozialistischen Landes haben mögen. Denn,
obwohl Greßmann sicher ein höchst eigenwilliger Dichter ist, ließen sich viele Beispiele von der Heimat-
poesie Johannes R. Bechers bis zu Eva Strittmatters
märkischen Liedern aufzählen, die sich vor bewußt
naiver Idyllik nicht scheuen und trotzdem nicht in
jedem Fall als Anachronismen abgetan werden können.
Wie Leo Nagel betont, ist das Idyll in der soziali-
stisch-realistischen Literatur "keine Zufluchtsstätte
des einzelnen, sondern nur als relativer Ruhepunkt,
Ort der Selbstbesinnung und Vorbereitung auf eine neue
produktive Lebenstätigkeit denkbar."[15] Die Qualität
vieler Gedichte Greßmanns besteht letztlich darin, daß
sie sich nicht in statischer Bildlichkeit erschöpfen,
sondern Spannungen sichtbar machen, ohne sie lauthals
zu verkünden. "Idyll als Ort der Besinnung bedeutet
eben kein Herausträumen aus der gegenwärtigen Welt,
sondern Besinnung auf sie."[16]

In diesem Sinne steigt das lyrische Ich in dem
Gedicht "An die Erde" "aus dem Raumschiff des Lichtes"
und sinkt "an die grüne zerklüftete Brust" der Erde:

        "Ganz anders als da draußen ist das hier",
            sage ich
        Und trinke als dein Gast eine Molle
        Und bummele mit dir die Schaufenster lang
        Oder mit der Fünf hinaus,
        Wald, dem Sänger, im Park zu lauschen,

Dem Schall seiner Schritte,
Seinen Worten . . .
Und ich fühle, wie eigenartig doch
die Sitte da ist,
Mit dir ein Mensch zu sein. (S. 40)

Mit diesen Beispielen ist der "Spielraum" von Greßmanns Werk längst nicht ausgeschritten. Da wären zum Beispiel die Verwertung von Sage, Märchen, Mythologie, das Thema des Todes und die Auseinandersetzung mit der literarischen Tradition der Klassik und auch der lyrischen Moderne zu nennen. Die beiden postum ebenfalls im Mitteldeutschen Verlag erschienenen Bände Das Sonnenauto (1972) und Sagenhafte Geschöpfe (1978) müßten in einer Würdigung des Gesamtwerkes herangezogen werden, die einer umfangreicheren Studie vorbehalten bleibt.

Um zum Schluß noch einmal auf die Biographie des früh verstorbenen Dichters zurückzukommen: Karl Mickel stellt in seiner kleinen Schrift "Zu Greßmanns Ehrengedächtnis" eine Verbindung her zwischen Greßmanns unermüdlichem Ankämpfen gegen die Krankheit und seinem poetischen Verfahren: "Er kämpfte um sich. Der Kranke ist die Krankheit: und wird gemieden; der Bote ist die Botschaft; der Vogel Frühling."[17] Festzuhalten bleibt, daß sich hier unter schwierigsten persönlichen Umständen eine eigenwillige poetische Stimme gemeldet und die lyrische Szene der DDR um ein Werk bereichert hat, dem wir unsere Aufmerksamkeit nicht versagen sollten.

University of Iowa

Anmerkungen

[1] Axel Schulze, "Aus Liebe zum Menschen," Neue Deutsche Literatur, 27, Heft 8 (1979), 135.

[2] Zitiert aus Holger J. Schuberts Nachwort zu Uwe Greßmann, Das Sonnenauto: Gedichte (Halle: Mitteldeutscher Verl., 1972), S. 101.

[3] Zitiert aus Adolf Endlers Vorwort zu Uwe Greßmann, Der Vogel Frühling: Gedichte, 2. Aufl. (Halle: Mitteldeutscher Verl., 1967), S. 4. Die Seitenangaben in Klammern beziehen sich im folgenden auf diese

Ausgabe.

[4] Uwe Greßmann, "Wie entsteht ein Gedicht?" in
Das Sonnenauto, S. 5-8.

[5] Brigitte Wormbs, Über den Umgang mit Natur:
Landschaft zwischen Illusion und Ideal, 2. verb. Aufl.
(Frankfurt/Main: Roter Stern, 1978), S. 11.

[6] Friedrich Schiller, "Über naive und sentimen-
talische Dichtung," Schriften zur Philosophie und
Kunst (München: Goldmann, 1959), S. 178.

[7] Schiller, S. 194.

[8] Schiller, S. 196-97.

[9] Konrad Franke, Die Literatur der Deutschen Demokratischen Republik, neubearb. Ausg. (München:
Kindler, 1974), S. 272.

[10] Das Sonnenauto, S. 8.

[11] "Aus Liebe zum Menschen," S. 137.

[12] Siehe Renate Böschenstein-Schäfer, Idylle, 2.
Aufl. (Stuttgart: Metzler, 1977), S. 21ff.

[13] Eckart Krumbholz, "Sehnsucht ins Große und
Weite: Fünf Sätze über Uwe Greßmann," Sinn und Form,
31, Heft 3 (1979), 696.

[14] Georg Wilhelm Friedrich Hegel, Vorlesungen
über die Aesthetik. Erster Band, Sämtliche Werke,
XII, hrsg. v. Hermann Glockner (Nachdr. Stuttgart-Bad
Cannstatt: Friedrich Frommann Verl., 1964), S. 350.

[15] Leo Nagel, "Zum Problem der Idyllendichtung,"
Weimarer Beiträge, 16, Heft 7 (1970), 107.

[16] Nagel, S. 108.

[17] Karl Mickel, "Zu Greßmanns Ehrengedächtnis,"
Neue Deutsche Literatur, 26, Heft 6 (1978), 115.

Die Lyrik von Joochen Laabs

Fritz H. König

"Was nun meine lyrische Produktion anbetrifft, so vollzieht sie sich nicht schüttladungsweise, sondern nur dosiert," schreibt Laabs.[1] Bisher hat er seinen Lesern zwei Dosen verabreicht: Eine Straßenbahn für Nofretete (1970) und Himmel sträflicher Leichtsinn (1978). Jeder Gedichtsammlung ließ er jeweils im folgenden Jahr einen ausgewachsenen Roman folgen: Das Grashaus oder Die Aufteilung von 35 000 Frauen auf zwei Mann (1971) und Der Ausbruch. Roman einer Verführung (1979). Außerdem hat er einen Band Erzählungen geschrieben: Die andere Hälfte der Welt (1974).[2] Mit anderen Worten, das bisherige Werk von Laabs und nicht nur die Lyrik hat den Vorteil, gut überschaubar zu sein. Diese Feststellung soll aber nichts Negatives enthalten; sie ist objektiv gedacht.

Laabs gehört zur großen Gruppe von Schriftstellern und Dichtern, die auf dem Umweg über einen anderen Beruf relativ spät zum Schreiben kamen. Der Beruf als Verkehrsingenieur erschließt die Welt technischer Bilder und Motive, naturwissenschaftliche Einsichten und Vergleiche, die das Milieu in seinen Werken bestimmen. Vom Stil her, von der Kühnheit des Bildes und auch teilweise von der Thematik her ist seine Lyrik der von Sarah Kirsch, Axel Schulze und Volker Braun artverwandt; seine Prosa, die sich mit der Rolle des Individuums in der sozialistischen Gesellschaft befaßt, erinnert an Werke von Erich Loest, Günter de Bruyn und Manfred Jendryschik.

Der Titel des ersten Lyrikbandes, Eine Straßenbahn für Nofretete, ist gleichzeitig auch der Titel eines der Gedichte in der Sammlung:

113

Ich möcht eine Straßenbahn sein.
Ihr steigt ein in mich (habt sogar
    gewartet),
mit den schwarzen Fingernägeln und den
    gelackten,
mit den Butterstullen und den Azeto-
    phentabletten,
Nofretete und Schwejk,
tretet euch auf die Füße und setzt euch
    nebeneinander,
setzt euch und seid ungeduldig,
seht auf die Häuserfassaden und horcht
    in euch.
So seid ihr und alle in mir.

Und wenn ihr aussteigt,
habt ihr mit den Perlonhemden etwas
    Staub am Kragen
und ihr mit den Schweißhemden etwas
    Lackduft in der Nase.
Aber alle seid ihr ein Stück weiter.

Ich möcht eine Straßenbahn sein.
                                (S. 29)

Meiner Ansicht nach bildet dieses Gedicht einen guten
Ausgangspunkt zur Diskussion der Lyrik von Laabs, denn
es enthält sowohl thematisch, metaphorisch als auch
formal gesehen wesentliche Ingredienzen, die vielen
seiner Gedichte gemeinsam sind. Es wird hier ein
gewisser alltäglicher Augenblick, eine an sich belang-
lose Situation, nämlich das Warten auf die Bahn, nach
der tieferen Bedeutung gefragt; aber nicht, natürlich,
nach der Bedeutung per se, sondern nach der Bedeutung,
die diese Situation für den Autor hat. Sie beherbergt
in sich den Impetus zur Anregung der Phantasie, zur
freien Assoziation. Viele der Gedichte nehmen ihren
Ursprung in der Atmosphäre eines Ortes, in seinem
genius loci; gleichgültig, ob das nun eine Landstraße
ist, eine Flugzeugkabine, römische Ruinen, die Wartburg, ein russisches Dorf oder der gedeckte Früh-
stückstisch. Immer leiten diese, an sich unwesent-
lichen, Lokalitäten hin zu Wesentlichem. Beispielsweise zu den Problemen zwischenmenschlicher Beziehungen oder zum Zweck, zum Wesen unseres Daseins
überhaupt.

    "Eine Straßenbahn für Nofretete" enthält die für
Laabs typischen Motive: die Faszination mit Verkehrs-
mitteln, in diesem Fall ein hyperbolischer Identifi-

114

kationsprozeß mit der Straßenbahn; sowie ein Hang zum Exotischen, eine Vorliebe für alle Arten von Reisen. Das antike Schönheitsideal und der kleine neuzeitliche Überlebenskünstler sind äußere Grenzzeichen, verkörpern die Spannweite des Publikums, das sich da in die Straßenbahn ergießt. Die beiden Namen werden unterstrichen durch die zwei vorausgehenden anaphorisch-parallelen Zeilen, in denen von "schwarzen Fingernägeln" die Rede ist und von "gelackten," von "Butterstullen" und "Azetophentabletten." Nachdem Nofretete und Schwejk (und einige andere) eingestiegen sind, tritt eine Mischung ein, eine Synthese, Symbiose--keiner dieser Ausdrücke trifft völlig zu, doch alle ein wenig. Da ist das Sich-gegenseitig-auf-die-Füße-Treten, das Nebeneinander-Sitzen, das Ungeduldig-Werden. Am Ende beim Aussteigen steigert sich dieses Zusammensein und Aneinanderreiben von der Wortwahl her nahezu zu einem pflanzlichen Befruchtungsvorgang, wenn es heißt: " [da] habt ihr mit den Perlonhemden etwas Staub am Kragen / und ihr mit den Schweißhemden etwas Lackduft in der Nase." Die Straßenbahn, der Dichter, hat diese Begegnung der verschiedensten Bevölkerungsschichten möglich gemacht. "Aber alle seid ihr ein Stück weiter," im Sinne von "habt ihr euch alle ein Stück weiterentwickelt, habt ihr voneinander gelernt, achtet ihr euch gegenseitig." Der am Ende wiederholte Wunsch "Ich möcht eine Straßenbahn sein" drückt meiner Ansicht nach weniger ein Streben aus, Werkzeug des Fortschritts, der gesellschaftlichen Weiterentwicklung zu sein, obwohl das natürlich auch mitschwingen mag. Vielmehr sehe ich darin das Verlangen nach menschlicher Begegnung, ohne die eine gesellschaftliche Weiterentwicklung nicht stattfinden kann. Außerdem scheint der Ausgangspunkt des Gedichts ein Zustand zu sein, dessen Gegenteil im Gedicht gefeiert wird: die Einsamkeit, das Alleinsein. Auch wenn die Fahrgäste mit anderen zusammen sind, sind sie trotzdem noch, wenigstens zeitweise, allein: "setzt euch nebeneinander / . . . / seht auf die Häuserfassaden und horcht in euch." Der Moment des In-uns-Horchens schließt Kontakte aus, und so kann die Gefahr bestehen, daß man inmitten von vielen Menschen doch schmerzlich allein sein kann, und umgekehrt, selbst wenn wir, wie die Straßenbahn, leviathangleich diesen menschlichen Mikrokosmos beherbergen könnten, wäre das Problem auch nicht gelöst, denn unsere gegenseitigen Beziehungen erreichen unweigerlich eine Mauer, eine Grenze, die wir nicht überspringen können, auch nicht in der Liebe.

115

Laabs bringt diese absolute Isolation zum Ausdruck in dem Gedicht "Wärn wir":

Wärn wir gemeinsam ins Bett gegangen,
wär der Schaden nicht halb so groß.
Unsere Illusionen wären vergangen,
und wir wären uns los.

Wärn wir über den andern hergefallen
mit Gier und Gebiß und Gebein,
hätten danach gedacht wie nach allen:
Bringt doch nichts ein.

Man kommt nicht weiter als bis an die
    Haut
und weder heraus noch hinein.
- Der Damm wär gesprengt, der den See
    gestaut,
entblößt der Stein.

So aber spürn wir des anderen Finger
immer noch voller Behutsamkeit,
glauben, er hätt aus dem Rippenzwinger
uns befreit. (S. 58)

Auch in der Liebe sind wir mitten im Zusammensein im Wesentlichen doch zum Alleinsein verurteilt.

Die Liebe, oder besser das andere Geschlecht, ist eines der Hauptthemen bei Laabs, beispielsweise in den ersten sechs Gedichten dieser Sammlung. Das erste, mit dem Titel "Die den Personalausweisvermerk tragen: Geschlecht--weiblich" (S. 6) ist eine Art Preisgedicht auf die Frau, in dem die Frauen immer wieder kollektiv angeredet werden. Die Situation wird am Ende des Gedichts ausgewertet, wo es u.a. heißt, "Für euch gilt keine Formel," d.h. der Frau wohnt ein gewisses Maß kreativer Unberechenbarkeit inne, eine fortdauernde Herausforderung: "Ihr fordert uns noch zum Zweikampf gegen uns selbst!" Daraus ergibt sich die logische Folgerung: "Wer vor euch versagt, versagt vor sich selber. / Wer vor euch besteht, dem ist auch die nächste Ausbaustufe an der Angara zuzutrauen." Mit anderen Worten, die Auseinandersetzung mit der Frau ist der Weisenstein unserer eigenen Werte.

Das zweite Gedicht, "Beschreibung der Selbstverständlichkeit bei der Durchsetzung des Glücks" (S. 8), gibt ein konkretes Beispiel zu den generellen Feststellungen im ersten Gedicht. Die Geliebte und

116

ihre Vorzüge werden mit der Weite der Welt verglichen.
Dieses Abwägen des externen Makrokosmos, der ganzen
Welttopographie, des Touristenrummels, mit den eher
bescheidenen Qualitäten des einen Menschen, der Geliebten, fällt dennoch zu ihren Gunsten aus, und so
ergibt sich nahezu zwangsläufig das dritte Gedicht,
"Beschreibung einer Schwierigkeit bei der Durchsetzung
des Glücks" (S. 10). Die Schwierigkeit dabei ist, daß
die Logik der Gedanken, die die Vorzüge der weiten
Welt, des beruflichen Erfolges erfaßt, nicht der der
Gefühle folgt. Aus dieser Diskrepanz resultiert
persönliche Tragik und auch die etwas bittere Forderung: "Sie sollten mal den Forschungsauftrag vergeben:
/ über die Notwendigkeit logisch zu fühlen." Im
vierten Gedicht, "Von unserer Liebe sprechen" (S. 12),
glätten sich die Wogen etwas. Die Liebe, die Gefühle,
werden akzeptiert: "Ist es ein Zufall, / . . . / . . .
/ daß ich in meiner Hand / deine Finger zähle, /
obwohl ich weiß, / es sind fünf?" Die Frage ist
natürlich rhetorisch, wie es von vornherein Rhetorik
war, die Liebe in Frage zu stellen, mit anderem zu
vergleichen. Und doch ist es eine Frage, ähnlich der
nach dem Sinn und Zweck des Daseins, die immer wieder
gestellt wird, gestellt werden muß, obwohl es klar
ist, daß es darauf keine, oder jedenfalls keine einfache Antwort geben kann. Im fünften Gedicht, "Ich
will an dich denken" (S. 14), werden wiederum Logik
der Umstände, das alltägliche Detail, mit der Un-Logik
des Gefühls kontrastiert. Das sechste Gedicht, "Du
und ich" (S. 16), bringt endlich vorübergehende Erfül-
lung und Frieden. Die feminine Unberechenbarkeit,
Instinktivität und Anmut werden im Symbol des Vogels
zusammengefaßt; das Statische, Schwere, Logische des
Mannes, in dem des Steines. Beide Symbole kehren auch
in den folgenden Gedichten immer wieder.

Die Gedichte von Laabs können hin und wieder
stilistisch romantische Anflüge haben; der Grundton
bleibt aber im Konkret-Alltäglichen haften. Dabei
bemüht sich Laabs fortwährend den Menschen in der
angemessenen naturwissenschaftlichen Perspektive zu
sehen, sowohl was seine Beziehung zum Ort als auch zur
Zeit betrifft. Indessen überrascht diese Perspektive
immer wieder, weil sie den Einzelnen mit den Äonen der
Geschichte und Vorgeschichte und mit dem Erdball, dem
gesamten Universum konfrontiert. Im Gedicht "Wir
haben zu essen, zu schlafen und beizuschlafen" fordert
Laabs: "Dann ist es höchste Zeit, daß wir uns ordent-
lich benehmen / und Ordnung reinkriegen in unsere
Kontinente-Beete nach einer halben Milliarde Jahre"

117

(S. 27).

Anläßlich seines dreißigsten Geburtstages fragt
er, was diese Zeitspanne schon ist im Vergleich zur
Unendlichkeit:

Dabei hat sich schon Hamurabi abge-
schunden. Mit Faustkeilen
aufs Gebirge losgegangen, mit Knüppeln
aufs Meer die Wikinger.
Und Dante ging auf die Hölle los und
Einstein auf den Himmel und Chaplin
auf seine eigenen Füße.
Und präpariert nur, vernietet und
furchtsam und selten springen wir
kurz mal über die Wolken,
brauchen wir doch noch immer zu jedem
Schritt die Erde.
Und das--Bilanz der Menschheit?
Im Raum von Millionen Lichtjahren!
Soll's wägbar sein?
Und gar nur ein einzelnes Leben!
("Der dreißigste Geburtstag," S. 49)

Etwas klingt hier Gottfried Benn an, der sich auch in
den Äonen verliert. Allerdings fehlt bei Laabs der
abgrundtiefe Pessimismus. Irgendwie geht das Leben
immer tröstlich weiter:

Und ich lausche. Da schallts:
Wir warten auf dich!
Winken vom Haus sie herüber, mit dem
Wischtuch die Mutter, der Junge
wirft den grellgelben Ball, und der
schlägt in den Kirschbaum,
zerprasselt die Stimmen der Blätter.
Fang! schreit der Junge.
Und ich verfolg, wie der Ball von Ast
zu Ast hüpft, strecke die Hände und
rufe:
Ich komme.
("Der dreißigste Geburtstag," S. 50)

Die Antwort auf transzendentale, metaphysische Fragen
liegt im Konkreten. Fragen, die sich aus gedanklicher
Logik ergeben, können nicht gradlinig auf der gleichen
Ebene beantwortet werden, sondern wie wir schon in der
Diskussion der Liebesgedichte gesehen haben, eher
durch die Un-Logik des Gefühls. Das sind die zwei
Seelen in der Brust, die fortwährend miteinander im

118

Widerstreit stehen, sich aber am Ende doch irgendwie
ergänzen, Teile eines Ganzen sind und dialektische
Exkurse fordern.

Im Verlauf der Gedichtsammlung werden immer
wieder die menschlichen Beziehungen nach ihrem Wesen
befragt, ausgelotet, so z.b. in einer Folge von fünf
Gedichten mit dem Titel "Reisebericht" (S. 51). Die
Reise führt uns auch in den folgenden Gedichten von
Orjol nach Indien, von der Kalahari nach Alaska. Mal
reisen wir im Flugzeug, mal im Zug, mal in der Straßenbahn. Immer ist das Verkehrsmittel Befreiungswerk-
zeug. Es befreit uns nicht nur von der uns anhaften-
den physikalischen Trägheit, sondern auch von unserer
angestammten nächsten Umgebung. Aus der Distanz
gesehen, gewinnt diese Umgebung die richtige Perspektive, und wir sind befreit, im Sinne von frei zu sein,
zu ihr zurückzukehren.

Mitten im Gedichtband Straßenbahn für Nofretete
steht das längste Gedicht, "Die Wartburg." Während
der erste und dritte Teil der Sammlung thematisch und
formell miteinander verknüpft sind, hebt sich der
zweite Teil, nur aus diesem Gedicht bestehend, davon
ab. Die Wartburg wird als Symbol und Katalysator der
geschichtlichen Ereignisse--besonders der jüngeren
Geschichte--in Deutschland gesehen. Viel Revolu-
tionäres klingt an: der frühe Kampf um mehr soziale
Gerechtigkeit in der Zeit der Bauernkriege, der späte
Kampf um endgültige soziale Gerechtigkeit seit dem
zweiten Weltkrieg. Parallel dazu Revolutionen und
Beständigkeit der Sprache und so nebenbei und nebenbei
auch: "Die Zäsur im Leib des Landes und immer noch
zweierlei Maß für / die Liebe, der Haß aufeinander
gerichtet, / besser sichtbar denn je, doch ich seh /
nur den Wald in argloser hügliger Fülle und denk einen
/ Lidschlag: Vielleicht ist's nicht mehr so. / Doch
wissen wir mehr als wir sehn . . ." (S. 44). Das
Gefühl des Erreichten östlich der "Zäsur" ist stark,
und die Hoffnung, daß es von der Wartburg "tausend
Jahre lang aufgesogen, bewahrt und ausgehaucht wird."

Von der Form her gesehen ist den Gedichten der
ersten Sammlung gemeinsam, daß sie, mit Ausnahme der
"Wartburg," ein bis zwei Seiten füllen. Die Langzeile
wird vorgezogen, mit häufigem Enjambement. Eine
Einteilung in Strophen (Abschnitt wäre ein besserer
Ausdruck) ergibt sich gewöhnlich zwanglos vom Inhalt
her. Mit anderen Worten nähern sich die Gedichte
häufig der Prosa und ähneln in dieser Hinsicht vielen

119

der Gedichte von Sarah Kirsch. Als technische Mittel
werden Alliteration, Lautmalerei, Wiederholung, Ana-
phern und Antithesen bevorzugt. Mit den Titeln tut
sich der Dichter ab und zu schwer; viele sind einfach:
"Du und ich," "Abends," "Die Wartburg," "Susi."
Andere aber geben auf barocke Art eine eher schwer-
fällige und doch in ihrer Ehrlichkeit bestechende
Inhaltsangabe des Gedichts: "Beschreibung der Selbstverständlichkeit bei der Durchsetzung des Glücks,"
"Muchak, Gemeinde- und Kirchenratsmitglied, nach
schwerem Abend bei Überwindung der Strecke zwischen
Gasthof und heimischem Hoftor" usw.

Das folgende Gedicht verdient besonders hervorge-
hoben zu werden wegen eines Zuges, der viele der
Laabsschen Gedichte attraktiv und zugänglich macht:
der Humor. Hier liegt er auf der Hand:

> Mond, matte Schweinsblase,
> eine Finsternis hier, daß man sich die
>   Beine brechen kann,
> und überhaupt die Sternspreu wieder
>   über der Himmelstenne verstreut,
> und der alte Mann schnarcht einfach in
>   der hintersten Ecke,
> läßt sich nicht sehn.
> Wie soll da Ordnung reinkommen?
>
> Da ist es wohl doch gut,
> daß sie die Raketen anschirren,
> um selbst nach dem Rechten zu sehn,
> und daß ich nicht für das Taufbecken
>   gestimmt hab,
> aber für die Straßenbeleuchtung.
>
> Jawohl, Mond,
> müdes, funzelndes Kälberauge.
> Es lebe die technische Revolution!
> Amen.   (Nofretete, S. 24)

Der Humor ist aber auch in vielen anderen Gedichten
zugegen, z.B. in "Guten Morgen." Da heißt es in der
vierten Strophe: "Kiefer runter, Kiefer rauf, Kiefer
runter-Marme-/lade hat kein Bewußtsein, sonst würde
sie anders / schmecken . . ." (S. 25). Weiter unten
heißt es von den Beinen, daß sie "Gesinnungslumpen"
sind, weil sie sich dem Verstand nicht unterordnen
wollen, und dann kommt die Bahn nicht, dafür aber die
Gedanken, und es wird gefragt, "ob das vielleicht ein
Ersatz sei?" Immer wieder werden wir mit solchen an

120

sich banalen Fragen, mit kindlichen Wünschen ("Ich
möcht eine Straßenbahn sein" oder "ich will Kolumbus
sein") oder mit lapidaren Feststellungen ("Und das ist
gut," "Ich komm") entwaffnet, bzw. es wird uns der
Teppich unter den Füßen weggezogen, denn sie scheinen
der Weisheit letzter Schluß zu sein, und es ist nicht
immer leicht, das zu akzeptieren.

   Die Sprache hat oft umgangssprachliche Züge.
Viele "e" werden synkopiert. Andrerseits wird sie
öfters mit technischen Spezialausdrücken angereichert
(Spannbetonkoeffizienten, der Öfner wagt den Abstich,
Azetophentabletten usw.), was eingedenk des früheren
Berufs des Dichters nicht weiter verwunderlich ist.
Angenehm fällt bei der Wortwahl auf, daß wenig
Effekthascherei dabei ist. Mangels eines besseren
Epithets möchte ich die Sprache als "ehrlich" bezeich-
nen. Innerhalb der Spannweite des angewandten Voka-
bulars geben sich "fünf biedere Sandbuckel" und das
"sternstaubige All" im gleichen Gedicht die Hand ("Wir
haben zu essen, zu schlafen und beizuschlafen," S.
27). Der Verdacht des Stilbruchs tritt dabei nicht
auf.

   Laabs fühlt sich dem amerikanischen Dichter
William Carlos Williams verbunden. Er hat sich darüber 1980 in einem kurzen Artikel geäußert.[3] Was Laabs
beeindruckt, ist Williams' extreme Wortökonomie und
die "Dichte" der Gedichte. Er faßt sein eigenes Credo
folgendermaßen zusammen:

> Poesie ist nicht sprachlich ästheti-
> sierte Information (worin sich die
> meisten Texte, die gemeinhin als Ge-
> dichte gelten, erschöpfen). Poesie ist
> der unausgesprochene Raum, den ein Wort
> oder die Verbindung mehrerer Worte um
> sich ausbreitet. Die Worte des Dich-
> ters--die Steine des Fundaments; wie
> sicher sie gefügt sind, wie gut ihr
> Material ist, davon hängt ihre Trag-
> fähigkeit ab und wie groß das Gebäude
> wird, das der Leser darauf errichtet.[4]

Nun, im Falle von Laabs wird das Gebäude schon von
Anfang an überdimensional, das läßt sich in Anbetracht
von weltumspannenden Reisen, von tausenden von Jahren
menschlicher Geschichte, dem unendlichen Weltall und
den Äonen der Entwicklung unseres Planeten gar nicht
vermeiden. Entscheidender scheint mir zu sein, daß

das Gebäude lebt oder wenigstens belebt ist, auch vom Dichter und Leser erlebt wird, und daß gegenüber der Megastruktur ein von Wimpern überschatteter kurzer Blick oder ein Grashalm nicht an Bedeutung verliert, im Gegenteil, durch die Kontrastwirkung ungeheuer an Bedeutung gewinnt. Formale Ähnlichkeiten zu den typisch engzeiligen, dürren Williams-Gedichten besteht sonst kaum, höchstens in ein paar Gedichten wie z.B. "Isländisches Liebesgedicht":

> Ich bin der Bottich,
> du drin der Hering.
>
> Und das Salz zwischen uns
> ist die Liebe,
> die uns haltbar macht
> - und zerfrißt. (S. 69)

Ähnlich dem bekannten mittelalterlichen anonymen Liebesgedicht "Ich bin dîn und du bist mîn" ist hier Perfektion gelungen. Da sind keine Abstriche oder Zusätze denkbar, und Interpretationsversuche sind zur Lächerlichkeit verurteilt. Jedoch sind Gedichte dieser kondensierten Art bei Laabs die Ausnahme und nicht die Regel.

Der zweite Gedichtband von Laabs, Himmel sträflicher Leichtsinn, ähnelt dem ersten vom Format her sehr: wiederum langzeilige reimlose ein- bis zweiseitige Gedichte und Gedichtfolgen. Der Grund für eine Dreiteilung der Sammlung ist hier noch weniger ersichtlich als im ersten Band. Laabs hat es nun aufgegeben, sich um Gedichttitel zu bemühen. Die erste Zeile dient immer gleichzeitig auch als Überschrift, was eine glücklichere Lösung zu sein scheint als die im ersten Band.

Im Ganzen herrscht in Himmel sträflicher Leichtsinn mehr Homogenität. Die Gedichte hängen nicht nur formal besser zusammen, sondern auch inhaltlich. Die Bildhaftigkeit dieser Gedichte lehnt sich stark an die in Eine Straßenbahn für Nofretete an. Da sind wieder die Ausflüge zurück in die Weltgeschichte, die Kontinenthüpferei, die Straßenbahn etwas weniger, das Auto etwas mehr; die Natur ist völlig unromantisch geworden. Die Thematik allerdings scheint sich verschoben zu haben. Es geht nicht mehr hauptsächlich um den Dialog, um die Verständigung, sondern um den Platz des "Ichs," um die Möglichkeiten, die Grenzen und den Sinn versuchter Selbstverwirklichung.

Diese Themen sind auch maßgebend im letzten Roman von Laabs, dem Ausbruch. Thomas und Hella lieben sich, versuchen, sich aus ihren Ehen zu lösen und werden zwangsläufig miteinander psychisch konfrontiert. Es ist sofort klar, daß die Kommunikationsmöglichkeiten Grenzen haben, daß die neue Situation nicht hält, was sie am Anfang zu versprechen schien. Nun beginnt für Thomas sein eigener, persönlicher Freiheitskampf, ein Kampf, sich von seinen eigenen Trieben, Gefühlen und traditionellen Denkweisen zu befreien, um zu einer anderen Daseinsform zu gelangen, zu einem anderen Lebenskapitel. Ob zu einem besseren bleibt dahingestellt. Der letzte Satz, "Es wird ein schöner Tag," muß nicht unbedingt als überaus optimistisch gewertet werden. Er signalisiert wohl eher einen neuen Anfang. Andrerseits ist das Ende, obwohl Thomas neben seiner Familie auch Hella verliert, nicht tragisch, denn Thomas verkraftet beide Tragödien. Er ist nun vielleicht etwas weiser, etwas älter, etwas resignierter. Aber diese Entwicklungen, wenn es überhaupt welche sind, sind nicht so wichtig. Entscheidend ist die Tatsache, daß Thomas sein Leben lebt, in der Gegenwart, in jedem Augenblick, daß er wenigstens versucht, selbst sein Geschick zu lenken und sich nicht nur dahintreiben läßt. Er setzt sich voll für sich selbst ein. 5

Im Gedicht "Nehmen wir bloß mal das Trampen" (S. 10) heißt es: "der Mensch ist doch keine Apparatur," und in einem anderen: "Kurz gesagt ich bin doch kein Auto" (S. 35)--und er möchte wohl auch keines sein. Die Zeiten, wo er eine Straßenbahn sein wollte, sind vorbei. Das Entscheidende ist, daß man selbst das Lenkrad in der Hand hält, auch wenn einem die Landkarte oder das Fahrverhalten der Karosse ein Schnippchen schlägt. Man muß etwas wagen, muß Entschlußkraft an den Tag legen, auch wenn sich vorher nicht alles genau vorausberechnen läßt; ein Gedicht, das dieses Anliegen konzis vorbringt: "Schneewittchen komm zu mir" (S. 29), endet mit der fröhlichen, zur Tat drängenden Aufforderung: "Ach, wir beißen einfach in den Apfel." Einfach in den Apfel beißen, den Ausbruch wagen, darauf kommt es an.

Gerhard Rothbauer nimmt das Titelgedicht dieser Sammlung vor, "Himmel sträflicher Leichtsinn," das mit der Frage endet "Wieviel Himmel braucht der Mensch?" und setzt diese Frage über eine Diskussion des Gesamtwerkes von Laabs. 6 Dabei stellt er fest, daß die letzten beiden Bücher, besonders der Gedichtband, mit Himmelsymbolik und himmelverwandten Bildern durchsetzt sind, und argumentiert recht überzeugend, daß der Himmel, der sich um den ganzen Erdball spannt, für Laabs und somit seine Leser erst die globale, die kosmische Perspektive zuläßt, die bereits früher erwähnt wurde, und die den Einzelnen, seine Taten, seine Beziehungen zum Kollektiv erst ins rechte Licht rückt. Natürlich ist der Himmel in dieser Hinsicht zentral, und natürlich ist die Frage nach der Lebensqualität eine rhetorische, weil sie in vager Relativität haften bleiben muß. Eben genug zu einem Leben, das Laabs "als Auseinandersetzung des Individuums mit der Umwelt und synchron damit als Auseinandersetzung des Individuums mit sich selbst" versteht.7

Wichtiger allerdings scheint mir die ebenfalls rhetorische Frage zu sein, die sich beinahe zwangsläufig aus der nach dem Himmel ergibt: wieviel sträflichen Leichtsinn braucht der Mensch? Es gehört wohl eine gute Dosis dazu, den Ausbruch zu wagen, in den Apfel zu beißen, den Beruf als Verkehrsingenieur an den Nagel zu hängen, homo ludens zu sein, der willens ist zur Kontinente-Hüpferei, zu Exkursen in die Vorzeit, der auch mal der Sprache die Zügel schießen läßt:

> Ein Schreibtisch--Barrikade;
> weißer Kittel--Talar der
>   Selbstlosigkeit,
> verändern den Menschen bis in die Gene:
> den Kopf voll und die Hose leer!
> ("Nehmen wir bloß mal das Trampen,"
>   S. 10)

Der Mensch sollte Zeit haben in den Himmel zu sehen. Er sollte auch mal Bilanz ziehen, beispielsweise aus dem letzten Jahrzehnt mit der Quintessenz: "Der Glaube erhalten--wars so ein gelungenes Jahrzehnt" (S. 80)--es hätte schlimmer kommen können. Doch ich will diese biographische Linie nicht weiterverfolgen. Laabs warnt davor:

> Die enge biographische Bindung ist für
> mich kein Dogma. Sie entspringt nicht
> zuletzt meinem erheblichen Bedürfnis
> nach Genauigkeit. Und ich kenne halt
> nichts besser als mich und die Umwelt,
> in der ich mich befinde. Wir werden
> sehen. Andrerseits muß ich aber sagen,

es klappt nicht, wenn das, was ich
schreibe, pur als mir Widerfahrenes
genommen wird. Weil es einfach nicht
zutrifft. Auch Gerhard Rothbauer hat
sich erheblich darin verheddert.[8]

Nun, Rothbauer dachte an die Prosa, bei der Lyrik ist
die Verhedderungsgefahr sowieso nicht so groß.

Sollte zum Vergleich der beiden Gedichtbände ein
Werturteil abgegeben werden, so ist das schwierig.
Der erste Band ist abwechslungsreicher, sowohl thematisch als auch formal. Man fühlt hin und wieder den
vergossenen Schweiß. Der zweite Band greift teilweise
dieselben Themen und Bilder wieder auf, aber ist
homogener, sprachlich geschliffener und eleganter.
Vor allen Dingen, die Ironie, die auch schon im ersten
Band anklang, taucht nun mehr oder weniger systema-
tisch in jedem Gedicht auf und verleiht somit dieser
ganzen Sammlung eine neue Dimension. In diesem Sinn
ist vielleicht eines der besten Gedichte dieses Bandes
"Das triste Furnier des Tisches." Hier erleben wir
noch einmal die Kommunikationsschwierigkeiten, die
zwischenmenschlichen Probleme, die exakte Beobach-
tungsgabe fürs Detail, den Willen zur Handlung und die
immanente Ironie:

Das triste Furnier des Tisches
belebst du mit blauem Steingut.
Klirrend zur Ordnung rufst du Messer
   und Gabeln.
Schaukelnd steigt der durchlichtete Tee
   ins Glas.
In deine sanften Lippen geraten
blutet sich aus die Tomate.
Aufgestört und wehrlos dem Zugriff
Zwiebeln in saftiger Nacktheit,
von deinem arglosen Blick gezeichnet,
schon ist das Schicksal der letzten
   Olive besiegelt.
Ohne zu zögern hervor aus dem Gatter
   der Wimpern
wechselt dein Blick auf mich. Doch
   munter
köpf ich das Ei. Sonntag morgens um
   neun.   (S. 71)

University of Northern Iowa

125

Anmerkungen

[1] Aus einem Brief von Laabs an Fritz H. König vom 26.2.81.

[2] Alle Bücher sind im Mitteldeutschen Verlag, Halle erschienen.

[3] Joochen Laabs, "Raum durch Worte," NDL, 28, Heft 3 (1980), 113 ff.

[4] Laabs, "Raum durch Worte," S. 114.

[5] Vgl. F.H. König, Buchbesprechung von Der Ausbruch, GDR Bulletin, 7, Heft 2 (1981), 9.

[6] Gerhard Rothbauer, "Wieviel Himmel braucht der Mensch? Zum Werk von Joochen Laabs," Weimarer Beiträge, 26, Heft 6 (1980), 74 ff.

[7] Ingrid Hähnel, "Interview mit Joochen Laabs," Weimarer Beiträge, 26, Heft 6 (1980), 51 ff.

[8] Hähnel, "Interview," S. 64.

Heinz Knobloch's Herr Moses in Berlin:
An Innovative Reclamation of the Jewish
Component of the GDR Cultural Heritage

Nancy A. Lauckner

The year 1979 brought the two hundred-fiftieth
anniversary of the birth of the eighteenth-century
philosopher Moses Mendelssohn, born on September 6,
1729. During the anniversary year there were the
customary celebrations and publications, many of which
took place in the GDR since Mendelssohn was born in
Dessau and spent most of his life in a part of Berlin
which now belongs to East Berlin. One of the most
unusual of the commemorative works published was a
book entitled Herr Moses in Berlin by the feuilleton-
ist Heinz Knobloch. It sold out rapidly, and a second
edition appeared in 1980. This is noteworthy because
the work is not a facilely narrated biographical novel
which would attract a broad readership. Although no
great literary achievement, the book deserves attention for its innovative approach and significant contribution to Erbeaneignung. Knobloch goes beyond the
limited scope of most commemorative works by using his
discussion of Mendelssohn as an opportunity to explore
and reclaim the Jewish component of the GDR cultural
heritage. To achieve this goal, he assembles an impressive collection of information on Mendelssohn,
Jewish culture and history, eighteenth-century Germany, Berlin, the Nazi past, and the contemporary
scene. The result is a tribute to Moses Mendelssohn
which vividly demonstrates how intricately the Jewish
contribution is woven into the German heritage.[1]

A brief investigation of the structure and narrative techniques of Knobloch's work is helpful before
examining his themes and purposes. From the outset he
underscores the feuilletonistic character of the book,
finally citing Ilja Ehrenburg: "Ich . . . halte den

Einfall des Zeitungsstils in die Romansphäre für ein legitimes Mittel, neue Formen des Erzählens aufzuspüren."[2] He states that he is writing neither a novel (p. 13) nor a biography (p. 16), and insists on permitting the content of his genreless work to determine its own form: "sich seine Formen mitzubringen oder selbst zu verschaffen" (p. 19). The result is a mixture of "Dokument + Essay + Fiktion" (p. 14) reminiscent of Christa Wolf's Kindheitsmuster and Johnson's Jahrestage,[3] yet far more documentary and less fictional than either of these works. Knobloch's description of his style as "phantasievoll-exakt" (p. 14) recalls Wolf's effort to achieve "phantastische Genauigkeit."[4] The documentary content of his book is impressive and extensive: it includes quotations from Mendelssohn's letters and literary works, from other authors about him, and from and about other contemporary authors; entries from lexica and other reference works; citations from the Talmud, rabbinical lore, and Jewish sayings; passages from novels, poetry, and songs; excerpts from newspapers, official announcements, and documents; and photographs of various Mendelssohniana. The essayistic aspects comprise "die dem Leser zugedachten Äußerungen" (p. 14), such as the author's feelings, experiences, intentions, and working methods; and his inclusion of the Nazi era and the present à la Wolf and Johnson. The fictional element is the least important; it contains anecdotes, occasional dialogue in dramatic form, humor, and just enough of a story line, based on Mendelssohn's life, to keep the action moving relatively chronologically and to provide the framework for the documentary and essayistic content. The character of this approach is well captured by the subtitle: "Auf den Spuren eines Menschenfreundes." Knobloch's effort to interpret Mendelssohn's significance might also have been effectively titled "Nachdenken über Moses M." or "Mutmaßungen über Moses."

The effect of this structure and these techniques is to slow the reader's progress by necessitating critical thought. Although Knobloch suggests that it may be "einer der Nachteile dieses Buches, daß es zum langsamen Lesen, Innehalten und Durchdenken nötigt" (p. 9), he intends his work to do just that. Writing, as he maintains (p. 14), for readers who want to distinguish between historical fact and the author's imagination, he forces the reader to work with him by doing some independent thinking, occasionally identifying with a character (p. 13), and playing with ideas suggested by the information provided (p. 14). Thus the reader is expected to contribute to the fictional and essayistic aspects of the work. Knobloch even solicits assistance with the documentary component by stating that the reader "kann und wird abschweifen. Es ist, wenn er will, ein archäologisches Buch. Lauter Ausgrabungen" (p. 15). By "digging up" information on Mendelssohn and the Jewish cultural contribution, the author hopes to inspire the reader to interrupt his reading periodically to investigate the present situation of the Jews in his own area, their history in Germany (p. 15), and Jewish culture in general (p. 457). Thus Herr Moses in Berlin serves as a personal workbook or do-it-yourself manual in the Jewish cultural heritage of the GDR.

The immediate purpose or theme of the book is to present Mendelssohn as one of the "Classicists" whom the GDR should claim and honor. Knobloch found that no one in his audiences had heard of this Mendelssohn (p. 15), and admits that even he scarcely knew his name when he began his research (p. 455). Since few people know more about Mendelssohn than his name and virtually only scholars read anything he wrote, the author is determined to see that his subject is not forgotten (p. 12). This effort to rescue Mendelssohn from oblivion is especially important for the GDR audience because Marx dismissed Mendelssohn as a "'Seichbeutel'" (p. 16) and "als Beispiel für den 'dem deutschen Bürger eingebornen "Kleinbürger"'" (p. 429). Although Knobloch considers such criticism "ein Grund mehr, sich für Herrn Moses zu interessieren" and ridicules the practice of consulting Marx before forming an opinion of someone (p. 16), he can cite statements by Lenin and Engels in favor of the Jews and against anti-Semitism (pp. 79, 346) to legitimate his interest in Mendelssohn. His position is not a dissident one, yet he does take pains to justify his portrayal of a man who was, after all, a "frühkapitalistische[r] Industriekaufmann" as an undeservedly unsung part of the GDR cultural heritage (p. 332).

Of course Knobloch provides basic biographical details about Mendelssohn, but more importantly he stresses certain aspects of his subject's life and work, and plays down others, to justify portraying him as a model part of that heritage. He readily admits that several facets of Mendelssohn's life are not exemplary to show that he is not praising non-socialist values. Mendelssohn's role as a capitalist indus-

trialist is not presented as a good economic example
(p. 332), yet Knobloch implicitly lauds him as a man
who did good work and who had to work hard in the
business world in order to make a meager living despite his desire to devote himself to philosophy (p.
110). He also illustrates Mendelssohn's integrity by
stressing his refusal to participate in a Jewish
counterfeiting scheme promoted by the king even though
an improved financial situation would have given him
more time for study (pp. 143-46). By concentrating on
these aspects of Mendelssohn's business career, he
depicts him as an honorable worker instead of a capitalist exploiter and thus enables GDR readers to
identify with him. Mendelssohn's piety and the reli-
gious nature of many of his works present another
problem, which the author confronts by making no
effort to portray religiosity as exemplary and by
admitting that Marx was right, "wenn er mit den 'Mor-
genstunden' nichts anfangen konnte" (p. 454). Rather
than condemning his subject's religious and philosophical views, Knobloch simply does not hold them up for
emulation; instead he presents him as a progressive
thinker for his day, both as an adherent of the Enlightenment philosophy and as an opponent of Orthodox
obscurantism. Thus, GDR readers can accept Mendelssohn's contributions as progress even though he never
reached the socialist goal.

Clearly, it is the human being Mendelssohn, not
the industrialist, devout Jew, or philosopher, on whom
the author focuses, as evidenced by the subtitle and
the suggestion that "der Mensch" Mendelssohn may serve
as a model for the socialist world (p. 332). Certainly Mendelssohn's overcoming of great personal odds
is presented as exemplary. Frequent references to his
poverty tend to legitimate him as a proletarian hero
even though he was a merchant. Admiration is also
solicited for his rising above his physical handicaps
of a deformed body and stuttering. His most serious
handicap, his being a Jew, receives the most attention. The incongruity between his intellectual accomplishments and the prejudiced treatment he was
accorded is repeatedly stressed. For example, he was
subjected to special fees exacted of Jews (p. 261) and
suffered the abuse heaped upon Jews in public places
(pp. 301f.). Knobloch is particularly incensed because Mendelssohn had to beg the king for the mediocre
status of "außerordentlicher Schutzjude" (p. 64) and
that the fee for this privilege be waived; he is also
indignant because Mendelssohn's wife and children

could have been banished immediately after his death (p. 178). That Mendelssohn surmounted all these hardships to become, as Schütz wrote, "'the philosopher of Germany'" (p. 377), an integral part of the Enlightenment, certainly establishes him as a model and justifies his place in the cultural heritage.

While he honors the purely personal achievements, Knobloch places greater emphasis on Mendelssohn's cultural contributions and service to others. He shows that the German and European Jews were the beneficiaries of Mendelssohn's efforts on behalf of political and intellectual emancipation. Mendelssohn made many contributions to Jewish intellectual advancement besides his philosophical works. The author cites his founding and editing of the "first modern Jewish magazine" (p. 94) and his translating of biblical texts. Mendelssohn himself saw his translation of the Bible into German printed in Hebrew letters as "'der erste Schritt zur Kultur'" (p. 288). By using the German alphabet for his later translation of Psalms, he further facilitated his Jewish readers' mastery of German (p. 403). Knobloch also mentions Mendelssohn's promoting the founding of "the first Jewish Freischule in Germany" (p. 323). He shows that these efforts for intellectual emancipation were coupled with equally important ones on behalf of political emancipation, citing Moritz Brasch's view that Mendelssohn's great service lay in educating the Jews to recognize their value as human beings and their consequent right to political emancipation (pp. 178-79). This attempt to raise the consciousness of the Jewish people was complemented by Mendelssohn's appeals for citizens' rights for Jews, tolerance, and abandonment of prejudice, in works directed to a general German and European audience as well as to Jews. Knobloch stresses that Mendelssohn did not limit his political service to theoretical writings, but intervened actively on behalf of individual Jews and Jewish communities that needed his help.

Knobloch further demonstrates, in ways that I will not enumerate here, that Mendelssohn contributed significantly to German as well as Jewish culture. Because of his accomplishments for German culture, the Berlinische Monatsschrift eulogized him as "'der Stolz und die Zierde unsrer Stadt'" (p. 448). Such recognition for a Jew reflects what Knobloch implicitly presents as Mendelssohn's most significant achievement, his contribution to changing the relationship between Jews and Germans. By promoting emancipation, he helped to prepare an atmosphere in which Jewish and German scholars could value each other as co-seekers of philosophical truth. Although he did not live to see political emancipation, his life and works exemplified the benefits which it would bring to German and Jewish culture. Knobloch even implies that Mendelssohn's pursuit of a changed relationship of Jews and Germans was revolutionary, citing a letter in which Mendelssohn described how the Jews must respond to efforts to prevent emancipation: "'Es müssen . . . immer mehrere unter uns aufstehen, die sich ohne Geräusch hervortun und Verdienste zeigen, ohne lauten Anspruch zu machen'" (p. 236). By concluding this section with the remark "Marx scheint diesen Brief nicht gekannt zu haben" (p. 236), Knobloch implicitly nullifies Marx's dismissal of Mendelssohn as a "Seich-beutel" and facilitates his own presentation of him as a model in his capacity as revolutionary Vorkämpfer of the progressive ideals of emancipation, tolerance, and the "'Sieg der Menschlichkeit über alle Vorurteile'" (p. 423), as Franzos wrote.

From this central focus on Mendelssohn's life and work, Knobloch develops several ancillary themes, sometimes digressing markedly from Mendelssohn, yet always shedding new light on the Jewish component of the GDR cultural heritage. One of the most important themes, Jewish culture and history, is essential for understanding Mendelssohn as a product of that back-ground. The author repeatedly explains facets of Jewish life which may be unfamiliar to his readers (p. 79), such as holy days, food and eating, circumcision, beard wearing, the Yiddish language, the charge of ritual murder, etc. He discourses at length on reli-gious matters, which require more detailed informa-tion. He devotes much attention to Jewish cultural history in order to acquaint his readers with this rich and largely unknown part of their heritage, for he is offering "Nachrichten aus unserer Vorgeschichte" (p. 176) and protesting "diese schreckliche Gleichgül-tigkeit gegenüber unserer Geschichte" in order to supplement and even correct previous training in Staatsbürgerkunde (pp. 332-33). Knobloch focuses mainly on the history of the German Jews, especially those in eighteenth-century Prussia. He stresses the power of the rabbis and their prohibition of secular learning; enumerates the various oppressive fines, taxes, and regulations imposed upon the Jews by the government; and traces the road to emancipation.

Besides trying to illuminate Mendelssohn's situation by these glimpses into the Jewish heritage, Knobloch also seeks to refute the Nazi claim that the Jews had made no cultural contributions ("Kulturtaten") in Germany (p. 154). He succeeds in that attempt by portraying not only the cultural contributions of Mendelssohn but also those of many other German Jews.

To counter any idea that the Jewish culture and history he is describing are alien to the German heritage, Knobloch develops another secondary theme: eighteenth-century German life. He records assessments of Mendelssohn by the latter's contemporaries and offers fascinating behind-the-scenes glimpses of the intellectual life of the day. Thus we meet Mendelssohn's friends Nicolai, Lessing, Ramler, Gleim, Herz, Bloch; his adversaries Lavater and Jacobi; as well as many others who were tangentially connected with him. Knobloch acquaints the reader with works from this period which are difficult to obtain in the GDR, among them Mendelssohn's Phädon (p. 192), his translation of the Old Testament (p. 280), and Lichtenberg's Timorus (p. 210), often citing extensive passages. He calls attention to authors whom he considers unjustly ignored contributors to the GDR heritage, explaining the achievements which entitle each a place in the cultural pantheon. These include Ephraim Moses Kuh (pp. 263-64) and "unseren Klassiker Lichtenberg" (p. 210). He also supplements works about the period by noting the names and contributions of people overlooked by reference books, such as Christian Wilhelm Dohm, who proposed citizenship for Jews (pp. 349-53).

Berlin, too, serves as an ancillary thematic focus. Since Mendelssohn spent most of his life there, Knobloch necessarily portrays eighteenth-century Berlin. He uses today's Berlin as an archaeological site for "excavating" memories connected with his other themes, much as the narrator of Wolf's Kindheitsmuster uses a visit to her former hometown to spark her memory. Thus, he often traces Mendelssohn's steps through Berlin, showing what he would have seen had he walked the same path in the nineteenth or twentieth centuries and comparing this with the appearance of the same places in Mendelssohn's day. Parks, buildings, parking lots, and the presence or absence of statues or commemorative tablets thus bear mute testimony to significant moments in Berlin's past and the degree to which they are still remembered (p.

103). Yet it is not the city itself but its splendid heritage which Knobloch celebrates, particularly the enrichment of Berlin's culture by the fruitful interaction of Jews and Germans. The undertone of mourning for this "[v]erklungene Berliner Kultur" (p. 370) is poignantly expressed in his description of its vitality just days before Hitler's assumption of power: he recalls the grand opening of the Berlin Jewish Museum on January 24, 1933, and a synagogue concert on January 29th at which Albert Einstein played a Bach violin concerto (pp. 369-70).

The author does not end his study of the Jewish component of German culture with the year 1933, but includes the Nazi era as another of his secondary themes. He does this in part because this period represents one stage of the history he is tracing, but, like Wolf in Kindheitsmuster, he also has a didactic purpose. He shares her view of the writer's moral duty to present this information, [5] asking "wer darf sich das leisten: weiterleben in Unkenntnis? Wer schreibt, der hat auch Chronistenpflicht" (p. 14). Like her, he wants to record this period for the benefit of youth,[6] who know "too little" about these events now that the older generation is dying out (p. 337). By including this era, he acts on his conviction that it is "ganz richtig, die Spuren der deutschen Geschichte nicht zu glätten" (p. 422), a practice which he condemns in frequent references to Grünanlagen planted where there should be historical markers (pp. 9, 176, 315, et passim). By discussing the Nazi era, he forces his readers to confront its attempt to eradicate the Jewish component of the German heritage and to reverse the gains which Mendelssohn and others had made in interweaving the two cultures.

Knobloch offers no organized account of the Nazi era, but provides glimpses of varied facets of that period. Some of the scenes derive from his experiences as a young boy in Nazi Germany; by "excavating" his memories following the principle "Lebensgeschichte meldet sich zum Weitergeben" (p. 17), he encourages his readers to do the same (pp. 15, 70), which is another technique he shares with Wolf.[7] In addition to personal experiences, he recounts many other facts and incidents related to the treatment of Jews in the Third Reich, such as the obligatory use of the names "Sara" and "Israel," book burnings, vituperation of the Talmud, Kristallnacht, and even the publication

134

stoppage of the Jubiläumsausgabe of Mendelssohn's works (p. 303) and the failure to observe the one hundred-fiftieth anniversary of his death in 1936 (p. 304). Most of these references are brief, yet Knobloch often betrays his feelings about the matters described with phrases like "die unmenschlichen Ereignisse" (p. 259) or "[e]ines schlimmen Tages" (p. 423). While he sometimes reflects on the fate of individuals in the Nazi era (p. 155), he seldom treats the extermination of the Jews directly, referring to it instead in asides, subordinate clauses and allusions, often with a biting undertone. Thus he describes how the pejorative word "Judenschule" is dying out: "es [das Wort] stirbt den Juden hinterher, die vor vielen Jahren sterben mußten und daher fast ausgestorben sind" (p. 326). This technique maintains distance from the worst horrors, forces the reader to think about the Jews' fate, and expresses the author's anger and sadness more effectively than a direct j'accuse.

To complete his portrayal of the Jewish contribution to the German cultural heritage, Knobloch includes the present as a final ancillary theme. This approach is reminiscent of Wolf's method in Kindheitsmuster; he even explains the use of contemporary events and concerns in a similar way: "Unweigerlich macht sich beim Schreiben täglich der heutige Tag bemerkbar und soll das auch. Die vergangene Woche gehört dazu wie das bisherige Leben" (p. 17).[8] Unlike Wolf, Knobloch confines his attention largely to the GDR and, by extension, to other socialist countries, referring seldom to western nations. Some of his remarks are only tenuously connected with the main concerns of his work. Of the contemporary references which are clearly related to his themes, some pertain to Mendelssohn. To foster empathy, he points out similarities between our lives and Mendelssohn's, mentioning letter writing (p. 180), constant interruptions (p. 181), prejudice against minorities (p. 359), contributing to charity (p. 388), and the experience of death (p. 444). Another group of references relates to remnants or aftereffects of the Nazi era in the present. He alludes to the persistence of Nazi melodies and texts in the memories of his contemporaries (p. 340)[9] and to isolated anti-Semitic incidents in the GDR (pp. 79-80, 112, 294), yet he also notes attempts to keep alive the remembrance of Nazi crimes by purposely not restoring certain ravaged buildings and statues (pp. 368, 422). Many references to the present concern efforts in the GDR to preserve

and commemorate the Jewish component of its cultural
heritage. Thus, he points to performances of Lessing's Die Juden (p. 73) and Nathan der Weise (pp.
308-309); to Nathan being assigned as obligatory
reading in school (p. 78); and to books and films
about the Holocaust which have become bestsellers (p.
79). He also mentions the postwar resumption of the
publishing of the Mendelssohn Jubiläumsausgabe (p.
303) and applauds the efforts to revitalize Berlin's
once strong Jewish cultural life, symbolized by the
opening of a 1650-volume library of the Jewish community on Oranienburger Straße (p. 368). Most such
references commend the GDR's response to its Jewish
heritage despite Knobloch's concern about the "indif-
ference" (p. 332) indicated by some failures to commemorate that heritage (pp. 363, 418) and about some
lingering prejudice. Clearly he sees progress being
made toward the "'Sieg der Menschlichkeit über alle
Vorurteile'. . . . ungeachtet alle Rückschläge und
Behinderungen" (p. 423).

Herr Moses in Berlin is Knobloch's contribution
to that ultimate victory by reclaiming the Jewish
component of GDR cultural history. He achieves this
goal by innovatively combining a focus on Mendelssohn
with ancillary themes which illuminate the Jewish
heritage from other angles and by employing a mixture
of fiction, documentation, and essay reminiscent of
Wolf's and Johnson's techniques. Guided by his rhetorical question "Was kann es schaden, wenn einer vom
anderen mehr erfährt?" (p. 282), he selects his material and develops his text by applying Mendelssohn's
own criteria: "Wird dadurch die Kenntnis der Menschen
berichtigt oder vermehrt? Das Nachdenken gestärkt?"
(p. 341). In accord with his desire for reader participation, he includes a selected bibliography for
those whom he has inspired to further study of the
Jewish cultural heritage. This author shares Knobloch's sentiments: "Ich wünschte, es wären viele" (p.
457).

The University of Tennessee, Knoxville

                              Notes

    [1] In this essay I differentiate between Jewish
and non-Jewish Germans by using the terms "Jews" and

"Germans." This is done solely to avoid repeated cumbersome circumscriptions. The terms should not be construed as having any other meaning.

[2] Heinz Knobloch, Herr Moses in Berlin: Auf den Spuren eines Menschenfreundes, 2nd ed. (E. Berlin: Buchverlag Der Morgen, 1980), p. 456. Subsequent references will appear parenthetically in the text. All translations are my own.

[3] Hans Mayer ("Der Mut zur Unaufrichtigkeit," rev. of Kindheitsmuster, by Christa Wolf, Der Spiegel, 11 April 1977, p. 185) discusses the similarity of Kindheitsmuster to Jahrestage and Wolf's penchant for writing works reminiscent of Johnson's.

[4] Christa Wolf, Kindheitsmuster (E. Berlin and Weimar: Aufbau, 1976), p. 354.

[5] Cf. Wolf's statements "daß diejenigen, die es [the Nazi era] miterlebt haben . . . , eine gewisse Pflicht haben, sich darüber zu äußern" and that "Berufsmoral" requires her to address this matter before going on to other topics ("Diskussion mit Christa Wolf," Sinn und Form, 28, No. 4 [1976], 861-62).

[6] See Hans Kaufmann, "Gespräch mit Christa Wolf," Weimarer Beiträge, 20, No. 6 (1974), 99.

[7] See Heinz Plavius, "Gewissensforschung," rev. of Kindheitsmuster, by Christa Wolf, Neue Deutsche Literatur, 25, No. 1 (January 1977), 144.

[8] The narrator of Kindheitsmuster says: "In die Erinnerung drängt sich die Gegenwart ein, und der heutige Tag ist schon der letzte Tag der Vergangenheit" (p. 10).

[9] Cf. Kindheitsmuster, whose narrator tries to no avail to forget the Nazi songs of her youth (p. 500).

Adaptations of Dramas and Myths of
Antiquity in GDR Drama

Gordon Tracy

In the 1960s and 1970s a number of GDR dramatists
turned their attention to ancient Greek dramas and
myths; a wave of adaptations and spectacular productions resulted. Peter Hacks, Heiner Müller, and
Stefan Schütz were the most productive, but Joachim
Knauth, Armin Stolper, and Karl Mickel also made
worthy contributions. Hack's Der Frieden (after
Aristophanes), directed by Benno Besson at the
Deutsches Theater in 1962, was the first in an impressive series of productions. Hack writes in his essay
"Kunst und Revolution" that "die Kommunisten ent-
schlossen sind, den Schatz an Gütern und Fähigkeiten,
den die veralteten Klassen akkumuliert haben, nicht
fortzuwerfen, sondern sich anzueignen und auf eine
höhere Stufe zu heben." [1]

In this essay I will first outline the importance
of antiquity for GDR dramatists and critics, then
discuss the themes which are of particular interest to
GDR dramatists and, on the basis of a few dramas,
examine their way of looking at antiquity.

Antiquity stands at the beginning of the cultural
and intellectual history of the occidental world. It
is generally considered a golden utopian age, and the
Germans have long been impressed by its "devastating
glory" (Hölderlin). The high artistic level, the
command of style and form, of the dramas of antiquity
is a decisive factor in their reception in the GDR.
They are also felt to be intellectually stimulating
and entertaining. Peter Hacks writes: "Die einzigen
nicht langweiligen Stücke, die je verfaßt worden, sind
die der Griechen." [2] All the basic questions of human
existence are considered in ancient Greek dramas and

myths: life and death, freedom and necessity, the relationship between individual and society, the perfection and imperfection of man. General human and social problems are also treated: war, peace, the gods, ideals, fate, the role of woman, and the family.

In the introduction to his Grundrisse der Kritik der politischen Ökonomie, Marx described the art and epic of antiquity as "norm and unattainable models."[3] He read Aeschylus in the original Greek every year and considered Aeschylus and Shakespeare the greatest dramatic geniuses that mankind has produced; he made frequent reference to antiquity in Das Kapital and other writings. Marx was impressed by what he considered the youthful charm of antiquity and found in it something of the naivety and truthfulness of the child, which he thought modern man should strive to regain. For Marx, antiquity was an essential part of the education and development of man. He believed that man, in absorbing art and knowledge, becomes rich, not because he possesses much, but because he is much. Intellectual wealth is the important thing.

Lenin, in an address before a congress of the Komsomol in 1920, said: "only through an accurate knowledge of the culture which has been created in the course of the entire development of humanity, only through a re-working of this culture can a proletarian culture be built."[4] The director Benno Besson expresses a similar view in connection with his production of Heiner Müller's Ödipus Tyrann: "Man bewältigt die heutige Wirklichkeit, wenn man mit der Art fertig wird, wie vergangene Kunst die Wirklichkeit bewältigt hat. Ohne diesen Umweg geht es nicht."[5]

The GDR critic Christoph Trilse considers the plays of antiquity eminently political and maintains that they present social totality.[6] The GDR director Ingeborg Pietzsch finds in ancient Greek plays "alle Grundmuster politischen Verhaltens" and adduces as examples: "die tyrannische Machtgier (eines Aigisth und einer Klytaimnestra . . .), die . . . Kampfbereitschaft (einer gedemütigten Elektra), der in die Tat verwandelte Widerstand (eines Orest . . .), die intelligente politische List und Vorsicht (des Erziehers). . . . "[7]

Antiquity presents an ideal image of man, and European humanism has its deepest roots in the ancient world. Marxists find Marx's ideals partly realized in

man of antiquity, whom they see as free, not yet
alienated, and in a productive and harmonious relationship with his fellowmen and nature. GDR dramatists express the Marxist concern for the development
of man, the cultivation of his individual strengths
and creative powers.

The GDR has, in common with antiquity, an inaugu-
ral or inceptive quality, and GDR society, like that
of antiquity, is undergoing radical change. In antiquity came the transition, after the long dominance of
families or clans (gentes), from original communism
(Urkommunismus) to the class and slaveholding society.
The GDR is now experiencing the second great upheaval,
the transition to a classless society. In antiquity
the patriarchate won out over the matriarchate, a
conflict which Trilse considers the oldest class
struggle on earth, a theme from the Urrevolution.[8]
Hacks describes it as a social struggle with nearly
agitprop dimensions:

> Die auf uns gekommene Version, der
> zufolge Orest der Ehebrecherin den
> verdienten Lohn erteilt . . . , ist
> eine Propagandafassung, in die Welt
> gesetzt von Ideologen der Männerherr-
> schaft. Für sie war der Muttermörder
> eine Art patriarchalischer Revolutionär
> . . . Alle Geschichten über das Haus
> Tantalos sind ursprünglich Geschichten
> über die Durchsetzung des Vaterrechts.[9]

The patriarchate is thought to be on the wane in the
GDR. Rudolf Schottlaender writes: "Die Geschlechts-
bevorrechtung gilt als menschenunwürdige Grundtorheit,
weil sie die eine Hälfte der Menschheit zurück-
setzt." [10]

In what he calls his classical plays, Hacks repeatedly considers the emancipation of humanity and
views it, in part, in the light of the emancipation of
woman. In his Omphale [11] and Adam und Eva,[12] he treats
new dimensions in the love between man and woman and
portrays a deep, fully experienced relationship, which
he sees as an aspect of socialist humanism.

Enjoyment of life and sensual pleasure are seen
in the GDR as increasingly important aspects of the
self-realization of man, of a future social harmony
and utopia. Trilse refers to Hegel's statement in his

141

Ästhetik that without having read Aristophanes "läßt sich kaum wissen, wie dem Menschen sauwohl sein kann."[13] Song, dance, and folk festivals appear in a good many GDR adaptations. There is also a new freedom in erotic matters. Trilse writes: "Die Befreiung der Liebe, die Legitimierung der Erotik, bei den Alten noch selbstverständlicher Anspruch, stehen hier und heute auf der Tagesordnung."[14] A freer, perhaps more hedonistic, way of life is seen as a sign of maturity and is intended to suggest the gaiety of life in the socialist society. In Knauth's Die Weibervolksversammlung, the president of the new gynocracy tears up the more austere new law governing sexual behavior, and one hears an urgent plea for the enjoyment of life.[15] In Hacks' Der Frieden Trygaios restores peace, in part, so that he can pursue his pleasures.[16] Lascivious and wise, Trygaios takes pleasure in his struggle for peace and his sexual exploits. The fun he has frees his emotions and works as a catalyst in his self-fulfillment. In general, Hacks' adaptations are celebrations and jocose-thoughtful spectacles which are meant to bring pleasure. Enjoyment of life, pleasure in work, and sexual pleasure are seen as aspects of peace, freedom, and the development of socialist man.

For Marx, the Greek gods and myths were symbols of man and of human powers. For the socialists, the gods, demigods, heroes, and revolutionaries are all great figures, all part of one and the same spectrum. In socialist society everyone is thought capable of becoming a great man. In GDR adaptations the gods are often anthropomorphized or secularized; they appear as noble supermen, as ideal humans (Jupiter in Hacks' Amphitryon),[17] as angry god-fathers who nevertheless prod humans into action (Zeus in Müller's Herakles 5),[18] or as all-too-human and corruptible (Zeus and Hermes in Hacks' Der Frieden).

Marx based his life on a Promethean devotion to struggle and defiance of the ruling gods and ruling classes. The Prometheus myth dominated his thinking from youth on, and the basic principle of his life was the line from Aeschylus' Prometheus Bound: "In a word, all gods are my enemies." In his dissertation Marx wrote that Prometheus was "the noblest saint and martyr in the calendar of philosophy." Prometheus is often revered in progressive circles as the ideal revolutionary figure.

One finds a second standpoint in the GDR reception of antiquity. While traditional reverence is shown for the ideal of beauty, the image of the beautiful human being, the high artistic quality--all humanist and utopian aspects of antiquity--some GDR theater people underline the ugly and inhuman aspects of antiquity: the bloody conflicts, power struggles, and predatory wars that were prominent in ancient Greek life and art. Hacks writes:

> Tantalos zeugte den Pelops. Pelops
> zeugte den Atreus und den Thyestes.
> Atreus zeugte den Agamemnon, Agamemnon
> den Orest. In den unmittelbaren Bege-
> benheiten dieser fünf Herren ereigneten
> sich die Schlachtung und Verspeisung
> von 6 Knaben . . . 2 der klassischen
> und beispielgebenden Fälle von Homo-
> sexualität, 2 Schändungen von Töchtern
> durch ihre Väter, 1 Vatermord, 1 Mut-
> termord, 1 Gattenmord, 1 Tochtermord,
> nicht zu rechnen Selbstmorde, Ehebrüche
> . . . Das Haus des Tantalos, das ist
> die Menschheit. Seine Greuel, das sind
> die Greuel der Klassengesellschaft.
> Ihr angeerbter Fluch ist das Eigentum,
> das sich, wie bekanntlich die böse Tat,
> ständig reproduziert.[19]

In Müller's adaptations, especially Philoktet, Ödipus Tyrann, and Prometheus (also Macbeth), barbarism is the basic theme. Müller intends the barbaric old world to have a frightening and disquieting effect.

The attitude toward antiquity, however, remains positive. Hack writes in a cunningly paradoxical way: "Die Welt Athens ist zerrissen genug für die Tragödie, harmonisch genug für die Komödie, zerrissen und harmonisch genug für äußerste Kunst."[20] Rolf Rohmer, the GDR theater scholar, speaks with confidence of the ability of GDR dramatists to interpret antiquity in a meaningful way and maintains: "unser Weltbild wird in überraschender Weise bestätigt . . . das humanistische Erbe kommt uns für das tiefere Verständnis unserer Gegenwart zugute. Dramatik dieser Art scheint mir . . . nicht nur legitim, sondern höchst notwendig."[21]

Proceeding thematically, I shall now consider

a number of adaptations more closely. First, those that deal with drastic social and political change. The most striking treatment of this theme is Joachim Knauth's Die Weibervolksversammlung, a rollicking comedy after Aristophanes in which the women establish a new social order and do away with the false war economy of the men. They disguise themselves as men with beards, walking sticks, and rough tunics, and go to early morning assembly. The men, without their clothes—and with no one to make their breakfast—miss the meeting, and the women rule the state. Their program: peace, the abolition of private property, an end to criminal activity, and festivals of joy. It is declared that "die Kinder gehören allen, denn bei diesem schönen Leben hat jedes mehrere Väter, . . . wodurch endlich unter uns ein Gemeinschaftsgefühl wächst" (p. 88) and that "frei und allgemein sind auch die Weiber" (p. 87). The rest of the play has to do with the problems and conflicts that result from the establishment of such a utopia, but it ends with a festive banquet, music, fireworks, and a Volksfest.

Hans Pfeiffer's Begegnung mit Herkules is full of proud pronouncements about man, history, and social progress.22 Kulle, the worker and "Kleinausgabe eines Herkules" (p. 130), says: "Wir errangen die größte Freiheit der Geschichte, die Freiheit über unsere Geschichte" (p. 131). Hercules wants to contribute to making " [u]nsere Welt bewohnbar . . . für ihre Bebauer" (p. 130) and Kulle points to the continuity of such strivings when he says to Hercules: "Wir liebten dich, wie seine Kindheit der Mann noch liebt . . . An die Stelle der Keule setzten wir den Hammer, den Zirkel und den Ährenkranz" (p. 164). There is frequent mention of the land of the Hyperboreans, a utopian land where the boundary between dreams and accomplishments disappeared, where dreams of peace, the hope for freedom, and the just distribution of wealth were realized. Hercules declares that such dreams and deeds have become reality in his temporary new home, the GDR. Hercules and Kulle must however still fight against things that are not altogether in order. The hydra and Cerberus are still in the land; the revolution is not complete. In his essay "Prämisse sozialistischer Dramatik," Pfeiffer advocates a "heraklitisch-faustische Welt" of constant change and readiness to change. 23

The second theme to be considered is that of the self-realization of man and the development of his

individual powers.   In Stolper's <u>Amphitryon</u>, a clever
imitation of the comedy by Plautus, man is assigned a
decisive role in the improvement of the world and of
conditions. [24]   As we hear in the play, man himself
should produce the hero and dragon killer.   Zeus says
to Amphitryon: "Doch wenn du tust, was ich hier laut
verkündete, / Wird dir der Himmel ewig dankbar sein"
(p. 63).   If man takes the initiative, the necessary
powers or historical processes will be activated.

Karl Mickel's <u>Nausikaa</u>, an imaginative and grotesque play that borders on the absurd, is interesting
for the questions it raises regarding personal relations, power relationships, and our attitudes toward
others. [25]   In an appendix to the play, Mickel poses
questions first raised in the play by the slave Knos-
sos and by King Alkinoos, who delivers a long, fiery
speech on the power of the glance of the other, the
eye of the neighbor.   Mickel also touches on human
rights and servitude as well as our relations with our
superiors.   To quote a few passages from the appendix:
"Sie kennen Ihren Chef; kennt Ihr Chef Sie? . . . Was
heißt das überhaupt: kennen? . . . Baut Ihr Chef Ihnen
goldene Brücken? oder läßt er Sie den Boden lecken:
Lecken Sie den Boden?"   (pp. 92-93).   Here Mickel
considers questions of authority and power in others
and of weakness, obsequiousness, and egoism in ourselves.   He also recommends a keen awareness of the
subtler aspects of the relationships between man and
servant, between man and man.

The title figure of Müller's <u>Prometheus</u>, who
loves men more than he loves the gods and wishes to
help them develop, appears as a productive revolutionary and a martyr to his efforts on behalf of man's
growth. [26]   Müller's <u>Ödipus Tyrann</u> is of great significance in connection with the development of man. [27]
Oedipus is seen as a heroic seeker after truth and as
creator of himself.   Karl-Heinz Müller writes: "Im
Stück wird der historische Punkt gezeigt, an dem das
Individuum aus der Gemeinschaft vortritt.   Das Stück
wurde aufgeführt zu einem Zeitpunkt, an dem das Individuum wieder eintritt in die Gemeinschaft und so
seine gewonnenen individuellen Kräfte freisetzen und
realisieren kann." [28]   Benno Besson says, in a discussion of his production of <u>Ödipus</u> which is included in
the Aufbau edition of the play: "Wir haben uns zunächst um den Werdegang von Ödipus und nicht um das
vorbestimmte Schicksal gekümmert." [29]   Besson also
speaks of the chiefly social elements that constitute

145

Oedipus' fate and of Oedipus' struggle for knowledge
and knowledge of himself: "Er . . . kommt zu dem
Schluß, er könne sich, sein Schicksal allein aufbauen.
Das ist eine revolutionäre Tat, eine große Haltung der
Figur" (p. 126). The struggle between Oedipus and
fate--between man and gods--is represented as a struggle between the individual and society. Besson and
his colleagues emphasize the great rational power of
Oedipus; they take the view that he blinds himself in
order to live in the world of absolute truth and pure
thought: "[er] findet oder erfindet das Reich der Ab-
straktion" (p. 125). They see in Oedipus' development
the dawn of abstract thought!

In his satyr play Herakles 5, Heiner Müller shows
the way in which work leaves its mark on the consciousness of man. Heracles is to clean the stall of
Augias, a task with which Zeus does not want to help
him. He builds a dam and, in spite of the thundering
threats of Zeus, diverts the river so that it will
perform the task. He also pulls down the sun so that
he can thaw the river which Zeus has frozen and, at
the end of the play, he pulls down heaven, rolls it
up, and sticks it in his pocket. This Heracles takes
on Promethean proportions.

In Hacks' Amphitryon it is again a question of
the individual and his possibilities. This clownish
and amusing chamber play is highly philosophical.
Hacks represents Amphitryon as a warrior who leads an
empty, formal existence. He loves war and the state,
and devotes himself to action in the public sphere.
He is for order and convention; Jupiter, on the other
hand, for beauty, love, productivity, and change.
These two are intended to represent two sides of man
which could complement each other and form a totality.
In response to criticism from his wife Alkmene, Amphitryon defends himself saying that he must contend
every day with practical life and is subject to its
wear and tear: "Es ist von solchem Ernst die Welt
beschaffen, / Daß nur ein Gott vermag, ein Mensch zu
sein" (p. 277).

In Hacks' Omphale Heracles and Omphale exchange
roles; they don the other's clothes and perform the
traditional roles of the partner. (There is no mention of such an exchange of roles in the old myths.)
Each wants to learn how the other experiences and
feels everything in order to achieve a complete one-
ness with the partner. Such empathy brings liberation

146

from one-sided, stereotyped sexual roles and, more importantly, is a step toward the emancipation of both partners as fully developed human beings. According to Hacks and Trilse, Heracles is a millenial figure who has absorbed the experiences and thought of a very long period of time. In connection with Omphale Trilse goes on to say:

Die Stufen der Fabel sind die Stufen
der Weltgeschichte und der Geschichte
des Menschen . . . Herakles ist Mensch-
heitssymbol: seine Taten symbolisieren
des Menschen Selbstbefreiung. Um die
Natur zu beherrschen, geriet er mit den
Göttern in Streit, die Menschen . . .
überwarfen sich, und der Mensch . . .
kam in Sklaverei, d.h. in Ausbeutung
. . . 30

The theme now to be considered is that of the position and role of woman and equality of the sexes. The women speak more freely and more self-assertively in these adaptations than in the Greek originals where they, apart from the great female figures Electra, Antigone, Ismene, Iphigeneia, Medea, and Lysistrata, usually appear as a chorus, occasionally as mute figures. In Knauth's Die Weibervolksversammlung the women become very effective persons of state, and one hears much scorn of men in this play. Praxagora says: "ihre Faulheit ist noch größer als ihre Brunst" (p. 84); and that is what makes them tolerable. Another woman in Knauth's play complains that she was late arriving at the meeting place because her husband made demands on her the whole night--a real slavery! The women in this play wish to undo, by means of feminine wisdom, the harm and chaos that male blindness has brought down on the world; the war economy of the men must be done away with!

In Stefan Schütz's Die Amazonen, Oreithyia and Antiope speak condescendingly of the male as a play-thing and an instrument of procreation that one needs to call on only once a year to keep the race alive. 31 Antiope speaks contemptuously of the "Penisbrut" (p. 17), but her powerful love for Theseus later annuls this view. In Schütz's Odysseus' Heimkehr Penelope is anything but chaste. 32 A real Machtweib, she manipulates the suitors and even her son Telemachus, all of whom lust after her sexual favors--and power.

Hacks' <u>Die Vögel</u>, a libretto for a comic opera
based on Aristophanes' utopian play, is a humorous but
thoughtful political fantasy about a never-never city
in the sky--somewhere between the here and the beyond
--where life is pure celebration of life and where
work and marriage are unknown.[33]   In this play, the
passion for change among the women is so great that
Liebinger says: "Dieses Geschlecht ist so unzufrieden
mit sich, daß es nur darauf sinnt, sich zu verändern"
(p. 160).   Hacks sees love between man and woman as
sensual love coupled with lively awareness (<u>Bewußt-
sein</u>) and a psychic harmony born of unselfishness.
For Hacks, love and concord have to do, in a decisive
way, with the improvement of social conditions; they
represent the attainable beauty of human relationships, truly human relationships, and are a factor,
even a catalyst, in the emancipation and self-
realization of the individual--the great human being.

     In Stolper's <u>Amphitryon</u> Zeus glorifies woman:
"der Olymp . . . seiner Weisheit tiefster Grund / Ist
das Verständnis schöner, kluger Frauen" (p. 62).   In
Hacks' <u>Amphitryon</u> the dignity of the woman and her
right to love and self-determination are stressed.
Hacks' Alkmene is a strong-willed woman who makes
strong demands.   Her cold, routine marriage seems
barren to her as a result of the appearances of Jupiter, the fiery, poetic lover.   In Hacks' <u>Omphale</u> the
love that Heracles seeks is a harmonious mixture of
vital sensuality and full understanding of the partner; it is a productively joyful, poetic love, not a
routine and unproductive belonging together.

     The last theme to be considered here is that of
the gods, the hero, and the great human being.   In the
prologue to Pfeiffer's <u>Begegnung mit Herkules</u>, where
the present and myth alternate and are seen as a continuum, one actor says: "Wo Götter Schicksal spiel-
ten, macht heut der Arbeiter Geschichte. Die Helden
werden demokratisiert" (p. 125).   Socialist man is
seen as the heroic successor of the gods.   In this
play Hercules glorifies the new man in the words:
"Ich bestand meine Taten, / Um unsterblich zu werden .
. . / Aber ihr verändert die Welt, weil ihr Sterbliche
seid. / Das ist größer. Das ist der heroische Sinn
eures Lebens" (p. 165).   Man no longer projects vir-
tues into divine figures but performs virtuous deeds
to his own advantage.   Hercules performs great deeds
in the play: he cleans the stall of Augias and fights
against the hydra, but these actions stand in a con-

148

trapuntal relationship to the accomplishments of Kulle
and his buddies. Demigods and men work together; they
are coordinate and complementary.

In his essay "Götter, welch ein Held. Zu 'Der
Frieden,'" Hacks speaks rhapsodically of the little
winegrower Trygaios, whom he sees as a great hero:

> . . . Trygaios. Der Besieger des
> Krieges, der Retter des Friedens, der
> Vertreiber der Kriegsgewinnler . . .
> der Beglücker des Volks . . . der große
> Trygaios, der glorvolle Trygaios, der
> Held Trygaios. Götter, welch ein Held!
> . . . Der Held hat erhabene Zwecke und
> platte Erfolge; Trygaios hat den plat-
> testen Zweck und den erhabensten Er-
> folg. Der Held geht aufs Ganze und
> gewinnt einen kleinen Teil; Trygaios
> will seinen kleinen Teil, und an dem
> hängt das Ganze. [34]

Here Hacks extols the modest but beneficent hero and
downgrades extravagant, lofty heroism. Trygaios, who
prods the chorus into pulling Eirene, the goddess of
peace, out of the well, is for him a hero of the
greatest stature.

In Hacks' Der Frieden, Zeus is referred to as the
god of the military. In Stolper's Amphitryon, Jupiter
is a hollow figure, a Scheingott, and representative
of the reactionary. In Hacks' Amphitryon, on the
other hand, Jupiter appears as Amphitryon's better
self and hero of the play. For Alkmene, Jupiter is
what Amphitryon once promised to become and could have
become. In Hacks' view Jupiter is "der vollkommene
Mensch unter den wirklichen Leuten wie Tarzan unter
den Affen." [35] Horst Laube writes that Hacks' Jupiter
is "ein Gleichzeitiges aus vermenschlichtem Gott und
vergöttlichtem Menschen" and that Hacks combines "das
menschliche und göttliche Prinzip zum Prinzip der
menschlichen Utopie." [36] Heracles in Hacks' Die Vögel
is, for a time, both god and shade, eternal and
temporal, immortal and mortal, hero and human; the
birds too see themselves as both--as truly great
beings.

In conclusion, I would like to refer to a statement of Peter Hacks concerning the greatness of Greek
drama. In regard to content and maturity of concep-

149

tion ("Reife des Entwurfs") he says that Goethe's Faust and Shakespeare are greater than Greek drama; but if the form and aptness for the genre ("Gattungsrichtigkeit") are the basis of comparison, the order of greatness is reversed: Greek classicism produced purer drama than Shakespeare and Shakespeare purer drama than Goethe.[37] One could perhaps add that GDR adaptations of Greek dramas and myths are among the best.

University of Western Ontario

Notes

[1] Peter Hacks, "Kunst und Revolution," in his Maßgaben der Kunst (Düsseldorf: Claassen, 1977), p. 174.

[2] Peter Hacks, "Der Fortschritt in der Kunst," Maßgaben, p. 250.

[3] Karl Marx and Friedrich Engels, Werke, XIII (E. Berlin: Dietz, 1964), p. 641. All translations from the German in this paper are my own.

[4] As quoted in Alexander Abusch, Humanismus und Realismus in der Literatur (Leipzig: Reclam, 1971), p. 38.

[5] Quoted from the "Gespräch" in Heiner Müller, Ödipus Tyrann (E. Berlin: Aufbau, 1969), pp. 169-170.

[6] Christoph Trilse, Stücke nach der Antike (E. Berlin: Henschel, 1969), p. 21.

[7] Ingeborg Pietzsch, "Die wilde Feuerseele. 'Elektra' von Sophokles am Staatstheater Dresden," Theater der Zeit, 32, No. 11 (1977), 7.

[8] Christoph Trilse, Antike und Theater heute (E. Berlin: Akademie, 1975), p. 58.

[9] Hacks, "Iphigenie, oder: Über die Wiederverwendung von Mythen," Maßgaben, pp. 104-105.

[10] Rudolf Schottlaender, Afterword, Stücke nach der Antike, by Christoph Trilse, p. 386.

150

[11] In Peter Hacks, _Vier Komödien_ (Frankfurt: Suhrkamp, 1971).

[12] Peter Hacks, _Adam und Eva_ (Düsseldorf: Claassen, 1976).

[13] Trilse, _Stücke_, p. 24.

[14] Trilse, _Stücke_, p. 23.

[15] In Joachim Knauth, _Stücke_ (E. Berlin: Henschel, 1973). Parenthetical references below are to this edition.

[16] In Peter Hacks, _Zwei Bearbeitungen_ (Frankfurt: Suhrkamp, 1963.)

[17] In Peter Hacks, _Vier Komödien_. Parenthetical references below are to this edition.

[18] In Heiner Müller, _Geschichten aus der Produktion 1_ (W. Berlin: Rotbuch, 1974).

[19] Hacks, "Iphigenie," _Maßgaben_, p. 106.

[20] Hacks, "Götter, welch ein Held! Zu 'Der Frieden,'" _Maßgaben_, p. 343.

[21] Rolf Rohmer, "Die Dialektik des Sündenfalls," _Theater der Zeit_, 28, No. 12 (1973), 37.

[22] Hans Pfeiffer, "Begegnung mit Herkules," _Neue Deutsche Literatur_, 14, No. 9 (1966), 117-165.

[23] _Neue Deutsche Literatur_, 14, No. 10 (1966), 144.

[24] In Armin Stolper, _Stücke_ (E. Berlin: Henschel, 1974).

[25] Karl Mickel, _Einstein/Nausikaa. Die Schrecken des Humanismus in zwei Stücken_ (W. Berlin: Rotbuch, 1974).

[26] In Heiner Müller, _Geschichten aus der Produktion 2_ (W. Berlin: Rotbuch, 1974).

[27] Heiner Müller. _Ödipus Tyrann. Nach Hölderlin_ (E. Berlin and Weimar: Aufbau, 1969).

[28] Karl-Heinz Müller, "Vorwort," Ödipus Tyrann, by Heiner Müller, p. 7.

[29] Quoted from the "Gespräch" in Ödipus Tyrann, by Heiner Müller, p. 100.

[30] Christoph Trilse, Das Werk des Peter Hacks (E. Berlin: Volk und Wissen, 1980), pp. 218-219. Hacks endows the monster and man-eater Lityerses with brutal qualities, both in his way of speaking and in his way of fighting. The poison gas that emanates from him in his fight with Heracles makes one think of modern warfare--and of Vietnam. Trilse says: "Lityerses ist . . . die Inkarnation des Ausbeuters aller Zeiten, Faschismus und Imperialismus inbegriffen" (p. 219).

[31] In Stefan Schütz, Heloisa und Abaelard (W. Berlin: Rotbuch, 1979), where it is titled Antiope und Theseus (Die Amazonen).

[32] Stefan Schütz, Odysseus' Heimkehr, Fabrik im Walde, Kohlhaas, Heloisa und Abelard (E. Berlin: Henschel, 1977).

[33] In Peter Hacks, Oper (E. Berlin: Aufbau, 1975).

[34] Hacks, Maßgaben, pp. 342-343.

[35] Hacks, "Zu meinem 'Amphitryon,'" Maßgaben, p. 352.

[36] Horst Laube, Peter Hacks (Velber: Friedrich, 1972), pp. 67, 69.

[37] Hacks, "Der Fortschritt in der Kunst," Maßgaben, p. 250.

Critical Editions East and West--
A Politics of the Comma?

David Lee

Critical editions of an author's works present
the reader with a text which has been examined by an
editor and cleansed, in so far as possible, of errors
and blemishes. The resultant text is presumably the
one the author wished to see in print and which would
have been printed had not human imperfection intervened in the form of printer's errors, sloppy proof-
reading, bowdlerization, or the like. Many critical
editions go a step further and examine the development
of the text in all its known versions to establish
which of them best corresponds to the author's true
intentions. This adds a historical dimension to the
critical one, thus the concept of the "historisch-
kritische Ausgabe."

When carefully done, critical editions are acts
of piety which not only pay obeisance to the glory of
the past but also preserve the heritage for the future. We could bask in the warmth of this statement
for a while, but sooner or later some pragmatic questions will confront us, particularly, "How much of the
past do you wish to preserve in a critical edition?"
or, in blunter form, "When is enough enough?" This
question is being answered in different ways in the
German Democratic Republic and in the Federal Republic, and the form the answer takes will have a significant effect on the literary scholarship of the
future, because it will determine the type of material
scholars have to work with. This paper discusses some
aspects of editing practice East and West and some of
the reasons which I believe have given rise to differences in philosophy about what a critical edition
should do. In considering these matters we will also
cast a glance at a controversy here in the U.S. which

paralleled an internal discussion in the GDR on editing principles.

In order to understand the issues involved we must start back in the Third Reich, when a professor from Tübingen, Friedrich Beißner, prepared the first volumes of his Hölderlin edition.[1] Beißner's contribution to editorial practice was to develop a much more elaborate system for the presentation of manuscript variants. Rather than printing isolated variants, Beißner attempted to provide insight into the genesis of the poems and the phases of growth through which they passed. In his introductory remarks to the critical notes, Beißner offered philosophical justification for his approach by quoting a statement of Goethe's: "Natur- und Kunstwerke lernt man nicht kennen, wenn sie fertig sind; man muß sie im Entstehen aufhaschen, um sie einigermaßen zu begreifen."[2]

Scholarship in the FRG has largely honored Beißner's aims and philosophy while rejecting his system, which has been judged by various analysts to be too subjective and unverifiable.[3] Beißner's efforts showed the way, however, and various attempts were made to create a system of representation which would adequately reproduce on the printed page the whole development of a poem as it could be deciphered from the messiest of manuscripts. To my mind, the most successful of these attempts was made by Hans Zeller in his edition of Conrad Ferdinand Meyer's works.[4] Zeller presents, as is customary, a description of all the text witnesses, and for each manuscript he defines the work phases or strata which are recognizable in it. Instead of printing just single words or phrases in his register of variants, he provides the entire text, using boldface type to signify the final version of the poem in that manuscript and standard type to indicate variants rejected by the author. Square brackets show strikeouts; lower-case italic letters-- a, b, c, etc.--set up a relative chronology of elements within a line unit or two-line unit. The page looks imposing, and the system is imposing as a creation, but it is more straightforward than it seems at first glance. After one has worked with it for a while, it becomes apparent that this is a clear and well-conceived method of presentation. Zeller's system has been used with some minor modifications in another major project, Walther Killy and Hans Szklenar's two-volume critical edition of Georg Trakl's poetry.[5]

One does not find anything similar to this being produced in the GDR, but the two Germanys have not always been so far apart in questions of editorial philosophy as they are today. Not long after the war some ambitious plans were made by the Deutsche Akademie der Wissenschaften zu Berlin. A new edition of Goethe's works was to appear under Academy auspices. The principal editor was Ernst Grumach. In 1950 Grumach published a very convincing article in which he detailed the inadequacies of the standard edition of Goethe's works, the Weimarer Ausgabe, which had set the critical norm for almost every popular Goethe edition for over sixty years.[6] Grumach had a staff of very talented co-workers, particularly Siegfried Scheibe, Waltraud Hagen, and Edith Nahler. They set about producing an edition which was to be systematic in the treatment of the texts, but unsystematic in the planned order of the works. They intended, as I understand it, to start with the works whose texts were most in need of reexamination and to proceed with further volumes as circumstances dictated.

The first volumes offered to the public for inspection were three in number. They contained the poems, prose, and paralipomena of the West-östlicher Divan.[7] The statement of editorial principles and register of variants was to follow in two volumes. At about the same time, a young academician at the Humboldt University, Hans Werner Seiffert, was finishing his Habilitationsschrift on the subject of editing practice.[8] He went on to edit Wieland's letters for the Academy, and the first impressive volume in this series appeared in 1963.[9] By then some seventeen additional volumes of the Academy Goethe edition had also been published.[10]

In retrospect, we can say that until the early 1960s scholars in both the GDR and FRG were operating on the same wave length and that they had the same basic idea of what a critical edition should be. This is not to say that there were not divergent opinions, but rather that the weight of authority lay with those who favored a highly detailed description of manuscript variants. A symbol of this closeness in spirit may be discovered in the fact that Hans Werner Seiffert laid the basis for Zeller's descriptive system in the C. F. Meyer edition or that Siegfried Scheibe, one of the editors of the Academy Goethe edition, contributed the long lead essay to a collection of articles on editing compiled by Hans Zeller and Gunter Martens.[11]

By the early 1960s there were storm clouds on the horizon, however. For one thing, Grumach's early volumes of the West-östlicher Divan published in 1952 had suffered a direct frontal attack from a German-American reviewer, Hans Albert Maier of the University of Connecticut. In two long articles, Maier charged that Grumach was destroying the rhythmic integrity—and, in many cases, thereby the sense—of Goethe's poems by changing the punctuation and by following versions of the text which were not authorized by Goethe.[12] Grumach had published one sample variant register for one Divan poem, but for the work as a whole there was no way to determine why he had done what he did with the poems.[13]

Grumach, who died in 1967, contributed much to Goethe philology, but various articles of his make me suspect that he was, unfortunately, the wrong man for the job of principal editor of such a large and important project. "The big discovery" is hard to come by in Goethe scholarship these days, and Grumach seems to me in several instances to be trying too hard, straining, in fact, to make that big discovery.[14] From the editor of a new critical edition of Goethe's works one demands, first and foremost, a keen, steady, judicious application of critical acumen. One would like to see ingeniousness confined to the system of presentation, and here, again, Grumach's model was not convincing. It crowded important and unimportant details into a small space without distinguishing between them.[15]

I do not know whether it was the critical attacks or internal difficulties or a combination of both that caused Grumach to step down as general editor, but by the early 1960s the Academy edition was no longer under his direction. The general philosophy, at first still intact, suffered a double blow shortly thereafter. First, Hans Albert Maier published a two-volume edition of the Divan—poems only—in 1965.[16] Although the work was published by Max Niemeyer Verlag in Tübingen, Maier acknowledged the help of Karl-Heinz Hahn, then director of the Goethe and Schiller Archives, in constructing the system used to describe the manuscripts and their variants. In general, the edition paid less attention to the genesis of the manuscript versions of the poems and to the physical properties of the manuscripts than was normal for

critical editions, and Maier's introduction indicated
no particular contact with the very lively discussion
of editorial practice going on in the Federal Republic
at the time. Most important, one now had a rival
edition of the _Divan_ which had appeared under the
intellectual sponsorship of Weimar. It was well
received, and reviews by several prestigious Goethe
scholars were very favorable.[17]

   One year after Maier's edition, a journal, _For-
schen und Bilden_, appeared. It was printed in Weimar,
carried the subtitle "Mitteilungen aus den Nationalen
Forschungs- und Gedenkstätten," and billed itself as
the first issue of a publication which would periodically deal with more theoretical aspects of the literary trade. As far as I know, no subsequent issues
appeared. The featured article was co-authored by
Karl-Heinz Hahn and by Helmut Holtzhauer, then director of NFGS.[18] The title of the article was provocative, "Wissenschaft auf Abwegen?" and it delivered a
well-thought-out attack on the whole course of modern
editorial practice, including that of the Academy
edition of Goethe's works. The authors argue that
editors have lost all sense of proportion, that the
availability of manuscript material has led them to
think, first, that the material must be included in a
critical edition and, secondly, that they must reproduce every last ink blot on it (p. 19). This practice
is judged to spring from a misplaced emphasis on
manuscript variants as the key to an understanding of
both the creative process and the meaning of a work
(pp. 13-14, 19). The authors reject the notion that
complicated variants can be recreated graphically with
any success, a criticism directed against Zeller and
his school (pp. 7, 14). Such information, they argue,
can better be communicated through photographic repro-
ductions. Their most significant suggestion is that a
detailed consideration of manuscript variants _not_ be
part of the obligations of the editor at all (pp. 12-
13). The editor, they feel, should be concerned primarily with preparing a critically sound text, and his
or her principal guide should be the _printed_ versions
of the work (p. 16). Art, they maintain, is a public
act: the artist places his work before society
through the medium of the printed text, and it is this
vehicle which creates the work for the public (p. 5).

   The theoretical arguments put forward by Hahn and
Holtzhauer have merit and are certainly well stated,
but there is also much that can be said for the oppos-

ing view. To elaborate on the justification for this
or that editorial philosophy would lead us beyond the
limits of this paper, which is concerned primarily
with the historical development of editing practice in
the FRG and GDR. My comments are thus restricted to
the practical effects of the position adopted by Hahn
and Holtzhauer.

The NFGS's editorial philosophy, articulated in
"Wissenschaft auf Abwegen?" has become a kind of semi-
official national policy, and the dominant institution
in the field of literary editions in the GDR is clearly Weimar. The Academy has continued to issue editions such as Wieland's letters, but the two volumes
in this series which have appeared since 1969 contain
only the letter texts without textual notes or commentary. [19] A few more volumes of the Academy edition of
Goethe's works were released in the early 1970s.
These volumes had been initiated earlier, and other-
wise the project has been laid to rest.

The prevailing attitude in the Federal Republic
on the question of major editions is that there is no
acceptable substitute for completeness. [20]   Users of
historical-critical editions prepared in the FRG or
Switzerland are encouraged by the nature of the text
notes to immerse themselves in the minutiae of the
work's development. The western position rests upon a
philosophy which emphasizes the individual sphere,
both of the creator and of the scholar who will examine the text. The GDR policy stresses the social
responsibility of the editor to preserve for society
texts which demonstrate progressive tendencies and
which are especially worthy of our attention. [21]
Readers of editions prepared in the GDR are encouraged
to turn their attention to matters other than the fine
points of stylistic development or complex questions
of dating which turn on the analysis of watermarks,
developmental phases of the manuscript, and the like.

Hahn and Holtzhauer do admit that manuscripts
must be examined to determine if they help in establishing the best text, and one of the major weaknesses
of their position is that they set no criteria to
justify the inclusion of one variant as opposed to
another. [22] Poem manuscripts would be the acid test of
their philosophy, but in the fifteen years that have
intervened since their article was published, no
critical notes to a volume of poetry have appeared to
instruct us on how they will deal with the problem of

selectivity. Maier's edition, with which the battle was joined, cannot serve as a model, since time has revealed various weaknesses in it, particularly in regard to its treatment of manuscripts.[23] Two separate editions of Heinrich Heine's works are currently being produced, one a collaboration between Düsseldorf and Paris, the other a cooperative effort of Weimar and Paris.[24] The textual notes for the Düsseldorf/Paris volume of Heine's poetry, which stand foursquare in the tradition of completeness, have been in print since 1975.[25] The text of the poetry volume of the Weimar/Paris edition has been around since then, but the notes have yet to appear. They should be in print in 1981 and they will offer an excellent chance to compare the two opposing philosophies of text preparation.

The present dichotomy between editorial outlooks in East and West began as an internal conflict between institutions in the GDR. An intriguing American parallel mirrors this conflict and helps to put the divergence in editorial philosophies more clearly in perspective. In 1968 Lewis Mumford unleashed an attack in The New York Review of Books on the critical edition of Ralph Waldo Emerson's Journals and Miscellaneous Notebooks.[26] Mumford's title, "Emerson Behind Barbed Wire," expresses clearly enough his attitude towards including diacritical marks in the text itself rather than printing them separately in a critical appendix. Mumford also used the occasion to deplore what he saw as the invasion of academic fascists into the wonderful and free world of the literary spirit. One letter in support of Mumford's position came from the dean of American critics, Edmund Wilson, who in the following year published a two-part blast in the same magazine entitled "The Fruits of the MLA [Modern Languages Association]."[27] In the early 1960s Wilson and Jason Epstein of Random House had proposed editions of great American authors in the tradition of the French Pléiade texts, i.e., the most important works in a single volume on thin paper. Wilson was piqued that the MLA's American authors project had snatched up funds from the National Endowment for the Humanities and was producing editions which in his view were weighed down with an impossible ballast of variants. Such editions were for him the seeds from which countless little Ph.D.s could grow, each a soulless product worthy of the inane tradition from which it had sprung. Delving further into this controversy, one discovers that the state of editing in the U.S. before the MLA project was abysmal in the extreme and that no decent editions of Twain, Hawthorne, Melville, Crane, and others were available. Coming from a European tradition, one is astounded to learn how primitive the situation here was.

Certainly there are political overtones and implications in the positions adopted in the GDR and FRG on editorial matters. The brief glance at the American situation shows, however, that the same type of divergence in editorial philosophy can occur without an ideological backdrop. The most significant "political" issues involved in such discussions are more likely to be those of various branches of the respective national literary establishments. Ultimately, I suspect, the whole question turns more on money than editorial philosophy. If the resources and the workers are available to produce detailed editions, then it makes sense to do so. If resources are limited, then one should, as in the GDR, choose the path which will guarantee the greatest number of texts to the greatest number of readers.[28]

University of Tennessee, Knoxville

Notes

[1] Friedrich Hölderlin, Sämtliche Werke: Hölderlin-Ausgabe im Auftrage des Württembergischen Kultministeriums und der deutschen Akademie in München, ed. Friedrich Beißner, 7 vols. in 14 (Stuttgart: Cottasche Buchhandlung Nachfolger, 1943-1977). This is the "große Stuttgarter Ausgabe." It shows different title pages; all volumes after Vol. 1 were printed by Kohlhammer Verlag.

[2] Goethe in a letter to Carl Friedrich Zelter from Aug. 4, 1803, as quoted by Beißner in Hölderlin, Sämtliche Werke, Vol. 1, Pt. 2, p. 318.

[3] See, for example, the discussion of Beißner's edition in Hans Werner Seiffert, Untersuchungen zur Methode der Herausgabe deutscher Texte, Deutsche Akademie der Wissenschaften zu Berlin, Veröffentlichungen des Instituts für deutsche Sprache und Literatur, 28 (Berlin: Akademie, 1963), pp. 141-52, esp. pp. 143-44.

[4] Conrad Ferdinand Meyer, Sämtliche Werke: Historisch-kritische Ausgabe, ed. Hans Zeller and Alfred Zäch, 15 vols. planned (Bern: Bentli, 1958 ff.). Vol. 2 (1964) contains Zeller's explanation of his system, pp. 88-111.

[5] Georg Trakl, Dichtungen und Briefe: Historisch-kritische Ausgabe, ed. Walther Killy and Hans Szklenar, 2 vols. (Salzburg: Otto Müller, 1969). Vol. 2 contains the editors' description of their system, pp. 29-43.

[6] "Prolegomena zu einer Goethe-Ausgabe," Goethe: Neue Folge des Jahrbuchs der Goethe-Gesellschaft, 12 (1950), 60-88; rpt. with revisions in Beiträge zur Goetheforschung, ed. Ernst Grumach, Deutsche Akademie der Wissenschaften, Veröffentlichungen des Instituts für deutsche Sprache und Literatur, 16 (Berlin: Akademie, 1958), pp. 1-34.

[7] Goethe, West-östlicher Divan, ed. Ernst Grumach, 3 vols., Werke Goethes, ed. Deutsche Akademie der Wissenschaften zu Berlin (Berlin: Akademie, 1952).

[8] See the citation in Note 3.

[9] C. M. Wieland, Briefe der Bildungsjahre (1. Juni 1750 - 2. Juni 1760), ed. Hans Werner Seiffert, Vol. 1 of Wielands Briefwechsel, Deutsche Akademie der Wissenschaften zu Berlin. Institut für deutsche Sprache und Literatur (Berlin: Akademie, 1963).

[10] Many bibliographical reference works list volumes of the Academy edition by individual title only. An overview over the progress of the edition is, however, provided under the heading "Goethe, Werke . . ." in Deutsches Bücherverzeichnis, ed. Deutsche Bücherei (Leipzig: Verlag für Buch- und Bibliothekswesen), Vol. 29 (1958), p. 1395; Vol. 35 (1964), p. 156; Vol. 41 (1972), p. 712.

[11] See Zeller's acknowledgment of Seiffert's help in Meyer, Sämtliche Werke, Vol. 2, p. 113. Scheibe's article, "Zu einigen Grundprinzipien einer historisch-kritischen Ausgabe," is in Texte und Varianten: Probleme ihrer Edition und Interpretation, ed. Gunter Martens and Hans Zeller (Munich: Beck, 1971), pp. 1-44.

[12] Hans Albert Maier, "Zur Textgestaltung des 'West-östlichen Divans,'" Journal of English and Ger-

manic <u>Philology</u>, 56 (1957), 347-81; 58 (1959), 185-221.

[13] Grumach's textual notes for the poem "Vier Gnaden" are reprinted in Seiffert, <u>Untersuchungen</u>, pp. 152-55. Seiffert does not cite the original place of publication, and I am unsure of it at this time.

[14] My comments are based on two longer articles by Grumach which deal in the first instance with a source, and in the second with different strata on a single manuscript leaf: "Prolog und Epilog im Faustplan von 1797," <u>Goethe: Neue Folge des Jahrbuchs der Goethe-Gesellschaft</u>, 14/15 (1952/53), 63-107; "Goethes Reinschrift der Hegire," in <u>Festschrift für Wilhelm Eilers: Ein Dokument der internationalen Forschung zum 27. September 1966</u>, ed. Gernot Wiessner (Wiesbaden: Harrassowitz, 1967), pp. 536-45. I explained some of my reservations about Grumach's attribution of sources in my dissertation, "The Genesis of Goethe's <u>West-östlicher Divan</u>: Hafis and the 'geselliges Lied'" (Stanford, 1968), pp. 14-25, 72-73.

[15] Cf. Seiffert's comments in <u>Untersuchungen</u>, pp. 154-55. Cf. also the comments of Karl-Heinz Hahn and Helmut Holtzhauer, "Wissenschaft auf Abwegen?: Zur Edition von Werken der neueren deutschen Literatur," <u>Forschen und Bilden: Mitteilungen aus den Nationalen Forschungs- und Gedenkstätten der klassischen deutschen Literatur in Weimar</u>, 1 (1966), 15. Hahn and Holtzhauer are speaking of the edition in general, which underwent several shifts in editorial policy, but their remarks certainly include Grumach's efforts.

[16] Goethe, <u>West-östlicher Divan: Kritische Ausgabe der Gedichte mit textgeschichtlichem Kommentar</u>, ed. Hans Albert Maier, 2 vols. (Tübingen: Niemeyer, 1965).

[17] Reviews by, for example, Albert Fuchs, <u>Études Germaniques</u>, 21 (1966), 251-53; Erich Trunz, <u>Germanisch-Romanische Monatsschrift, Neue Folge</u>, 17, or Vol. 48 of the entire series (1967), 103-08; Ewald Rösch, <u>Wirkendes Wort</u>, 19 (1969), 287-88.

[18] See Note 15 for complete citation. The article by Hahn and Holtzhauer is on pp. 2-22. Further references to the article will be given in parentheses in the text.

[19] Vol. 2: Anmerkungen zu Band I (Briefe vom 1.6.1750 - 2.6.1760), ed. Hans Werner Seiffert (1969); Vol. 3: Briefe der Biberacher Amtsjahre (6. Juni 1760 - 20. Mai 1769), ed. Seiffert and Renate Petermann (1975); Briefe der Erfurter Dozentenjahre (25. Mai 1769-17. September 1772), ed. Annerose Schneider and Peter-Volker Springborn (1979). This is not to imply that the Akademie der Wissenschaften is no longer engaged in producing large-scale editions. The multivolume edition of Georg Forster's Werke: Sämtliche Schriften, Tagebücher, Briefe (Berlin: Akademie, 1958 ff.) shows clearly that this is not so. The approach to major literary figures, however, has changed discernibly.

[20] A convincing restatement of the dominant tendency in the Federal Republic can be found in Manfred Windfuhr's "Herausgeberbericht" in the impressive new Düsseldorf Heine edition: Buch der Lieder: Apparat, ed. Pierre Grappin, Vol. 1, Pt. 2 of Heine: Historisch-kritische Gesamtausgabe der Werke, ed. Manfred Windfuhr (Hamburg: Hoffmann und Campe, 1975), p. 1210.

[21] Hahn/Holtzhauer, pp. 16-17.

[22] Hahn/Holtzhauer, p. 16.

[23] See the criticisms of Maier's treatment of the printed editions of the Divan in Wilhelm Solms, Interpretation als Textkritik: Zur Edition des West-oestlichen Divans, Poesie und Wissenschaft, 15 (Heidelberg: Stiehm, 1974), pp. 32-34 and 38-47. I have discussed Maier's treatment of watermarks in "Zum Stand der Wasserzeichenforschung in der Goethe-Philologie--mit besonderer Berücksichtigung des West-östlichen Divans," which is scheduled to appear in the newly founded Yearbook of the North American Goethe Society in 1982.

[24] Besides the edition cited in Note 20, there is the Säkularausgabe: Werke, Briefwechsel, Lebenszeugnisse, ed. Nationale Forschungs- und Gedenkstätten der klassischen deutschen Literatur in Weimar and the Centre National de la Recherche Scientifique in Paris (Berlin and Paris: Akademie and Editions du CNRS, 1970 ff.). Thirty-one of a planned fifty volumes have appeared so far, with the commentary on the first volume of poems promised for this year (1981), Gedichte 1812-1827: Kommentar, ed. Hans Böhm.

[25] See Note 20.

[26] Lewis Mumford, "Emerson Behind Barbed Wire," The New York Review of Books, 10, No. 1 (Jan. 18, 1968), 3-5.

[27] Wilson's letter appeared without title in The New York Review of Books, 10, No. 5 (Mar. 14, 1968), 35. "The Fruits of the MLA: I. 'Their Wedding Journey'" and "II. Mark Twain" appeared in Vol. 11, No. 5 (Sept. 26, 1968), 7-10, and Vol 11, No. 6 (Oct. 10, 1968), 6-14. The MLA response, which combined letters from The New York Review of Books, a reprint from another journal, and an original statement by the Executive Secretary of the MLA, was published as a pamphlet: William Gibson et al., Professional Standards and American Editions: A Response to Edmund Wilson (New York: Modern Language Association of America, 1969).

[28] The economic question is one which is openly acknowledged by all parties. See Hahn/Holtzhauer, p. 18, or Windfuhr, Heine, Vol. 1, Pt. 2, p. 1257.

Erwin Racholl--A GDR Joseph K.?

Linda Thomas

    A recent story by Klaus Schlesinger, "Die Spal-
tung des Erwin Racholl,"[1] shows that Kafka's influence
is alive and well in the GDR and gives rise to the
hypothesis that this is so because his methods are
more capable of treating certain problems of life
there than those of the officially favored aesthetic
theory. Like Joseph K. in Kafka's Der Prozeß,[2] the
protagonist in Schlesinger's story is brought to trial
for no real crime and forced to examine all aspects of
his past and present life. In telling the story,
Schlesinger not only touches upon themes typical of
Kafka, such as guilt, fear, isolation, and helplessness, but also employs stylistic devices characteristic of Kafka.

    Despite an easing of the total ban on works by
Kafka in the GDR and the apparent acceptance by certain Marxist literary critics of his relevance for
socialism at the Kafka conference in Czechoslovakia
(1963), the official attitude towards Kafka has been
quite consistently one of rejection. In the West,
this conference has been viewed as acknowledgement by
the socialist world of Kafka's topicality for socialist society.[3] Volume Eleven of the Geschichte der
Deutschen Literatur, published in the GDR in 1977,
suggests, on the other hand, that Kafka's importance
for socialism was recognized by only a few at the
conference and that they were misguided. In fact,
this literary history shifts the emphasis to the
negative and states that Marxist critics at the conference questioned, rather than accepted, Kafka's
relevance for socialism:

        Das Werk FRANZ KAFKAS, in dem sich die
        Ohnmacht und Ratlosigkeit des Autors

angesichts der imperialistischen Wirklichkeit auf faszinierende Weise wider-
spiegelt, wurde von einigen Kongreß-
teilnehmern als auch für die sozialistische Gesellschaft aktuell bezeichnet. ERNST FISCHER, der Prager Literaturwissenschaftler EDUARD GOLDSTÜCKER
und andere begründeten diese Aktualität
damit, daß es auch im Sozialismus Erscheinungen von Entfremdung gäbe, wie
sie Kafka gestaltet habe. Sie stützten
sich dabei auf Diskussionen bürgerli-
cher und revisionistischer Ideologen
über den von Marx analysierten Vorgang
der kapitalistischen Entfremdung der
Arbeit. Dabei war dieser Begriff ver-
wässert und auf die unterschiedlichsten
gesellschaftlichen Erscheinungen und
schließlich auch auf die sozialistische
Gesellschaft angewandt worden, in der
die objektiven ökonomischen Ursachen
der kapitalistischen Entfremdung der
Arbeit beseitigt sind. Marxistisch-
leninistische Theoretiker hatten eine
solche Ausweitung dieses Begriffs ver-
schiedentlich zurückgewiesen. In Li-
blice stellten marxistische Literaturwissenschaftler diese Aktualisierung
Kafkas in Frage und forderten eine konsequent historische Betrachtungsweise,
die allein der bedeutenden Leistung des
Dichters gerecht werde. . . . In der
Deutschen Demokratischen Republik wur-
den die ideologischen Infiltrations-
versuche des Gegners entschieden be-
kämpft.[4]

As this quotation indicates, only Kafka's ability
to describe alienated man in "imperialist reality" is
accepted in official GDR criticism. The supposed
impossibility of alienation in socialist society is at
the core of the problem concerning Kafka's pertinence
for the GDR. The Kulturpolitisches Wörterbuch (1978)
adheres rigidly to the position that socialism and
alienation are mutually exclusive: "Der Sozialismus
ist die Aufhebung der Entfremdung. . . . Die Errich-
tung der Diktatur des Proletariats und der Sieg der
sozialistischen Produktionsverhältnisse . . . sowie
die objektive Überwindung des Gegensatzes von Individuum und Gesellschaft--entzieht der E [ntfremdung]

166

allen sozialen Boden."5   As long as this position is
maintained, the works of Kafka can never be considered
germane to the problems of those living in a socialist
society.

Regardless of these official pronouncements,
Kafka has influenced a number of GDR writers, such as
Rolf Schneider and Günter Kunert. Klaus Schlesinger's
story, written and published in the GDR, indicates
that writers there continue to be influenced by him.
These writers obviously find his methods well-suited
to describing the real world, be it the world of
socialism in the GDR or that of "imperialist reality."

The events of Schlesinger's story are as follows:
on his thirty-fifth birthday, Erwin Racholl learns of
his promotion. Paradoxically, this positive turn of
events prompts immediate physical reactions of nausea
and dizziness. After an almost sleepless night,
Racholl is on his usual subway ride to work when the
train mysteriously fails to stop at the expected place
and he soon finds himself in West Berlin. Resolved to
make his way back to East Berlin immediately, Racholl
begins to wander apparently aimlessly through the
city, but slowly becomes cognizant of the feeling that
he is moving toward a subconscious goal. Eventually
he comes to a bar where he senses that he is at the
end of his search. This is confirmed by a stranger
who informs him that he has arrived late. Racholl is
shoved into a back room where a trial takes place.
During the trial, which is presided over by his immediate superior at work, Racholl is compelled to consider the events of both his personal and professional
life. In the end, he passes a negative judgement on
himself and comes to the realization that he is divided into two irreconcilable people. The story ends
back on the subway in East Berlin with Racholl asking
a fellow passenger where they are headed. The man
lowers his paper and Racholl is not surprised to see
himself.

The dilemma of the protagonist in both the Kafka
and the Schlesinger stories is stated climactically in
the first sentence. Kafka's Prozeß begins: "Jemand
mußte Josef K. verleumdet haben, denn ohne daß er
etwas Böses getan hätte, wurde er eines Morgens verhaftet" (p. 11). One of the most noteworthy features
of Kafka's style, the contradiction between an extraordinary event and the pragmatic way of relating it,
is already apparent in this first sentence. The same

167

description could be applied to the beginning of Schlesinger's story: "Am 27. April, dem Tag seines fünfunddreißigsten Geburtstages, war Racholl auf dem Höhepunkt seiner Laufbahn, am 28. April, schon einen Tag später, an deren Ende" (p. 5). Kafka maintains this tension throughout, while Schlesinger only employs it occasionally and most noticeably here.

Erwin Racholl and Joseph K. find themselves at an important milestone in life: Joseph K. is arrested on his thirtieth birthday; Racholl's trial begins on his thirty-fifth birthday. Both are forced in the course of the trial to deal with problems which they have avoided until now, and both are forced to pass judgement on themselves. Both find themselves guilty: Joseph K. condemns himself to death; Racholl judges himself unfit to accept his new promotion. But while Joseph K. goes to his death, Racholl is declared innocent by his superior, who explains: "Wir müssen das Land mit den Leuten aufbauen, die wir haben" (p. 98).

In both stories the ordeal begins as the protagonists awaken. In fact, Joseph K. is arrested in bed. When Racholl's ill-fated journey to West Berlin begins, he has just gotten up. Despite his fatigue, or perhaps because of it, Racholl's senses are heightened; he sees colors and contours more sharply than usual. The proximity of the nighttime world of dreams and the daytime world of normal existence results in confusion. Are the extraordinary experiences of Joseph K. and Erwin Racholl to be attributed simply to dreaming? Despite his having named the collection of stories Berliner Traum, Schlesinger makes some effort to dispel the notion that Racholl could be dreaming. Toward the end of his trial, Racholl pleads with his superior to tell him that he is dreaming. An unknown person replies: "Der denkt tatsächlich, er träumt!" (p. 92). Racholl falls asleep on the subway on his way to work and at various times during his trial. There is at least one dream sequence during the trial, which would be a dream within a dream if the whole story were to be regarded as such.

Much more important than the question of whether Racholl is actually dreaming or not is the dreamlike atmosphere which pervades the entire story and is reminiscent of Kafka. Schlesinger creates this mood by an overall lack of logical and causal connections. Things occur which have nothing to do with the plot.

People appear inexplicably and act in curious, irrational ways. Events which begin as everyday, matter-of-fact occurrences slip into the absurd. For example, in Racholl's world of divided Berlin, the simple act of ordering a drink at a bar causes complications: upon his arrival at the West Berlin bar where his trial is to take place, Racholl is about to order a drink when he realizes to his shame that his money is worthless in that part of the city. To save himself he orders something he assumes the bar doesn't have:

> . . . er verlangte, indem er mühsam
> Wort für Wort, Silbe für Silbe in das
> Gesicht des Wirtes sprach, eine Scho-
> kolade, nein, keinen Kakao, eine Scho-
> kolade: Ich trinke nur Schokolade. Der
> Wirt sah ihn fassungslos an. Racholl
> reckte sich. Er spürte, daß er dem
> Wirt für diesen Moment überlegen war.
> (p. 23)

In the same scene, an incident takes place which appears to be totally unrelated to the situation and which thus conveys the dreamlike atmosphere so typical of Kafka's writings, in which illogical occurrences are commonplace:

> Jetzt fiel ihm auch das Sprechen leich-
> ter, und er fügte seiner Bestellung
> hinzu, daß es dort, wo er herkomme,
> eine Selbstverständlichkeit sei, Trink-
> schokolade im Angebot zu führen, ganz
> gleich, welche Preisstufe ein Restau-
> rant habe, das sei eben der Vorzug des
> Gesellschaftssystems, in dem er,
> Racholl, zu leben das Glück habe, und
> wenn der Wirt die gleichen Vorzüge
> genießen wolle, brauchte er nur . . .
> Racholl konnte nicht zu Ende sprechen.
> Mit einem Tempo, das er dem massigen
> Wirt nicht zugetraut hätte, sprang
> dieser hinter der Theke hervor und warf
> sich mit seinem ganzen Gewicht auf
> einen Mann, den Racholl bei seinem
> Eintritt in die Kneipe als einen stumpf
> ins Bierglas glotzenden Mittdreißiger
> wahrgenommen hatte. (p. 23)

As the reader later learns, the man is having an epi-

leptic fit. Despite this rational explanation, the
incident has nothing to do with the rest of the story
and thus appears as absurd as some of the totally
irrational events in Kafka's works. After this episode, which results in only a brief interruption in
the conversation between Racholl and the bartender,
things return to a normal, everyday level until
Racholl confesses that he is from East Berlin, where-
upon events take another Kafkaesque turn:

> Dann sind Sie es also! sagte der Wirt.
> Nun war aller Respekt aus seiner Stimme
> verschwunden. --Wer soll ich sein?
> fragte Racholl. Der Wirt trat, ohne zu
> antworten, hinter seiner Theke hervor,
> packte Racholl am Arm und schob ihn in
> Richtung einer Tür im Hintergrund der
> Kneipe. --Kommen Sie, sagte er, Sie
> werden schon erwartet. (p. 26)

The shadowy, hallucinatory mood in both Kafka's
novel and Schlesinger's story is enhanced by a contradiction between the location in which the event takes
place and the event itself. Neither trial is held in
the sober surroundings one would expect. Joseph K.'s
trial is conducted in the attic of a tenement apartment house; Racholl's, in a bar, where loud music is
playing in the background and people are dancing. The
table at which the "judge" is seated is located on a
platform intended for an orchestra. The treatment of
the defendants contributes further to the unreal
atmosphere. Neither Racholl nor Joseph K. enjoys the
attention usually accorded the defendant in a trial.
In fact, no one even notices them at first. This
emphasizes their insignificance and the absurdity of
the whole situation. Schlesinger writes of Racholl:
"Er stand in einem Raum, der voller Menschen war.
Merkwürdigerweise beachtete ihn niemand" (p. 27).
Kafka describes Joseph K.'s situation as follows: "K.
glaubte in eine Versammlung einzutreten. Ein Gedränge
der verschiedensten Leute--niemand kümmerte sich um
den Eintretenden--füllte ein mittelgroßes, zweifen-
striges Zimmer . . ." (p. 47). This ludicrous situation, in which the central figure is ignored, continues as Schlesinger describes what happens to
Racholl: "Offenbar wurde jemand aufgefordert näher-
zutreten, aber wer und wohin, ging aus dem Satz nicht
hervor, und erst als Racholl von einem Vorüberlaufen-
den zu Boden gestoßen wurde, kam ihm, in der Zeit, die
er brauchte, um nach einer Stuhllehne zu greifen und

sich aufzurichten, der Gedanke, daß die Aufforderung
möglicherweise ihm selbst gegolten habe" (p. 28).

Because the reaction of the audience in both
trials is often inappropriate and exaggerated, it too
seems to belong more to the world of dreams than to
reality. When Racholl is asked how long he has been
at his present job and he answers "Neun Jahre," some
of those standing around clap (p. 33). Racholl lowers
his eyes shyly. When he tells about giving up smoking
and not yielding to the temptation to begin again,
some of the observers laugh. He later admits having
been in that bar before and they frown and glance at
him with distrust (p. 38). Some laugh maliciously
when he admits that he was once there with a friend
(p. 39). During his first interrogation, Joseph K.
says: "Mag ich zu spät gekommen sein, jetzt bin ich
hier" (p. 48). This prompts clapping from the audience. Joseph K. is asked if he is a house painter, to
which he responds that he is a clerk in a large bank.
The answer evokes "ein Gelächter, das so herzlich war,
daß K. mitlachen mußte" (p. 49). Kafka continues:
"Die Leute stützten sich mit den Händen auf ihre Knie
und schüttelten sich wie unter schweren Hustenan-
fällen" (p. 49).

It is not only in the creation of this dreamlike
mood that Schlesinger and Kafka are on common ground,
but also in the themes they treat. Kafka's world view
is based on a deep pessimism, and one can draw the
same conclusion about Schlesinger on the basis of this
story. There is as little hope in "Die Spaltung des
Erwin Racholl" as there is in Der Prozeß. Both authors depict the common man at the mercy of mysterious
forces. Both heroes are disturbed by their conscience
and confronted with the problem of justice. Neither
Joseph K.'s nor Racholl's guilt is caused by any real
crime, but is due simply to the circumstances in which
they live. In both cases, they are alone against society, seeking help but seldom finding it. The result
is a feeling of fear and isolation.

According to Wilhelm Emrich, Joseph K. represents

. . . the average citizen of modern
society. And also, for that very reason he harps on his innocence. For not
one of these average citizens would
ever charge himself with any sort of
guilt that could not be established

171

legally or in accordance with the conventional moral code. Not one of these
citizens suspects that it is just this
ordinary citizen's existence of his
that constitutes his real guilt.6

Joseph K.'s guilt is never clearly defined, except to
say that he does not know the law: "Sieh, Willem, er
gibt zu, er kenne das Gesetz nicht, und behauptet
gleichzeitig, schuldlos zu sein" (p. 16). Emrich
maintains that Kafka intends to show that all of
earthly existence is a "vast judiciary system," but
that only those who know nothing about such a tri-
bunal, who know nothing about an inner law and who
consider themselves innocent are caught up in it.7
Emrich comments further that the court is the expression of Joseph K.'s own inner state: "in this court
he has to come to terms with himself alone, he has to
attain clarity about himself. . . ."8

Schlesinger makes it clear that Racholl's trial
is an expression of his inner state and that it is for
the purpose of attaining clarity about himself. After
Racholl has confessed things long kept to himself, he
is told that his superiors were already aware of his
transgressions (p. 97). Unlike Joseph K., Racholl is
caught up in his trial not because he considers himself innocent, but because he considers himself
guilty. Furthermore, in contrast to Joseph K.,
Racholl's guilt is quite tangible. It stems from
three different sources: in addition to the guilt he
suffers merely because of his presence in West Berlin,
part of it has to do simply with his being German,
while the other aspect is unique to his situation as a
citizen of the GDR. The most immediate cause stems
from once having helped a friend escape to the West.
It is this feeling of guilt and the fear attached to
it that cause the physical reaction of illness in
Racholl when he learns of his promotion. He has not
only committed an act contrary to the laws of his
country, but has concealed this information at work
for fear of not being promoted. Paradoxically, rather
than having a sense of atonement for never correspond-
ing with his friend after his departure, Racholl
suffers further from a contradictory feeling of guilt
for having abandoned him. His human instincts and his
sense of duty as a citizen of the GDR are in conflict.

Racholl fears that he joined the Party for professional advancement and in an attempt to overcome

his feelings of isolation rather than out of political conviction. His behavior during the June 17th uprising also haunts him. At his factory the workers were asked to vote on whether or not to end the strike and he found himself raising his hand twice—once for ending it and once for continuing it (p. 88). Racholl considers himself a socialist and a revolutionary, yet he finds himself in total disagreement with young West German socialist revolutionaries whom he encounters in a dream sequence during his trial. Here he is suddenly in the uncomfortable position of taking a conservative stance similar to what one would expect of a West German of his age. The young West Germans advocate the theoretical socialism espoused in the GDR and he must explain why the theory cannot be put into practice (p. 52).

As a German, Racholl has been unable to come to terms with the past. His conscience does not permit him to divorce himself from responsibility for the German crimes against the Jews despite the official GDR position that the present socialist society is not accountable for those crimes, which are attributed to the old imperialist, capitalist society. He is unable to reconcile the past because of the many conflicting and mutually exclusive influences he experienced growing up. As a child he liked Hitler, played Keitel in war-crime games with his friends, and pretended at the same time to be a Russian soldier fighting the Americans (p. 74).

As a result of the trial, which has forced him to examine all aspects of his past and present beliefs and behavior, Racholl experiences a complete alienation from himself:

> Ich sehe mich nach dieser Untersuchung
> als zwei völlig verschiedene Personen,
> die ich beim besten Willen nicht in
> Übereinstimmung bringen kann. . . .
> Wenn es so wäre, daß ich Dieser bin und
> Jener war, sagte Racholl, dann wäre
> alles einfacher. Aber das Komplizierte
> ist, daß ich glaube, ich bin Dieser und
> Jener, verstehen Sie? (pp. 96-97)

Racholl's division is a mental manifestation of the physical split of his city and country. That this is a fate shared by his fellow citizens is evidenced by the incident on the subway at the end of the story when he sees himself in the passenger sitting opposite him. At an earlier point in the story Schlesinger makes it clear that Racholl's dilemma is not to be regarded as an isolated incident. Near the end of his trial someone remarks that Racholl is a problematic character. Another unidentified person replies that this would not be so dangerous if it were not a mass phenomenon (pp. 94-95).

One of the criticisms of Kafka in the GDR has been that he offers no acceptable solutions to the problems he raises. Similarly, Schlesinger's story ends with a question to which there is no answer. In the final scene on the subway, Racholl asks the passenger who looks like him the metaphysical question "--Wissen Sie, wohin es geht?" (p. 103). One is reminded of Kafka's parable "Gib's auf!" in which the main figure begs the policeman to tell him the way. Like Kafka, Schlesinger has not told his reader the way. Instead he has only depicted the human results of the political division of his country--a problem to which there seems to be no solution and thus a problem very much at home in the world of Franz Kafka.

Randolph-Macon Woman's College

Notes

1 Klaus Schlesinger, "Die Spaltung des Erwin Racholl," in his Berliner Traum (Rostock: Hinstorff, 1977).

2 Franz Kafka, Gesammelte Schriften (Berlin: Schocken, 1935), III. Further references are to this edition and will appear in the text in parentheses.

3 See, for example, Hans-Dietrich Sander, Geschichte der Schönen Literatur der DDR (Freiburg: Rombach, 1972), p. 233.

4 Horst Haase et al., Literatur der DDR, Vol. XI of Geschichte der Deutschen Literatur, 2nd ed. (E. Berlin: Volk und Wissen, 1977), p. 510.

5 Manfred Berger et al., Kulturpolitisches Wörterbuch, 2nd ed. (E. Berlin: Dietz, 1970), p. 167.

[6] Wilhelm Emrich, *Franz Kafka* (New York: Ungar, 1968), p. 318. This is an English translation of the original German.

[7] Emrich, p. 319.

[8] Emrich, p. 323.

Literature and Its Uses:
Günter de Bruyn's Preisverleihung
and Märkische Forschungen

James Knowlton

As a prolific writer of eminently readable prose, Günter de Bruyn has been accorded a good deal of attention by critics and reading public alike. His first novel, Der Hohlweg (1963), was awarded the Heinrich Mann Prize of the GDR, and his subsequent fiction has also been received well, in both East and West Germany.

This study deals with the theme of literature and its uses in de Bruyn's two most recent novels, Preisverleihung (1972) and Märkische Forschungen (1978). This theme has played a significant role in much of de Bruyn's fiction as well as in his critical writing. Karl Erp, the hero of Buridans Esel (1968), to give an example, is by no coincidence a librarian, and the discussions concerning the reception and use of literature have an important function in the novel since they often reflect the aspirations and ideals, both conscious and subconscious, of the characters.

De Bruyn is also known for his parodies of GDR literature.[1] Literary parodies, assuming they take the literature they parody seriously, can have an important epistemological function in that they call into question the modes of expression employed as well as the world view portrayed in the parodied work of literature. Critics and other readers have also discovered a wealth of concealed literary quotes in de Bruyn's prose fiction--quotes from Jean Paul, Theodor Fontane, and Arno Holz, to name a few. In a certain sense, these quotes serve as a kind of subtle coming-to-grips with the GDR's literary heritage (Erbe).[2] But, in a greater sense, the use of literature in

literature points to the function of literary reception as personal experience, as the personal appropriation of new and differing modes of perception. Our
view, indeed our knowledge of the world, is often the
result of indirect experience, of the appropriation--
frequently through literature--of others' perceptions.
Literature is viewed as a vehicle which mediates between personal subjectivity and the world of objects.
If this is the case, the reading of literature has an
important function in shaping our experience of the
world. But this, in turn, opens up a whole range of
questions concerning access to literature: who is involved in the reception of which literary works under
what circumstances? These are key themes in Märkische
Forschungen and Preisverleihung.

Preisverleihung is the story of the Universitäts-
assistent Teo Overbeck, who is given the task of
holding the laudatory speech on the occasion of the
bestowal of a literature prize on a novel written by
an old friend--a friend Teo has not seen for some
seventeen years. In fact, Teo's earlier relationship
with the author, Paul Schuster, is the reason why Teo
was selected to give the speech--and why Teo assented
without having read the book. After reading Paul's
novel, Teo finds that he cannot praise it: "Wem nützen
denn hochgelobte Ladenhüter, preisgekrönte Staub-
fänger?"[3] For Paul's book, as Teo sees it, mindlessly
reflects official perceptions of the world, offering
nothing new to its readers. Teo is confronted with
the contradiction which underlies de Bruyn's novel: a
book is praised and awarded a prize solely because of
its political view, its harmony with official political positions, not because of any inherent literary
quality.

Teo's friendship with Paul had begun when Teo, a
student at an Arbeiter- und Bauern-Fakultät, was
working as an Erntehelfer in the Mark Brandenburg. In
the village pub, Paul, a local fisherman, had narrated
the story of his family's flight to the Federal Republic and his own return a short time later. Why did he
return? he was asked. His only reason, he assured his
listeners, was a girl friend whom he deeply loved.
But Teo's youthful ideological tunnel vision was only
able to comprehend Paul's return as an expressly political act. As their relationship developed, Paul
moved to Berlin to live with Teo, and Teo encouraged
Paul to write his story down. However, Paul's honest
rendering of the experience seemed politically wrong

to Teo, who initiated a protracted struggle with Paul
in an attempt to change the book to fit prevalent
ideological precepts. Teo's fervor and his intellectual superiority were victorious. The manuscript
underwent several revisions. Using his personal
contacts, Teo arranged to have a publisher review
Paul's book, Die Rückkehr. It was tentatively accepted for publication, but at the key meeting where the
editor explained to Paul why he was interested in publishing the manuscript--the reasons were largely po-
litical--Paul realized that the book was "no longer
his own" (p. 27). He then withdrew the manuscript and
set out on a monumental drinking binge, at which point
the contact between the two friends was lost. The
matter was further complicated when Teo married Paul's
girl friend, Irene, who was expecting a child from her
relationship with Paul (Teo was involved in the production of Paul's novel, but not in the "production"
of his own child!).

In the intervening seventeen years Paul worked as
a free-lance journalist, time and time again sacrific-
ing his keen writing skills and his natural honesty to
the whims and desires, to the political norms of his
editors. His texts were often altered to the extent
that they expressed the exact opposite of what he had
written. Paul's standard of living increased, his
hunger for success was gratified, but his self-esteem
suffered--until one day he discovered his old manuscript. Driven by an insatiable desire for recognition, he began rewriting and revising his novel. By
now, Paul's talents had been coopted so often that he
was hardly capable of distinguishing between honesty
and success. The new version of the novel was slick
and pleasing, it pandered to both the officially
desired view of the world and the wishes of a mass
reading public. In short, it was tailored for success, which it received in abundance.

Teo agreed to speak at the ceremony celebrating
Paul's literary prize with the old manuscript in mind.
He is shocked when he reads the published novel, but
his attempts to extricate himself from this difficult
situation are met with disapproval from all sides.
His wife Irene is concerned about Teo's academic
success, which she sees threatened if he refuses to
speak. And his immediate superior, Professor Liebscher, a man who clearly understands for whom he is
working, sees dangerous political tendencies in Teo's
attitude: "Damit sind die Positionen für Liebscher

179

klar. Der hier vor ihm sitzt [i.e., Teo] ist einer,
dem das eigene Seelenheil mehr bedeutet als das Wohl
aller, ein Kleinbürger . . . ein Subjektivist, der das
Heil der Welt in heilen Seelen sucht" (p. 59).

Teo could, of course, exercise an additional
option and publicly criticize the book. Indeed, that
is his intention as he spends a day trying, strug-
gling, to prepare a speech. His attempts fail, however, and Teo is forced to attend the event without a
complete set of notes. The speech is a singular
catastrophe, exceeding by far the allotted time, with
no main train of thought and no logical development,
an embarrassment to all present. For the reader it
becomes increasingly clear that Teo's seemingly cha-
otic meanderings are the attempt at a compromise, a
compromise between personal conviction and social-
political necessity. This is symbolically expressed
in a comical scene where Teo, in a hurry to get to the
ceremony, unthinkingly jumps into what he believes to
be his dress shoes. Only at the auditorium does he
notice that he is wearing one dress shoe and one
leisure shoe--a good illustration of Teo's dilemma,
his vacillating between public and private existence.

Preisverleihung is a book about the conditions
surrounding the production and use of literature in
the GDR. Both Paul's writing and Teo's speech are
compromises, both acquiesce to social pressure. But
in neither case does external coercion play a decisive
role in the decision. This is the key. The system of
social domination has become internalized. Teo's
decision to sacrifice his cherished personal honesty
and compromise his evaluation of Paul's book is clearly a sign of the prevalence, indeed the radical domination of the state-dominated public sphere over the
private sphere, of an officially conceived view of the
world over personal conviction.

Teo is convinced that all good literature is
autobiographical, that the honest rendering of personal perceptions is a precondition of good literature. He says: "Wirken kann ein Buch nur durch voll-
ständige Aufrichtigkeit; denn nur wenn der Autor sich
mit seinem Werk identifiziert, kann der Leser dessen
Gedanken und Gefühle zu eigenen machen" (p. 115), and
"das Entscheidende aber lernt man nicht, das lebt man,
das ist man, und deshalb sind Entscheidungen, die man
im Leben trifft, auch Entscheidungen über die Bücher,
die man schreiben wird" (p. 128).4 Inherent in these

statements is an indictment of GDR society, of the ideological domination over private existence. The genesis of Paul's book and Teo's speech shows that personally held ideals often cannot be realized. More importantly, they point at a root of alienation in this society; they expose the chasm between personal ideals in the private sphere and conflicting demands in the public sphere. At the end of the day, in the privacy of his own home, Teo summarizes "die Lehre des Tages" for "his" daughter: "Wahre Übereinstimmung mit der Gesellschaft kannst du nicht erschleichen. Du kannst nur geben, was du hast . . ." (p. 137).[5] But why should this be necessary? Why, in a socialist society, must public needs be in conflict with private needs?

Radical honesty and compromise are also important elements of de Bruyn's next novel, <u>Märkische Forschungen</u>.[6] But here de Bruyn takes a different tack. <u>Märkische</u> Forschungen is the story of two men, the village schoolteacher Ernst Pötsch and the university professor Winfried Menzel, whose research about the fictitious writer Max von Schwedenow brings them together in a problem-filled relationship.

Max von Schwedenow, whose life spanned the period defined by the French Revolution and the Wars of Liberation, died, according to the few existing documents and biographies, in 1813, a hero on the field of battle as a member of the <u>Freikorps</u>. His life shows many of the radical bourgeois revolutionary tendencies praised by Marxist historians and literary scholars alike. It is this ideological aspect which motivates Menzel's interest. And Schwedenow is, for all practical purposes, unknown. The last edition of his works appeared around the turn of the century, and his name appears only in the most scholarly reference works. Menzel, an extraordinarily ambitious social climber, endeavors to discover this gifted democratic author for a general reading public--and to make a name for himself at the same time. Not that Menzel is unknown; on the contrary, he is a man with a wide-ranging network of connections. And these connections have been good to him. He is a well-know TV personality and the director of his own institute, the ZIHIHI (Zentralinstitut für Historiographie und Historiomatie), more commonly known as MP (Menzel's <u>Pfründe</u>), over which he reigns like a feudal despot. Needless to say this carries over into a near-feudal life style. As the novel begins, Menzel's monograph, <u>Ein</u>

märkischer Jakobiner, a scholarly monstrosity of truly
German proportions, is essentially ready for publication. While on an excursion through the historical
sites related to Schwedenow's life, he chances to meet
Ernst Pötsch, an unpublished expert on Schwedenow's
life. Menzel, enthralled with Pötsch's detailed
knowledge and by his unassuming, i.e., unthreatening
manner, invites Pötsch to join the ZIHIHI as an
Assistent--under the condition that he complete his
Ph.D. under Menzel's guidance.

Menzel and Pötsch are about as different as two
people can be, and their divergent personalities are
clearly reflected in their scholarship: "Denn Pötsch
liebte, was ihm nahe war, und nahm es dadurch in
Besitz, daß er es so genau wie möglich kennenlernte.
Stand Menzel gleichsam auf einem Aussichtsturm und
schaute durch ein Fernrohr in die Weite, so Pötsch,
mit Lupe auf platter Erde, wo jede Hecke ihm den Blick
verstellte. Sein Wissen war begrenzt, aber innerhalb
der Grenzen universal" (p. 14). Where Menzel's work
is motivated by a clearly defined view of history and
supported by an elaborate theoretical framework,
Pötsch collects and sorts data without historical and
theoretical mediation. The primary motivation for
Pötsch's enthusiasm for Schwedenow stems from an
interest in local history--both Pötsch and Schwedenow
come from the same town. But there is another important motivation: "Pötsch fühlte sich dem Mann ver-
wandt. In Schwedenows Dichtung fand er sich selbst.
Seine Gefühle waren dort formuliert, seine Sehnsüchte
beschrieben, seine Gedanken vorgedacht. Pötsch sah in
Schwedenows Romane und Gedichte wie in einen Spiegel--
und war von sich entzückt" (p. 15).

De Bruyn treats both characters with a touch of
irony, but what he has sketched here is no less than
two distinctly different and conflicting ways of
dealing with literature: the ideological and the
personal. Where Menzel's work is suspiciously selec-
tive, containing only those biographical data and
literary works which support his thesis, Pötsch's
research, unburdened by ideological considerations,
aims at filling in many of the gaps in Schwedenow's
life. Menzel, for example, uses the name "Max Schwedenow," leaving out the problematic "von." And Menzel
has bestowed upon Schwedenow "das ehrenvolle Prädikat
'kleinbürgerlich-revolutionärer Demokrat fronbäuerli-
cher Herkunft'" (p. 24)--this image being the underlying thesis of Menzel's book. But Pötsch is not

convinced, and further research indicates--although Pötsch is never able to prove this beyond doubt--that Schwedenow was, in fact, Maximilian von Massow, son of a Prussian colonel who was the administrator of the Royal Prussian Forstamt in Schwedenow, and that he had simply assumed the nom de plume "Max von Schwedenow" in the meaning of "Max aus Schwedenow." Of course, the fact that Max was of old nobility is still no reason for concern. His books, after all, are the final arbiter of his liberal convictions, and here there can be no doubt: Max was a fervent admirer of the French Revolution and was later active in the revolutionary nationalist movement in Germany. But then Pötsch makes a final--and for his career catastrophic--discovery: Max's date of death is incorrect. It seems that he did not die in 1813 on the field of battle, as Menzel had reported, but rather in 1820 in Berlin. Although Pötsch is unaware of it, this discovery, if published, could knock holes in Menzel's thesis: that Max Schwedenow gave his life for the revolutionary cause. Menzel's subordinates in the Institute warn Pötsch that his work could be harmful to his career, but Pötsch, obsessed by the naive belief that all scholarly endeavors are motivated by the desire for truth, refuses to comprehend the approaching conflict with Menzel, who, as yet, has not seen Pötsch's results.

Finally Pötsch stumbles across the missing link: he proves that Massow left the military in 1815 and moved to Berlin, where, at the time of his death in 1820, he was nothing less than the vice-president of the Ober-Zensur-Kollegium, the official censorship organ of the government. Thus Pötsch is able to draw a final, if tenuous conclusion, the irony and danger of which he never grasps: "Eindeutig . . . nahm der 'Märkische Jakobiner' seine Jugend-Progressivität zurück und denunzierte nun in ekelhafter Weise revoltierende Studenten als Jakobiner" (p. 81).

Inspired by his new discoveries and still unmindful of their consequences, Pötsch completes an essay entitled "Die Suche nach einem Grab," and, in a key scene in the novel, presents it to Menzel at Menzel's birthday party. Of course, Menzel is too busy stroking his important guests to read anything on the spot, and, in a touching scene in which he offers Pötsch the "Du," he bares his character, his weakness, his compulsion to compensate to Pötsch, whom he considers to be his best friend. Here he explains why his book means so much to him: "Warum, meinen Sie, habe ich dieses Buch geschrieben? 600 Seiten, zehn Jahre Arbeit. . . . Nur darum, weil ich die Flüchtigkeit aller anderen Erfolge erkannt habe. Bleibendes stiften nur Bücher" (p. 108).

The stage is set for the final confrontation. Pötsch's work clearly contains the negation of Menzel's thesis. But Pötsch, still unaware of the possible consequences, has, in the meantime, quit his job at the village school, uprooted his family, and arranged to move to Berlin to take up work at the Institute. On the following day, Menzel drags Pötsch into his private office and proceeds to condemn the essay (a birthday present!), using words like "Mangel an Bedeutsamkeit," "Detailbesessenheit," "Kleinkariertheit," "zweiter Aufguß des Positivismus," finally concluding that the study contains "gefährliche Thesen eines Hobby-Historikers, die zu beweisen er nicht fähig ist" (p. 122). It is characteristic of Menzel's critique that not one of the items listed has anything to do with the content of the essay. He merely disqualifies the form.

When Pötsch submits his manuscript to various journals, Menzel sets his connections in motion and has it rejected. Pötsch persists and prepares his study for a talk in the Urania lecture series--a series directed by Menzel. Menzel had arranged and announced the lecture, before having read Pötsch's essay. Now it is too late to cancel. Before the talk begins, Menzel attempts conciliation. He explains to an uncomprehending Pötsch that this essay could only be understood as a counter project to the <u>Märkischer Jakobiner</u>. Finally he comes to the core of the matter: "Dir geht's um ein Phantom, das du, wie ich dich kenne, Wahrheit nennst. Mir geht es um viel mehr: um Sein oder Nichtsein in Wissenschaft und Nachwelt" (p. 140). When Pötsch insists on continuing, Menzel, in his introductory remarks, attempts to discredit the article on political grounds, obliquely referring to certain "Kleinigkeitskrämer" and "Detailfetischisten" who, when viewed objectively, are only capable of driving Schwedenow "in die Fänge der Reaktion" (p. 142). And the sheer power of Menzel's presence, his overwhelming eloquence, so overshadows Pötsch's presentation that its significance is overlooked and never comprehended by those present. Pötsch is defeated, Menzel prevails. [7]

In both novels de Bruyn denounces the ideological dominance of the public sphere over the private, of ideology over truth. In both cases, Pötsch's undoing and Teo's failure to uphold his ideals, reigning forms of social domination prevail over privately, individually conceived truth. Both books share an underlying skepticism concerning the uses of literature in this socialist society. In both we find the unholy dominance of the ideological in the reception of literature, both contemporary literature, as in the case of Paul Schuster's book, and historical, as in the case of Max von Schwedenow. Schuster's novel fulfills an officially and thus "objectively" perceived necessity; it mediates a view of the world which complies with that of officialdom. So it is praised and rewarded. Teo's objection that this novel reflects "paper and not the world" (p. 143) is consequently perceived to be a dangerously subjective and politically deviant view. The key here, however, is not that Teo is forced to acquiesce, but rather that he has unconsciously conformed. His compromising reception of Paul's novel is clearly the process of unreflected acquiescence to social pressure, of conforming. If literature indeed is a vehicle which mediates between objective reality and subjective individuality, then its reception here must be regarded as a mode of domination by which an official view of the world gains access to personal perception.

Pötsch's reception of a historical figure and his literature, on the other hand, maintains an objective quality which clashes with the subjective needs of a powerful public figure, Professor Menzel. Menzel, in turn, reflects the need of the public sphere for historical and political self-legitimation. However, in this case, the modes of social domination are more forcefully expressed: Pötsch is muscled out and isolated, Menzel's view dominates.

University of Northern Iowa

Notes

[1] Maskeraden. Parodien (Halle: Mitteldeutscher Verlag, 1966). In two articles de Bruyn discusses the uses of literature parodies: "Das unartige Kind der

Zeit. Gedanken zur Literaturparodie." Sonntag, 18, Nr. 6 (1964); "Über Literaturparodie," in his Im Querschnitt. Prosa, Essays, Biographie (Halle: Mitteldeutscher Verlag, 1979). De Bruyn also edited an anthology of literature parodies under the name Das Lästerkabinett. Deutsche Literatur von Auerbach bis Zweig in der Parodie (Leipzig: Reclam, 1979).

2 Bernd Allenstein discusses de Bruyn's use of literary quotes in greater detail, "Günter de Bruyn," in Kritisches Lexikon zur deutschsprachigen Gegenwartsliteratur, ed. Heinz Ludwig Arnold (Munich: edition text und kritik, 1978 ff.), p. 6.

3 Preisverleihung, in Im Querschnitt, p. 61. Page references, which will be indicated parenthetically in the text, are to this edition.

4 This corresponds to de Bruyn's view of literature. In one essay he notes: "Erst längere literarische Praxis hat mich an das Wunder glauben gelehrt, daß Eigenstes, genau dargestellt, sich als Allgemeines erweist" ("Der Holzweg," Im Querschnitt, p. 328). In an essay on Thomas Mann's Tonio Kröger, de Bruyn expands on this: "Diese Möglichkeit allgemeiner Wirkung beruht auf dem Beispielhaften, daß der Künstler seinem individuellen Fall zu geben vermag. Scheinbar paradoxerweise wird das aber nicht erreicht durch Allgemeinheit der Darstellung. Ganz im Gegenteil: Gerade das Konkrete, Individuelle, Zeit- und Ortsgebundene kann einer Geschichte die Genauigkeit und Stimmigkeit geben, die sie exemplarisch macht und damit nacherlebbar . . ." (Im Querschnitt, p. 357-58).

5 Rulo Melchert points out: "Es ist bezeichnend genug, daß nicht im 'öffentlichen Vortrag', sondern erst im [privaten] 'Küchenvortrag' die Kritik Teos an Pauls Roman gelingt," "Günter de Bruyn, Die Preisverleihung," Sinn und Form, 25 (1973), 1312.

6 Märkische Forschungen. Erzählung für Freunde der Literaturgeschichte (Frankfurt/M: Fischer, 1979). Parenthetical references in the text are to this edition.

7 At least one GDR literary scholar, Bernd Leistner, felt compelled to defend the honor of his colleagues: "Einmal mehr wird ein Literaturwissenschaftler zum saturierten Ignoranten abgestempelt und damit als 'würdiger' Anwalt eines kategorischen Im-

perativs attackiert, dessen Pflichtgebot nicht das der Moral ist," "Günter de Bruyn: Märkische Forschungen," Weimarer Beiträge, 26, Nr. 3 (1980), 142.

GDR Literary Influences on the FRG
Werkkreis Literatur der Arbeitswelt

William Walker

In the concluding lines of his 1974 poem "Aufruf
des Werkkreises," Panos Voglis states: "Des Volkes
Rede ist die Tat / Bring seine Taten zum Reden."[1]
Although Voglis is referring to the need for dissemi-
nation of strike reports to the public, the spirit of
the poem is characteristic of the philosophy of the
FRG Werkkreis Literatur der Arbeitswelt (WLA), which
was founded in 1970 as a "parteiunabhängige, gemein-
nützige Organisation an der Seite der Arbeiterklasse
und ihrer Gewerkschaften."[2] In over thirty regionally
based WLA workshops, laborers and white-collar employees interact collectively with professional writers, critics, and journalists to develop and promote
workers' literature. With the assistance of such
professional writers and critics as Erika Runge,
Angelika Mechtel, Peter Schütt, Josef Büscher, Richard
Limpert, Lilo Rauner, Peter Fischer, and Peter Kühne,
the WLA aims at creating a socially critical body of
literature, including paperback books, articles for
union newspapers, and other regional publications,
which will elevate the workers' consciousness and
subsequently induce social change in the interest of
the working class.

Among the more intriguing aspects of the WLA is
the degree to which GDR literary theory and practice
may have influenced the development of the WLA. As
early as 1974 Ingeborg Gerlach observed: "Die Frage
nach dem möglichen Vorbildcharakter der Bitterfelder
Literatur für den Werkkreis ist nie expressis verbis
gestellt worden."[3] The question, though posed, still
remains unanswered, and I would like to address this
issue by investigating the origins of the WLA to
determine whether a direct link exists between the WLA

189

and GDR literature, specifically as reflected in the 1959 directives of the Bitterfeld Conference.

The remarks of a co-founder of the WLA, Erasmus Schöfer, indicate that the WLA emerged in part as a reaction to the Dortmund Group 61, an association of writers and workers which focused, as its 1961 Programm states, on the "literarisch-künstlerische Auseinandersetzung mit der industriellen Arbeitswelt der Gegenwart und ihrer sozialen Probleme."[4] In a 1970 essay Schöfer observed: "Der Werkkreis für Literatur verdankt sein Entstehen der Kritik an der Praxis und Theorie der Gruppe 61 und damit im Grunde der Gruppe 61 selbst, die ja als erste die industrielle Arbeitswelt als einen Gegenstand, als ein Thema der Beschreibung bekanntgemacht hat."[5] By 1968 the Group 61 was being assailed by many of its members, including Erika Runge, Josef Büscher, Günter Wallraff, and WLA cofounders Peter Schütt and Erasmus Schöfer, because of the Group 61 leadership's resistance to change, a factor which ultimately would necessitate founding the WLA. As Heinz-Ludwig Arnold characterized the situation:

> Jüngere, der Gewerkschaft nahestehende
> Mitglieder kritisierten die ideolo-
> gische Offenheit der Gruppe und ihr
> schlechtes Verhältnis zu den Gewerk-
> schaften; beklagt wurde die Verbürger-
> lichung der in der Gruppe geförderten
> Literatur; verlangt wurde eine poli-
> tisch radikalere Stellungnahme im Sinne
> der außerparlamentarischen Opposition
> und die stärkere Beteiligung von Arbei-
> tern an der Gruppenarbeit. Diese
> Forderung wurde verbunden mit einer
> massiven Kritik an den in der Gruppe
> gängigen traditionellen Literatur-
> formen.[6]

Finally, Schöfer indicted the Group 61 for maintaining "eine Trennung von der Arbeiterdichtung der Nachweltkriegszeit und der DDR sowie den schreibenden Arbeitern auch hierzulande."[7]

Peter Schütt, described by Heinz-Ludwig Arnold as "der geistige Mentor des Werkkreises," referred in 1972 to the pre-World War II German proletarian literary tradition, including the literary activities of German workers during the 1920s, as an indispensable contribution to the development of the WLA. He observed that the proletarian literary heritage was preserved and developed in the GDR and acknowledged the intermediary role of the GDR in communicating this heritage to the FRG: "Wir sind darauf hingewiesen worden durch Veröffentlichungen, durch Diskussionsbeiträge, durch den Rat der Genossen in der DDR."[8]

In what specific areas can one ascertain the influence of pre-World War II workers' literature, as transmitted by the GDR, on the development of the WLA? The first area of influence entails collective group activity and reciprocal criticism. The method of literary production in the WLA, which involves the collective interplay of professional writers, journalists, critics, and workers from the inception of a work to publication, has as its earliest model the Bund proletarisch-revolutionärer Schriftsteller (BPRS), founded in 1928 by Johannes R. Becher and Kurt Kläber, among others. Prior to 1928 Becher had also been instrumental in creating the Proletarische Feuilletonkorrespondenz (PFK), which provided journalistic assistance to Arbeiterkorrespondenten in the preparing of documentary works for mass distribution to workers. The BPRS was the first organized body in Germany to stress the interaction of workers and writers in the creation of a genuine proletarian literature. The goal of the BPRS, the establishment of proletarian-revolutionary literature as a dominant force within the larger literary tradition, was to be achieved by means similar to those later used by the WLA; their method was "durch praktische Ratschläge und vor allem durch die scharfe Waffe der Kollektivkritik die schreibenden Arbeiter zu befähigen, aus den einfachen Agitationstexten Kurzgeschichten oder kleinere Erzählungen zu formen und die dadurch einem größeren Publikum lesbar zu machen."[9] The concept of collective production and reciprocal criticism was underscored by Walter Ulbricht at the 1959 Bitterfeld Conference in his remarks on the value of the BPRS for GDR workers' literary circles: "Glaubt einer der Genossen Schriftsteller, daß es möglich ist, große Kunstwerke zu schaffen ohne jede Kollektivität der Arbeit? Das ist nicht möglich."[10]

A significant influence of the BPRS on the GDR workers' circles during the Bitterfeld era involves the method of publication and distribution of group-produced materials, a method employed by the WLA as well. The BPRS used as many progressive, worker-oriented publication organs as possible in order to create a broad Basisöffentlichkeit. The Communist Party press played an important role in the publication of such BPRS journals and newspapers as Die Rote Fahne and Die Linkskurve. The BPRS also relied heavily on union and neighborhood newspapers, estimated in 1929 to number 700. The BPRS was also responsible for the publication of the series Der Rote-Eine-Mark Roman, inexpensive paperback novels designed to educate the working masses and satisfy their need for relevant, enjoyable literature. As with the BPRS, the vast bulk of literature produced by the Bitterfeld writers' circles appeared either in union-sponsored Zirkel collections, as exemplified by the three-volume Deubener Blätter, or in government-sponsored journals, such as the monthly journal ich schreibe, published by the Zentralhaus für Kulturarbeit der DDR. Although the WLA has produced two informational journals, INFO and Werkstatt, on a regular basis since 1970, the major WLA publication organs have been factory journals and union newspapers. As Jürgen Albrechts stated:

> Hier wird in kontinuierlicher Arbeit
> betriebsnahe Information gegeben, die
> von den Betriebsangehörigen gemacht
> wird, die die Kollegen direkt erreicht
> und mit der sie auch etwas anfangen
> können. Zweites wichtiges Mittel sind
> die Gewerkschaftszeitungen, die von den
> Einzelgewerkschaften herausgegeben
> werden, aber auch z.B. die 'Welt der
> Arbeit' als Wochenzeitung des DGB.
> Diese Zeitungen erreichen immerhin rund
> 7 Millionen Kollegen.[11]

The WLA has also attempted to reach the larger reading public by publishing since 1971 over 500,000 copies of inexpensive short-story collections, novels, and documentary reports which treat a wide variety of themes relating to the workers' everyday lives.

An additional link between the BPRS, the Bitterfeld writers' circles, and the WLA concerns the role of literature as a means of promoting social, political, and economic change favorable to the working class. Johannes R. Becher's Proletarische Feuilletonkorrespondenz had been the first group in Germany to pursue this goal, which Berta Lask described as: "Literatur zu fördern, die das Leben des Proletariats

schildert, das Klassenbewußtsein weckt, den wirtschaftlichen und politischen Kampf vorwärts treibt."12
Lask pointed out stages in the creation of proletarian
literature which were later acknowledged by the BPRS,
the GDR Bitterfeld writers' circles, and the WLA: one
must first inspire the writer to reflect on the nature
of his/her social, political, and economic circumstances; second, the writer elevates the consciousness
of the reader by sharing that newly perceived awareness of the workers' situation. In this way, it is
possible to transform the ideological perspective of
the workers.

The first stage, the educating of the aspiring
writer in regard to the nature of his/her social
circumstances, was clarified as early as 1921 in the
"Leitsätzen zur Bildungsarbeit der KPD": "Der Kampf
des Proletariats um seine ökonomische und politische
Befreiung ist deshalb zugleich ein Kampf um die Befreiung des proletarischen Denkens und Fühlens von den
überkommenen Formen der bürgerlichen Weltanschauung
und Lebensführung."13   At the 1959 Bitterfeld Conference this idea was particularly stressed.   Alfred
Kurella stated: "Der Kopf muß wissen, was die Hände
tun";14   Walter Ulbricht observed as well that the
first stage in the creation of a socialist German
national literature had to begin with the collective
self-enlightenment of the members.15   The official WLA
position on educating the worker/writer clearly echoes
the sentiments of both the Communist Party during the
Weimar Republic and the GDR Bitterfeld directives:
"Der sozialistische Schriftsteller muß sich das Wissen
seiner Zeit über die gesellschaftlichen Verhältnisse
angeeignet haben.   Damit er mit seinen Waffen gut
kämpfen kann, muß er den Kampfplatz kennen."16

The BPRS, the GDR writers' circles, and the WLA
each recognized that the primary goal of the worker/
writer, after a period of collective training in
ideological issues, is to shape a socialist perspective in the readership.   Johannes R. Becher was emphatic in his belief that the writer who took pen to
hand was not an "ordinary minstrel," but a person with
a cause to explain and defend: "Es war das proletarische Bewußtsein, Klassensolidarität, das ihm Herz
und Hirn bewegte . . . für die Aufgaben des Klassen-
kampfes, für die Vorbereitung der proletarischen
Revolution."17   It was the task of the Bitterfeld
Conference as well to determine how the writers "bei
ihrer Tätigkeit an der Durchführung der sozialisti-

schen Umgestaltung, insbesondere bei der sozialistischen Bewußtseinsbildung der Arbeiterklasse und der
Bevölkerung der DDR mithelfen könnten. . . ."[18] Not
only did Erasmus Schöfer admit that the WLA could be
defined as "eine breitangelegte demokratische Bewegung
mit zweifellos sozialistischen Zielen,"[19] Peter Schütt
went a step further by remarking: "Es kann uns nur
helfen, daß wir uns mit unseren literarischen Darstellungen am konkreten Sozialismus orientieren, an der
DDR und an der Sowjetunion. . . ."[20]

In accordance with their goal of promoting socialist consciousness, the BPRS, the GDR writers'
circles, and the WLA became aligned with as many
different proletarian mass organizations as possible.
Although the BPRS recognized the leading role of the
KPD in directing and sustaining its activities, Becher
preferred to think of the BPRS as "überparteilich"; he
believed a more general pro-socialist, anti-fascist
stance was of overriding importance for fulfilling the
BPRS mission.[21] And, while the SED provides the most
direction and support, the GDR writers' circles have
also worked with other socialist constituencies,
including the labor unions, in their effort to create
a socialist culture. The WLA has also avoided affili-
ation with any one political party and has directed
its efforts primarily toward aligning itself with the
labor unions, as well as with the Jungdemokraten, the
SPD, and DKP.

A major issue remained imprecisely defined during
the short lifespan of the PFK and BPRS: the role of
the writers' circles in the creation of a socialist
culture. This question was clarified later in the GDR
Bitterfeld writers' circles and transmitted in the
form of a direct influence to the WLA. In his address
at the 1959 Bitterfeld Conference, Walter Ulbricht
observed that a genuinely socialist national culture
had yet to materialize in the GDR, and that it was the
task of professional writers and workers to create
"jene Kultur, die ihrer Form nach national und ihrem
Inhalt nach eine sozialistische Kultur ist."[22] Not
only could literature, as Ulbricht observed, acquaint
GDR readers with the significant spiritual, moral, and
ideological developments taking place in the GDR, but
literature could assist also in eradicating any lingering remnants of capitalist ideology.

The WLA has repeatedly asserted its role in
improving social and economic conditions and in cre-

ating a democratic socialist culture in the FRG. A 1972 issue of INFO states:

> Beide Forderungen, die Demokratisierung der Kultur und die Demokratisierung der Wirtschaft und Gesellschaft sind Forderungen der Arbeiterbewegung, die eines Tages erreicht werden sollen. Diese Forderungen sind sozialistisch: denn erst mit der Vergesellschaftung des privaten Besitzes an Produktivvermögen wird auch die Vergesellschaftung des kulturellen Reichtums möglich sein.[23]

The creation of a democratic socialist culture, as the WLA has observed, can be successful only "wenn der Zusammenhang gesehen und praktisch hergestellt wird. In diesem Zusammenhang muß die Arbeit des Werkkreises und seiner Werkstätten verstanden werden."[24]

The primary focus of the BPRS had been to create a militant, anti-fascist Kampfliteratur for purposes of promoting a revolution in Germany; it remained the task of the GDR, with considerable assistance from the Soviet Union, to define more precisely the form and content of a workers' literature within a socialist cultural context. These definitions later had a significant influence on the development of WLA theory and practice.[25]

In regard to literary form, Ulbricht declared in 1959 that brigade diaries, reportage, and other forms of documentary literature should form the nucleus of GDR socialist culture. The FRG critic Ingeborg Gerlach interpreted the promotion of documentary literature as a means of influencing worker productivity: "Das Brigadetagebuch soll die Arbeitsproduktivität günstig beeinflussen, indem es die einzelnen Brigademitglieder zu sozialistischen Menschen erzieht und zu einem Kollektiv vereinigt, das sich seiner Verantwortung bewußt wird und das Leben des Betriebes mitbestimmt."[26] The fact remains, however, that documentary forms were regarded as a preparatory step toward more complex literary forms. As the GDR Handbuch für schreibende Arbeiter notes, involvement with documentary forms of literature allows the worker/writer sufficient time to develop both as a writer and as a socialist personality, "um seinen Blick zu schärfen, um beobachten zu lernen, um tiefer in die Realität einzudringen."[27] In his Bitterfeld address

Ulbricht conceded that fiction, as opposed to documentary literature, "in meisterhafter Gestaltung immer wegweisender wird für die Entwicklung unserer sozialistischen Nationalkultur."[28]

The WLA has also encouraged the production of concrete, localized documentary texts written in an informational fashion as a means of contributing to the objective presentation of socialist culture and of providing the necessary pre-stage in the writer's ideological and artistic ripening process. As Peter Kühne and Erasmus Schöfer explain: "Auf diese Weise versucht der Werkkreis, die materiell-technischen Probleme der Arbeitswelt als gesellschaftlich bewußt zu machen."[29] At the same time it shows "den Ausweg aus der Ausbeutungssituation in der Überführung des privaten Produktivvermögens ins Gemeineigentum."[30] Peter Schütt cited Willi Bredel as a model for the novice writer, since Bredel's writing demonstrates in exemplary fashion the progression from documentary forms to more complex fictional literary forms: "In seinem Werk sieht man die schrittweise Entwicklung von der kleinen literarischen Form, von der Reportage bis hin zum Roman. Er zeigt, wie auch wir zu den größeren literarischen Formen kommen können."[31]

In light of the importance attached to fiction in both the GDR and FRG writers' circles, a focus on the totality of the worker's world as potential subject matter has emerged in both groups. At the 1959 Bitterfeld Conference Ulbricht noted the importance of the writers' drawing subject matter from the totality of life: "Der Auftrag besteht darin, daß sie das Neue im Leben, in der gesellschaftlichen Beziehung der Menschen, in ihrem Kampf um den sozialistischen Aufbau, um die sozialistische Umgestaltung des gesamten Lebens künstlerisch gestalten."[32] This point has been underscored on several occasions by Peter Schütt, namely that FRG workers' literature cannot restrict itself to "proletarian reserves": "Der Werkkreis . . . darf sich nicht selbstgenügsam auf das Thema 'industrielle Arbeitswelt' beschränken. Gestaltungswürdig ist das ganze Spektrum unseres Lebens--aus der Sicht der arbeitenden Menschen."[33] Significantly, this position made it possible for both the GDR and WLA writers' circles to include white-collar employees, even high-level management, in the process of literary production.

An additional concern of GDR literary theory and

practice has become manifest in WLA literature: the nature and function of realistic writing, as well as the vision of a "new man" and "new social order" to emerge in that literature. A fundamental expectation of socialist realism throughout its development in the GDR has been that the writer create a truthful representation of social reality by exploring the social, economic, and political laws which operate beneath the observable surface of reality. Günter Wallraff, in his address to the 1970 WLA Congress, stressed exactly this interpretation of literary realism as it should apply to the WLA: "Phantasie auf Veränderung hin ausrichten heißt, sich nicht damit begnügen zu beschreiben, wie es ist, sondern in der exakten Beschreibung mit durchblicken lassen, wie es anders sein könnte, und gleichzeitig nach den Ursachen und Verantwortlichkeiten fragen, weshalb es so bedrückend ist, wie es ist." [34] Later, as a consequence of the 1972 WLA Congress, the central issue of realistic writing was addressed again, and the similarity with GDR literary realism is apparent: "Realistisch schreiben heißt für den Werkkreis, nicht die Wirklichkeit 'abfotographieren', sondern die Oberfläche durchdringen und zeigen, was hinter den Fakten steckt, welche wirtschaftlichen und politischen Zusammenhänge bestehen." [35] Walter Ulbricht maintained at the Bitterfeld Conference that variety in literary form is an integral part of realism; the WLA conference concluded in a similar fashion that all proven or new forms of realistic creation should be used. [36]

Another aspect of GDR socialist realism in WLA theory concerns <u>Antizipation</u>, the anticipation of the "new man" and "new society" which would emerge in the socialist order. In his Bitterfeld address Ulbricht was extremely critical of earlier GDR novels which dealt with such issues and problems as mastery of technology and the fulfillment of quotas. He recommended that the writers portray "wie die Menschen in ihrer täglichen Arbeit wachsen, wie die Arbeiter unter Führung der Partei die Aufgaben lösen, wie sich neue Beziehungen zwischen den Menschen entwickeln, wie sich der neue Mensch formt." [37] Ulbricht envisioned a "new man," who, by having resolved the division between spiritual and physical activity, could make culture the province of the working class. As a consequence of exposure to this type of literature, the reader, in his view, would be motivated to emulate the story's hero and/or try his own hand at resolving ideological issues in an artistic manner.

197

The 1972 WLA Congress came to strikingly similar conclusions in regard to the role of literature in defining future society and the "new man": "Weiterhin soll das 'realistische Schreiben' sich nicht nur begrenzen auf die 'tatsächliche Realität' (Was ist? Warum ist es so?), es soll und muß sich auch ausdehnen auf die Gestaltung der 'möglichen Realität' (Kann es auch anders sein? Wie könnte es werden?)."[38] Peter Schütt acknowledged: "Für die Menschenbild-Problematik können wir, glaube ich, viel von der DDR lernen."[39] In Schütt's opinion, the task of the WLA would be much the same as that faced in the GDR: one must create positive heroes who are masters of their destinies as opposed to individuals who are imbued with doubts and pessimism: "gesucht werden Herren ihres Schicksals . . . erkennende, handelnde, die Verhältnisse verändernde Menschen."[40]

When contemplating the manner and conditions in and under which GDR literature may have had an impact upon the WLA, a literary circle functioning within a radically different ideological environment, it is instructive to keep in mind the remarks made by Peter Schütt as he discussed the implications of transferring aspects of the GDR workers' circles to the FRG Werkkreis: "Man kann nichts aus der DDR 'übernehmen', denn inzwischen liegt eine ganze Epoche, dazwischen liegen sozusagen Generationen Kampf der DKP, die uns bevorstehen."[41] While the Bitterfeld writers' circles have fulfilled their historical mission of contributing to the creation of a socialist culture in the GDR and are no longer a significant force in GDR literature, the WLA remains an active, growing, and dynamic force within the FRG, as evidenced by the recent Fischer Verlag series of novels (for example, Herbert Somplatzki's Muskelschrott), short-story collections (Neue Stories), and documentary reports (Der rote Großvater erzählt and Mein Vaterland ist international). It remains to be seen whether the WLA, which has been in existence for only eleven years, will be successful in creating the necessary level of consciousness among the FRG workers as a pre-stage in collectively changing the political, economic, and social conditions of the FRG worker in the interest of the entire working class.

Bradley University

Notes

[1] Panos Voglis, "Aufruf des Werkkreises," Werkstatt, Nr. 1 (September 1974), p. 2.

[2] Cited in Peter Kühne and Erasmus Schöfer, "Schreiben für die Arbeitswelt," Akzente, 17, Nr. 4 (August 1970), 335.

[3] Ingeborg Gerlach, Bitterfeld: Arbeiterliteratur und Literatur der Arbeitswelt in der DDR (Kronberg/Ts.: Scriptor, 1974), p. 161.

[4] Aus der Welt der Arbeit: Almanach der Gruppe 61 und ihrer Gäste, ed. Fritz Hüser et al. (Neuwied: n.p., 1966), p. 13.

[5] Erasmus Schöfer, Kultur und Gesellschaft, Nr. 7/8 (July 1970), p. 24.

[6] Heinz-Ludwig Arnold und Ilsabe Dagmar Arnold-Dielewicz, Arbeiter-Literatur in der Bundesrepublik Deutschland (Stuttgart: Klett, 1975), pp. 15-16.

[7] Erasmus Schöfer, Süddeutsche Zeitung, 7 Nov. 1969, p. 8, col. 9.

[8] Ursula Reinhold, "Interview mit Peter Schütt," Weimarer Beiträge, 18, Nr. 2 (1972), 61.

[9] Werkkreis Literatur der Arbeitswelt Dortmund, Informationspapier Arbeits-Literatur, April 1974, p. 9. Available in archives of the Stadtbücherei Dortmund.

[10] Protokoll der Autorenkonferenz des Mitteldeutschen Verlages Halle (Saale), 24 April 1959, p. 109.

[11] Jürgen Alberts, "Politisches Referat zur 6. Delegiertenversammlung des Werkkreises Literatur der Arbeitswelt," speech presented at the WLA conference in Dortmund, May 1974.

[12] Cited in Elisabeth Simons, "Der Bund proletarisch-revolutionärer Schriftsteller Deutschlands und sein Verhältnis zur kommunistischen Partei Deutschlands," in Literatur der Arbeiterklasse, ed. Irmfried

Hiebel (E. Berlin: Aufbau, 1971), p. 143.

[13] "Leitsätze zur Bildungsarbeit der KPD. Entwurf des Reichs-Bildungsausschusses," Die Internationale, No. 18-19 (1921), p. 681.

[14] Protokoll der Autorenkonferenz des Mitteldeutschen Verlages Halle, p. 17.

[15] Protokoll, p. 109.

[16] Werkkreis Literatur der Arbeitswelt Dortmund, p. 14.

[17] Simons, p. 165.

[18] Protokoll, p. 94.

[19] Erasmus Schöfer, "Für die aktive Solidarität der Hand- und Kopf-Arbeiter," Referat zur Eröffnung der Werkstättendiskussion bei der Mannheimer Tagung des Werkkreises Literatur der Arbeitswelt, November 1970 (unpublished manuscript in Stadtbücherei Dortmund).

[20] Reinhold, p. 52.

[21] Gerald Stieg and Bernd Witte, Abriß einer Geschichte der deutschen Literatur (Stuttgart: Klett, 1973), p. 165.

[22] Protokoll, p. 97.

[23] Werkkreis Literatur der Arbeitswelt, INFO, August 1972, p. 21. Available in archives of the Stadtbücherei Dortmund.

[24] Ein Baukran stürzt um, ed. Karl Bredthauer et al. (Munich: Piper, 1970), p. 18.

[25] Elisabeth Simons cites the following areas which were addressed by the BPRS, but not ultimately clarified until the GDR Bitterfeld Conference: "Fragen der qualitativen Besonderheit der proletarisch-revolutionären Literatur, des Zusammenhangs von Parteilichkeit und schöpferischer Freiheit, von Parteilichkeit und Wahrheit, der Bedeutung schreibender Arbeiter für die Entstehung der proletarisch-revolutionären Literatur, die Rolle der wissenschaftlichen Weltanschauung für den sozialistischen Schriftsteller, die Frage nach

der geeigneten schöpferischen Methode, nach der Nutz-
barmachung des literarischen Erbes und der bürgerlichen Literatur für die Sache des Proletariats" (p.
188).

[26] Gerlach, p. 52.

[27] Handbuch für schreibende Arbeiter, ed. Ursula
Steinhaußen et al. (E. Berlin: n.p., 1969), p. 110.

[28] Protokoll, p. 62.

[29] Kühne and Schöfer, p. 335.

[30] INFO, August 1972, p. 7.

[31] Reinhold, p. 62.

[32] Protokoll, p. 96.

[33] Peter Schütt, "Literarische Aktionseinheit,"
Universal Zeitung, 30 March 1972, p. 5.

[34] In Sachen Wallraff: Berichte, Analysen, Mei-
nungen und Dokumente, ed. Christian Linder (Reinbek
bei Hamburg: Rowohlt, 1977), p. 19.

[35] Werkkreis Literatur der Arbeitswelt Dortmund,
p. 8.

[36] INFO, August 1972, p. 21.

[37] Protokoll, p. 100.

[38] Werkkreis Literatur der Arbeitswelt Dortmund,
p. 8.

[39] Reinhold, p. 50.

[40] Schütt, p. 5.

[41] Reinhold, p. 52.

A New German Language?
Language Change and Lexicography
in the GDR and FRG

H. Jochen Hoffmann

Working with GDR source materials is often frus-
trating for students of the GDR, who are frequently
confronted with unfamiliar words, acronyms, and other
abbreviations. Until recently, the problem was com-
pounded by the lack of dictionaries and other reference works with which the meaning of a given word
could be determined. In recent years, however, several new lexica and detailed linguistic studies have
appeared, which, when carefully used, can be of considerable aid.

The task of analyzing meanings and preparing new
lexica has been undertaken for the most part by FRG
and GDR linguists--until now Anglo/American scholars
have played only a minor role in the study of GDR and
FRG language development.[1] The most significant
studies have been produced by linguists associated
with major centers of language research in the two
Germanies and by independent scholars drawing on
resources painstakingly collected over the years. Two
works compiled in the West, the Bibliographie zum
öffentlichen Sprachgebrauch in der Bundesrepublik
Deutschland und in der DDR (1976) and Michael Kinne's
Texte Ost - Texte West (1977), give an indication of
the direction and variety of both FRG and GDR research.[2] In this study I will provide a brief survey
of the most important research and of current GDR-
related lexicography; I will also investigate the
differing attitudes of FRG and GDR linguists toward
their subject and to the theory of the emergence of a
separate national language in the GDR.

During the 1950s and 1960s language changes in

the East which did not parallel those in the West drew much attention in the FRG media. Research in these years tended to focus on developments in the GDR since linguists in the FRG often considered FRG language as the norm and any changes in the East as an undesirable deviation.3 During the 1960s, to overcome this one-sided methodology and biased interpretation, reputable linguists such as Hugo Moser, Werner Betz, and Herbert Bartholmes began to examine language changes on both sides of the German/German border. Their work demonstrated significant efforts to go beyond the superficial and invective-filled discussions about language conducted for the most part by FRG journalists and politicians.4

In 1964 the Forschungsstelle für öffentlichen Sprachgebrauch (FÖS) was founded in Bonn, on the initiative of Hugo Moser, who also served as its first director. The FÖS, which was a branch of the Institut für deutsche Sprachforschung (Mannheim) until 1980, developed into a major center for research on the development of GDR and FRG language, as its many scholarly contributions show.5 Manfred W. Hellmann, who succeeded Moser as the head of FÖS, ranks among the most knowledgeable investigators of German/German language development.

One of the major projects of the institute in Bonn, and perhaps the most pertinent to our topic, is a study called "Ost-West-Wortschatzvergleiche," which was conducted from 1976 to 1980, when funding for the project was terminated. In contrast to past studies, which were often based on insufficient evidence or such one-sided sources as speeches, party programs, media excerpts, or Duden lexica, researchers at the FÖS attempted to achieve a greater degree of objectivity by looking at language changes in the public sphere over an extended period of time. The Forschungsstelle chose eighteen volumes of what it considered representative national and regional newspapers of the GDR and FRG spanning the period from 1949 to 1974. The inclusion of regional as well as national newspapers was thought to be necessary, particularly in the case of the GDR, in order to balance the more programmatic, propagandistic national papers against regional and local dailies. In the FRG, the selection of Die Welt as a national daily was balanced by adding the Frankfurter Rundschau when changes in the editorial policy and quality of Die Welt came about as a result of its merger with the

Springer Press in 1969.[6] Since direct access to the GDR language area and language users is limited for FRG linguists, the study relied on the wide variety of texts and language styles represented in newspaper writing for its investigation of contemporary GDR language. The computer-stored texts and the word lists already compiled provide much source material and verifiable data for lexicography and other research on comparative language development.

Perhaps the most tangible and useful result of the work of the Forschungsstelle is the first GDR-specific dictionary: Kleines Wörterbuch des DDR-Wortschatzes by Michael Kinne and Birgit Strube-Edelmann, two associates of the Forschungsstelle.[7] The Kleines Wörterbuch des DDR-Wortschatzes provides for the first time a list of GDR neologisms and also new definitions of familiar words which have changed their meaning in the different ideological and social system. In spite of its limited scope--it lists only eight hundred lexical items and terms of contemporary usage--, this dictionary serves as an example of an exciting and fruitful new direction of scholarship in lexicography and language usage.

In 1969 a research center for linguistics was established in the GDR: the Zentralinstitut für Sprachwissenschaft der Akademie der Wissenschaften der DDR (ZISW) in East Berlin. Since 1974 the work of the Zentralinstitut has centered increasingly on contrastive studies of spoken and written language in the two Germanies. Not surprisingly, some of its reported findings have resulted in major debates in the West. One hotly debated hypothesis of GDR linguists, alluded to above, is that a single German national language no longer exists. Using data collected for the major research project of the Zentralinstitut, the Wörterbuch der deutschen Gegenwartssprache, GDR linguists are attempting to show a separate development of the German language in the GDR.[8] The GDR linguist Gotthard Lerchner drew considerable attention by claiming that there is now a fourth German language variant, in addition to those spoken in the FRG, Austria, and the German-speaking part of Switzerland.[9] Lerchner argues that the socially determined aspects of the German language differ substantially in the GDR and FRG. He asserts that the elimination of social classes and of class-determined differences in education has changed the conditions and the experience on which language is based.[10] Changes in socio-economic conditions result in changes in communication. In his words the new language phenomena in the GDR are "sprachliche Reflexe auf neuentstandene soziale Kommunikationsbedingungen völlig neuer Qualität."[11] The continued claim of one national language suggests, as he maintains, an absence of historical processes and assumes a static concept of language.

It should be noted that the GDR-centered language research being conducted by Lerchner and the Zentralinstitut coincides with the emphasis on the theory of two separate German nations which was officially proclaimed at the Eighth Party Congress of the SED in 1971 and reaffirmed at the Ninth Party Congress in 1975.[12] This theory of the emergence of a socialist German nation in the GDR, as opposed to the bourgeois German nation in the FRG, would receive greater credence if it could be supported by evidence in the area of language. In the FRG, on the other hand, the sharing of a single national language is used as proof of the existence of one German nation--in keeping with the FRG view of "Zwei deutsche Staaten - eine Nation." FRG critics of the GDR language hypothesis, especially Manfred Hellmann, point out that Lerchner's thesis is flawed: 1) because his far-reaching conclusions are not supported by the evidence cited; and 2) because he does not give criteria which would make it possible to determine when we are dealing with a national language variant and when not.[13]

Hellmann's conclusions about East/West language changes are detailed and have significance for the hypothesis of the emergence of a second German language. Looking at all aspects of language, he finds that the German grammar system remains stable and unaffected by the separation into two distinct and different social systems.[14] Changes in syntax and style, on the other hand, are evident to the careful observer. GDR sentence structure, especially in political texts, shows the use of more nouns and is more abstract than comparable texts in the West. The genitive case is used with increasing frequency, resulting in wordiness and the cumbersome style which is often criticized or ridiculed, even in the GDR. Common examples would be: "Der Stellvertreter des Vorsitzenden des Ministerrats der DDR" or "auf der 4. Gesamtstaatlichen Fachtagung des Deutschlektorats des Kultur- und Informationszentrums der DDR (in) Prag."[15]

According to Hellmann, however, the only signif-

icant language change, and one which could have consequences for effective communication between people
from the GDR and FRG, is taking place in the area of
vocabulary. Differences in vocabulary in the FRG and
GDR derive, to a certain extent, from the linguistic
influence of the United States and the Soviet Union,
respectively. Language usage in the FRG shows a high
frequency of Anglo/American words and neologisms. The
adoption of Russian words into GDR language has been
less; the common assumption that changes in the GDR
economy led to a massive russification of language in
the GDR is an oversimplification which can be put into
better perspective by recognition of the far more
extensive influx of Americanisms in FRG language. 16

   From the many examples recorded in the Kleines
Wörterbuch des DDR-Wortschatzes and in the various
articles by Hellmann, I have selected neologisms or
vocabulary differences in two areas: first, ideology
and politics; and second, commerce. 17 (I have omitted
from consideration the basic international vocabulary
of Marxism-Leninism which came into use prior to
1945.) The western assertion that new compounds and
word combinations in the GDR often take on propagandistic meaning must be balanced by the recognition
that the same can be maintained for the FRG. Such
word creations from the GDR as Arbeiter- und Bauern-
Staat, sozialistischer Staatsbürger, and sozialistische Staatengemeinschaft can be matched by a list
from the FRG: mündiger Bürger, freiheitlich-demokra-
tische Grundordnung, atlantische Partnerschaft. 18 The
particular origin and usage of these terms may require
tracing through up-to-date reference works. Of more
immediate interest is the vocabulary shared by both
Germanies, but defined differently--in keeping with
the differing ideologies and socio-political systems.
Not surprisingly, the terms Demokratie, Sozialismus,
Freiheit, and Eigentum mean something radically different in the GDR, where so-called progressive definitions for these and similar terms are continuously
commented upon and interpreted by the media in an
attempt to encourage their incorporation into daily
usage.

   We find the highest frequency of word changes and
neologisms in the area of commerce. These changes
have resulted from the emergence of the socialist
economic system in the GDR and the accompanying need
to name or define new activities, relationships, or
positions. Thus in the GDR we find terms like Kader-

leiter, Betriebsparteiorganisation, Neues ökonomisches System der Planung und Leitung der Volkswirtschaft, or such abbreviations as KAP, VVB, and LPG, which have no equivalent in the West.

Another reason for differentiation in terminology is the integration into different international economic systems, COMECON and the European Economic Community. A short list restricted to compounds formed from "Inter-" in the GDR and from "Euro-" in the FRG might include:

Interport	Europort
Intervision	Eurovision
Interflug	Euratom
Intershop	Eurodollar
Intertank	Eurocheque
Interchem	Euro-Kommunismus.

The scope of this paper unfortunately necessitates the deletion of other areas which merit comment and investigation, in order to turn briefly to the question of communication. At what point does communication between people from different states become inhibited? Regional variants are known to interfere at times with effective communication between, let us say, a farmer from the North Sea coast and one from Bavaria. Once these two meet face to face, processes can be employed to make communication possible, namely repetition, question, and explanation. Communication may, however, be impaired when these mechanisms do not come into play, for example, when a reader in the FRG is confronted by a GDR text dealing with ideology, politics, or commerce. Many terms from these areas also appear in GDR literature, requiring the reader to place them in their socio-political context. Those educated in GDR affairs may be aided by their political sophistication, but what about the general populace in the West? The reader in the GDR, assisted by an awareness of FRG language usage stemming from the availability of FRG radio and television programs in the GDR, may be in a somewhat better position. Many scholars now concur that, given certain topics, situations, or personal circumstances, communication between individuals from the two states can become difficult to the point of being at least partially impaired. In an article in the recent Lexikon der Germanistischen Linguistik, Hellmann asserts: "Wortschatz- und Gebrauchsunterschiede sind so erheblich, daß--bei meist unzureichender Kenntnis der Lebensum-

stände der Partner im anderen Staat--mit Verständi-
gungsschwierigkeiten partiell zu rechnen ist." 19

Given the realities of two political and economic
systems and the constraints placed on verbal interaction, the dependence on reference works and lexica
quickly becomes evident. The general reader as well
as the scholar trying to assess and compare language
usage in the GDR and FRG must be aware of the limitations inherent in the available reference works. The
research and the lexica produced by the Duden publishing houses, the Forschungsstelle für öffentlichen
Sprachgebrauch in Bonn, and the Zentralinstitut für
Sprachwissenschaft in East Berlin offer incomplete,
often politically biased and contradictory data.
Discipline-oriented dictionaries from the GDR, such as
the Kulturpolitisches Wörterbuch, now in its second
edition, or the Wörterbuch zum sozialistischen Staat
are of help in that they provide background information and GDR-specific definitions. 20 However, given
their informational and educational intent, their
definitions tend to be wordy, self-serving, and often
propagandistic.

It has been more common practice for scholars to
turn to the two Duden lexica published separately in
Mannheim (FRG) and Leipzig (GDR) to determine language
differences and change, as did Fritz J. Raddatz in his
introductory chapter in Traditionen und Tendenzen
(1972), excerpts of which appeared six years later in
a long article in Die Zeit. 21 Reliance on the Duden
may, however, lead to erroneous conclusions. New
listings of political or ideological vocabulary in the
GDR Duden reflect the SED's attempt to encourage
people to accept new lexical items. Listing them does
not prove usage by the GDR populace, however, since
GDR dictionaries often do not tell us how a word is
used, but how it is supposed to be used. Walther
Dieckmann, one of the first FRG scholars to focus on
what he called "the East-West problem in the area of
language," warned as early as 1967: "Der Ost-Duden
ist ein Instrument politischer Sprachlenkung, und wer
ihn nicht als solches erkennt, wird ihn falsch inter-
pretieren." 22 Dieckmann observes in the same article
that the FRG Duden also contains readily apparent
flaws and biases: it too lacks political neutrality,
often overlooking even the most commonly known lexical
items originating in the GDR. 23 For example, the term
Volksdemokratie, although frequently used in the FRG as
well as in the GDR, does not appear in Der Große Duden

209

of 1970.[24] GDR critics, for their part, have not only noted the lacunae of GDR vocabulary in the Mannheim Duden but also the retention of such lexical items as Armenhaus, Arbeitgeber, and Armenrecht, which have disappeared from the GDR because, according to the official view, social and historical developments have eliminated the conditions and thereby the need for such words.[25] Instead of Armenhaus or Arbeitgeber, the Leipzig Duden lists words like Arbeiterstudent or Aktivist which imply functions germain only to a socialist society.[26] These editorial practices mirror the manipulation of language in the public sphere, and they can be found on both sides of the German/German border. As Gustav Korlén has noted: "wir sollten uns nichts vormachen lassen: Sprachlenkung ist keine Erscheinung, die lediglich für die östliche Welt zu verzeichnen wäre."[27]

The FRG publisher's tendency to assign a normative function to Der große Duden by denying the existence or legitimacy of language developments in the GDR has fortunately changed in the climate of improved German/German relations since the 1970s. In its new and ambitious project, Das große Wörterbuch der deutschen Sprache in sechs Bänden (Volumes I to V have been published thus far since 1976), Duden departs radically from its previous editorial practice.[28] The editors of the new Mannheim Duden decided to take into account a broader range of language levels and style, for example Umgangssprache as used in the soccer stadium or the neighborhood pub, and regional variants. Most importantly, "distinct language units" ("sprachliche Besonderheiten") from the GDR, as well as the FRG, Austria, and German-speaking Switzerland are now included. Thus, for the first time, language changes and neologisms originating in the GDR are incorporated. But they are carefully labeled "sprachliche Besonderheiten" to indicate that the changes which have taken place are all part of one common German language.[29] Commenting on their new practice in the introduction to Volume I, the editors of the Mannheim Duden explain: "Dieses Wörterbuch hat die Aufgabe, die deutsche Sprache in ihrer ganzen Vielschichtigkeit darzustellen und damit auch bewußt zu machen."[30]

To give a brief illustration of the Mannheim Duden's new editorial practices: the word Produktion received only cursory mention in Der große Duden (1970); variants and compounds were omitted. In Das große Wörterbuch der deutschen Sprache, the word Produktion fills an entire column and includes seven GDR compounds or definitions, among them Produktionsfonds and Produktionsgenossenschaft. Das große Wörterbuch distinguishes between pre-war and post-1945 word formations now used in the GDR by giving their origin or etymology, from Marxist theory or the Soviet Union, for example. It does not however always systematically include all compounds, variants, or definitions.

The six-volume dictionary prepared by the Zentralinstitut für Sprachwissenschaften in East Berlin, the Wörterbuch der deutschen Gegenwartssprache, tends to be more complete than its western counterpart. In listing vocabulary known and used in both states, careful distinction is made between differences in meaning which have come about as a result of changed social and ideological conditions (e.g., Staat, Partei, Proletariat, Revolution). Neologisms to label activities, institutions, etc., within each social system are also listed and defined (e.g., Neuererbewegung, Volkseigentum for the GDR, or Management and Showgeschäft for the FRG). The user should be aware, however, of a major shift in editorial policy starting with Volume IV, which was published in 1975. The entries in the last three volumes (Volumes IV, V, VI) reflect a strict Marxist-Leninist view of class struggle: "Das Wörterbuch . . . wird vom 4. Band an den gesamten Wortschatz konsequent auf der Grundlage der marxistisch-leninistischen Weltanschauung darstellen."[31] Definitions point with increased emphasis to the social conditions responsible for the formation of neologisms and compounds unique to the FRG or to the GDR. This new editorial practice reflects the more recent work by GDR linguists and the Zentralinstitut für Sprachwissenschaft, which, in the wake of the two nation theory, questions the continued existence of one national German language.

Since the existence of a new socialist language variant in the GDR has not yet been definitively established, it may be premature to assert the emergence of a second German language distinct from the one in the FRG. To deny the existence of a significant number of lexical items unique to the GDR would be equally injudicious in the face of mounting research evidence to the contrary. Students and scholars who deal with GDR literature, history, politics, economics, etc., need to be aware of the very real potential for misunderstanding and misinterpret-

211

ing GDR texts; they need to become familiar with the tools which can be used to help avoid this dilemma. The lexica and studies on language change recently published in both Germanies are useful resources, especially when combined with at least some recognition of their biases, omissions, and limitations.

Smith College

Notes

[1] Anglo/American contributors to GDR/FRG language research include: M. Folsom and H. Rencher, "Zur Frage der sprachlichen Unterschiede in der BRD und der DDR: Zwei statistische Studien," Deutsche Sprache, No. 1 (1977), pp. 48-55; Jürgen Eichhoff, "Zu den Unterschieden und Differenzierungstendenzen im 'neutralen' Wortbestand der Bundesrepublik und der DDR," in Akten des V. Internationalen Germanistenkongresses, ed. Leonard Forster and Hans-Gert Roloff (Cambridge, 1975), II, 95-104; Derek Lewis, "East German--A new Language?" GDR Monitor, 1, No. 1 (1979), 28-34.

[2] Manfred W. Hellmann, ed., Bibliographie zum öffentlichen Sprachgebrauch in der Bundesrepublik Deutschland und in der DDR (Düsseldorf: Schwann, 1976); and Michael Kinne, ed., Texte Ost - Texte West (Frankfurt/M.: Diesterweg, 1977). Kinne's collection of articles, some excerpted, is primarily a reader intended for classroom use.

[3] See Manfred W. Hellmann, "Sprache zwischen Ost und West - Überlegungen zur Wortschatzdifferenzierung zwischen BRD und DDR und ihren Folgen," in Sprache und Kultur: Studien zur Diglossie, Gastarbeiterproblematik und kulturellen Integration, ed. Wolfgang Kühlwein und Günter Radden (Tübingen: Gunter Narr, 1978), p. 20.

[4] Hellmann, "Sprache zwishen Ost und West," p. 20.

[5] Research aims of the FÖS, as well as of its counterpart in the East, the East Berlin Zentralinstitut für Sprachwissenschaft der Akademie der Wissenschaften der DDR (ZISW), are described by Hellmann under the heading "Sprache" in the DDR Handbuch, ed. Peter Christian Ludz and Johannes Kuppe, 2nd ed.

(Cologne: Wissenschaft und Politik, 1979), p. 1024.
See also the brief report on the beginning phase of
the two centers by Randall L. Jones, "German Language
Research in East and West," Die Unterrichtspraxis, 3,
No. 2 (1970), 96-100. The research conducted by the
FÖS is outlined in Manfred W. Hellmann, "Wie unter-
schiedlich ist die Sprache in Ost und West? Über die
Arbeit der Bonner Forschungsstelle für öffentlichen
Sprachgebrauch," Mitteilungen des Instituts für
deutsche Sprache, No. 7 (1980), pp. 27-33.

[6] See Hellmann, "Sprache zwischen Ost und West,"
pp. 25 f.

[7] Michael Kinne and Birgit Strube-Edelmann,
Kleines Wörterbuch des DDR-Wortschatzes (Düsseldorf:
Schwann, 1980).

[8] Akademie der Wissenschaften der DDR. Zentralinstitut für Sprachwissenschaften, Wörterbuch der
deutschen Gegenwartssprache, 6 vols. (E. Berlin:
Akademie, 1964-1977). See the introductions to Volume
I and Volume IV.

[9] Gotthard Lerchner, "Die deutsche Sprache und
das 'wirkliche Leben.' Nationalsprachliche Varianten," Forum, 30, No. 3 (1976), 10-11. Also in Kinne,
Texte Ost - Texte West, pp. 30-34; see in particular
p. 34.

[10] As quoted in Kinne, p. 32.

[11] As quoted in Kinne, p. 34.

[12] The evolution of this theory is discussed under the heading "Nation und nationale Frage" in the
DDR Handbuch, pp. 748-750. See also Wilhelm Schmidt,
"Thesen zum Thema 'Sprache und Nation,'" Zeitschrift
für Phonetik, Sprachwissenschaft und Kommunikations-
forschung, 25, No. 4/5 (1972), 448-450; and Erich
Honecker, "Zügig voran bei der weiteren Verwirklichung
der Beschlüsse des XIII. Parteitages der SED," Neues
Deutschland, 29 May 1973, pp. 5-7.

[13] Hellmann, "Sprache zwischen Ost und West," p.
16.

[14] Hellmann, "Sprache zwischen Ost und West," p.
29.

[15] As quoted in Hellmann, "Sprache zwischen Ost und West," p. 17.

[16] See the well-documented study by Broder Carstensen and Hans Galinski: Amerikanismen der deutschen Gegenwartssprache, 3rd ed. (Heidelberg: Carl Winter, 1975). First published in 1965.

[17] For a more detailed discussion of these and other areas, see Hellmann, "Sprache zwischen Ost und West," pp. 30-35.

[18] Hellmann, "Sprache zwischen Ost und West," p. 31.

[19] Manfred W. Hellmann, "Deutsche Sprache in der Bundesrepublik Deutschland und der Deutschen Demokratischen Republik," in Lexikon der Germanistischen Linguistik, 2nd rev. ed. (Tübingen: Max Niemeyer, 1980), p. 525.

[20] Kulturpolitisches Wörterbuch, 2nd. ed. (E. Berlin: Dietz, 1978. Wörterbuch zum sozialistischen Staat (E. Berlin: Dietz, 1974).

[21] Fritz J. Raddatz, Traditionen und Tendenzen. Materialien zur Literatur der DDR (Frankfurt/M.: Suhrkamp, 1972). Fritz J. Raddatz, "Abkindern oder abzahlen? Brauchen wir bald deutsch-deutsche Simultan-Dolmetscher?" Die Zeit, No. 40, 29 Sept. 1978, p. 45, cols. 2-5, p. 46, cols. 1-5.

[22] Walther Dieckmann, "Kritische Bemerkungen zum sprachlichen Ost-West-Problem," Zeitschrift für deutsche Sprache, 23, No. 3 (1967), 136-165. Quoted in Kinne, p. 43.

[23] Dieckmann, as quoted in Kinne, p. 43.

[24] Der große Duden in zehn Bänden, Vol. X (Mannheim: Dudenverlag, 1970).

[25] Willi Steinberg, "Der geteilte Duden," in Freiheit. Organ der Bezirksleitung Halle der SED, 12 May 1967, p. 10, as quoted in Kinne, Texte Ost - Texte West, p. 21.

[26] Steinberg, as quoted in Kinne, p. 21.

[27] Gustav Korlén, "Führt die Teilung Deutschlands

zur Sprachspaltung?" in Der Deutschunterrrricht, Vol. 21, No. 5 (1969), p. 14.

[28] Das große Wörterbuch der deutschen Sprache in sechs Bänden, I, 1.

[29] Das große Wörterbuch, I, 1.

[30] Das große Wörterbuch, I, 1.

[31] See "Vorbemerkung," in Wörterbuch der deutschen Gegenwartssprache, IV, iv.

"Unreserved Subjectivity" as a
Force for Social Change: Christa Wolf and
Maxie Wander's Guten Morgen, du Schöne

Linda Schelbitzki Pickle

In "Berührung," her foreword to the oral testimony collected and edited by Maxie Wander in Guten
Morgen, du Schöne, Christa Wolf writes: "Rückhaltlose
Subjektivität kann zum Maß werden für das, was wir
(ungenau, glaube ich) 'objektive Wirklichkeit' nennen.
. . ."[1] She is quick to add, however, that this can
happen "nur dann, wenn das Subjekt nicht auf leere
Selbstbespiegelung angewiesen ist, sondern aktiven
Umgang mit gesellschaftlichen Prozessen hat" (p. 212).
Those familiar with Wolf's own work will sense that
she is addressing not only the subjectivity of the
personal testimony of the women Maxie Wander interviewed, but also, indirectly, GDR criticism of the
subjectivity of her own work, and defending its value,
along with the testimony of these other GDR women, as
a force for social change.[2] She sees in Maxie Wander's collection, I believe, an answer to the GDR
literary establishment's call for "realism" in literature: namely, a concept of realism which does not
exclude the subjective interaction of the self with
the text. And she claims that such subjective, individual confrontations with the realities of socialist
society can provide the impetus for changing those
aspects of GDR society which do not yet correspond to
the socialist ideal, in this case, the continued
presence of attitudes and structures which place
higher value on stereotypically male behavior patterns, spheres of activity and social constructs, in
spite of legal guarantees of equal treatment of the
sexes.[3] By implying a connection between her own literary work and the personal non-literary testimony of
other women in her society, Christa Wolf is asserting
a new aesthetic ideal of "unreserved subjectivity."

217

This and the distinction suggested here between male objectivity and female subjectivity will be explored below. I will examine thematic and formal connections between Maxie Wander's Guten Morgen, du Schöne and Christa Wolf's work. And, finally, I will attempt to determine whether the potential for social change which Christa Wolf claims for such personal and literary subjectivity can be demonstrated.

Thematic parallels between Guten Morgen, du Schöne and Christa Wolf's work are not difficult to identify. Maxie Wander speaks in her "Vorbemerkung" of "das Bedürfnis der Frauen nach Selbstverwirklichung." [4] The problem of self-realization of the individual within modern socialist society has been at the center of Christa Wolf's work. Almost without exception, the protagonists through whose experiences she has examined this problem have been women: Rita in Der geteilte Himmel (1963), Christa T. and the narrator of Christa T. (1968), the narrator of "Unter den Linden" (1969), the scientist in "Selbstversuch" (1974), and Karoline von Günderrode in Kein Ort. Nirgends (1979) and "Der Schatten eines Traumes," the essay accompanying the text of Günderrode's works, which Wolf edited under the same title in 1979.

Wolf has long recognized that the difficulties of attaining self-realization are still acute for women in GDR society. In an interview with Hans Kaufmann in Weimarer Beiträge, she speaks of the legal basis as a mere "Vorstufe, die wir erklommen haben und von der aus neue radikale Fragestellungen uns weiterbringen müßten." [5] Maxie Wander's book testifies to the fact that the attitudes toward women have not yet changed dramatically in the GDR. These interviews also often point out the new areas of radical questioning of which Christa Wolf speaks. Many of the women interviewed refer to the conflict between the opportunities their society affords them and the role expectations of women in a still basically paternalistic society. One of the women, Karoline, tells movingly of the mental and physical breakdown she suffered after fifteen years of a marriage in which she was expected to do all the work in the house--"Vom Boden bis zum Keller alles Frauensache!" (p. 203), care for five children with little money and no day-care centers, and work now and then, for the sake of the money but also so that she would not always have to live as a housewife, "so losgelöst vom Leben" (p. 204), as she puts it. Her husband cannot cope with the house and children when she collapses; he evades his responsibilities and even gets another woman with child. Karoline finally gains her self-confidence and independence by becoming a "Jugendfürsorgerin." She still lives with her husband, who would welcome her quitting work because then she would again be dependent on him and he would regain the upper hand in their relationship (p. 206). Other women interviewed (Petra, p. 61; Uta, p. 71) indicate that traditional sex roles are still prevalent among younger people as well. Twenty-four-year-old Uta quotes her lover as saying that women do not really want equality, by which he seems to mean the "freedom" of being sexually and emotionally uncommitted but which she understands as the sharing of housework (p. 80). There are problems in the area of work as well: the need for women to be attractive as well as capable in order to gain acceptance and recognition from their male colleagues (Doris, pp. 31f.); professional jealousy between husband and wife (Lena, p. 174); greater pressure on women than on men to prove themselves on the job (Katja, p. 141).

To a large extent, the women in Guten Morgen, du Schöne correlate the problems they have in realizing themselves fully with difficulties placed in their way by men or by traditional male value systems. They criticize men's excessive rationalism, their selfishness, and their refusal to treat women as equal human beings, particularly when this manifests itself in men's unwillingness to really know women (Steffi, p. 147; Petra, p. 61; Lena, pp. 169, 178; Erika, p. 166). Ruth's statement might serve as one of the more extreme examples of this latter criticism: "Man muß Männern wirklich immer was vorspielen, sonst verschreckt man sie. Ich habe noch keinen gekannt, der dahinterkommen wollte, wie ich wirklich bin und warum ich so bin. Die haben alle was Bestimmtes mit mir vorgehabt" (p. 48). Similarly, Christa Wolf makes "typically" masculine behavior (selfishness, rationalism) the object of her critical analyses of what is wrong in man-woman relationships. Kostia in Christa T., Peter and the doctor loved by the narrator in "Unter den Linden," Professor Barzel in "Neue Ansichten eines Katers," the project director in "Selbstversuch," Brentano and Savigny in Kein Ort. Nirgends are examples. And in her later works, beginning particularly with the three stories in Unter den Linden, Christa Wolf presents the desire of women to be "known" by men as individuals "free of the sexual identity as a woman"[6] as an integral part of women's self-realization, of their "Subjektwerden," as she puts it in "Der Schatten eines Traumes," for example: "Gekannt werden, der inständige Wunsch von Frauen, die nicht durch den Mann, sondern durch sich selber leben wollen. . . ."[7]

Some of the women interviewed in Guten Morgen, du Schöne make a connection, as does Christa Wolf, between traditional male behavior and values and materialistic, hierarchical regimentation. Ruth speaks of her step-brother, whom she calls "ein kleiner Spießer . . . ein Mensch ohne einen eigenen Gedanken, nur mit dem Drang nach viel Geld, was darzustellen, Sicherheit zu haben." She goes on: "Dabei ist der in einer leitenden Stellung. Ich frage mich manchmal: Welche Gesellschaft bauen wir eigentlich auf?" (p. 57). Margot, a theoretical physicist, has gained success in her career by exercising authority and domination, behavior expected of her in her "male" profession. But now she says: "Wenn man sich aber lange auf Leistung trimmt, zerstört man etwas Wichtiges in seiner Persönlichkeit" (p. 185). Moreover, she sees this as detrimental to her functioning productively in society: one loses sight of the connection of one's activities to ultimate social goals, and this causes further atrophy of one's inner life and isolation of the individual within the socialist "brotherhood" (p. 189).

In Christa Wolf's work we find the same negative effects of the acceptance of "male" values (above all, rationalism, hierarchism, and materialism) on socialist society. Christa T.'s inability to feel useful in her society is one example; the negative change which Anders undergoes after becoming a man in "Selbstversuch" is another. More recently, Wolf has traced the origins of the division of the world into rational and irrational spheres, and of work into men's and women's work, to the rise of capitalism at the beginning of the bourgeois era. Her analysis of the period of German Romanticism in Kein Ort. Nirgends and "Der Schatten eines Traumes" concludes that contemporary society, even in the GDR, has much to learn from this earlier time. In "Berührung" she speaks of the state as "Über-Mann" (p. 217) and of her world as "diese Männerwelt" (p. 219), but she also asks, as she did in the 1974 interview with Hans Kaufmann (p. 93), if women should really want to be integrated into "jene hierarchisch funktionierenden Apparate" of society as it has been constituted by men (p. 219). Instead, like at the end of "Selbstversuch," she claims that women's long-accustomed subjectivity and desire for love and sharing rather than authority and dominance can be a powerful force that will change men, too, as women seek new ways of living in order to realize all aspects of their being.[8]

Some of the women in Maxie Wander's book also proclaim the superiority of (female) subjectivity and cooperation. Ruth criticizes "socialistic conformity" and traces it back to its nineteenth-century bourgeois roots of emotional inhibition, false pride, and suspicion of others (pp. 20f.). She contrasts that with the spirit of solidarity which animated the women, children, and old men left behind in her building during the war. Other women speak of the importance of subjectivity, of personal involvement in their lives and work (Barbara, p. 45; Erika, p. 167; Katja, p. 141). Lena makes the most complete statement of the need for subjectivity in order to break down the isolation of the individual in a hierarchical society. She consciously foils the expectations of others who want to see in her an authority figure: "Diesen ganzen Autoritätszauber halte ich doch für eine Farce, für die kein vernünftiger Mensch Bedarf hat" (p. 175). Moreover, Lena clearly connects self-assertion and self-realization with social effectiveness and purpose: "Ich sehe die Selbstverwirklichung des einzelnen eigentlich nur in einem sinnvollen Verhältnis zur gesellschaftlichen Selbstverwirklichung" (p. 180). And this is accomplished by using all one's energies, both intellectual and sensual: "Man wird nicht nur mit dem Kopf, sondern mit seinem ganzen Körper begreifen, daß man alles einsaugen muß, damit unser Lebenssaft nicht austrocknet" (p. 182). It would be hard to find in Christa Wolf's own works a more direct expression of her belief in the interrelatedness of subjectivity, self-realization, and social change.

The final thematic parallel between the texts collected in Guten Morgen, du Schöne and Christa Wolf's work is that of sisterly sharing, which Wolf herself sees in the Wander interviews: "Schwesterlichkeit, die, so scheint mir, häufiger vorkommt als Brüderlichkeit," "ein Selbstbewußtsein . . . das nicht zugleich Wille zum Herrschen, zum Dominieren, zum Unterwerfen bedeutet, sondern Fähigkeit zur Kooperation" ("Berührung," pp. 209, 220). The narrator's "search" for Christa T. is an example of the loving attempt to know the other person that women have so

often missed in men. Similar relationships exist
between the narrator of "Unter den Linden" and the
young girl who falls in love with the narrator's
friend Peter, and between Bettina Brentano and Karoline von Günderrode, as Wolf discusses in her afterword to the new edition of Bettina's epistolary novel
Die Günderode. [9] In Guten Morgen, du Schöne, the most
important example of this is the implicit relationship
which Maxie Wander establishes with each of her inter-
viewees. The reader perceives the women's need to
make themselves known to her. Often there is increasing self-revelation as the interview continues,
and a greater insistence on honesty with oneself and a
greater assurance that Maxie Wander knows and understands as this process goes on. The interviews with
Ruth, Angela, Erika, and Lena show this in paricular.
Steffi ends hers by saying: "Schau, im Grunde genommen ist alles, was ich dir erzählt habe, das, was du
schon weißt. Du brauchst mich nur anzuschauen, guckst
in meine Augen, und wir verstehen uns" (p. 151). The
emphasis on honesty, on self-knowledge, and on sharing
carries over into the reader's relationship with the
text as well, at least for female readers, something
else which Guten Morgen, du Schöne has in common with
Christa Wolf's work. We are called upon to truly know
those who speak in the work, to become involved with
them subjectively, and through this to know and realize ourselves more fully as well. The male reader's
reception of the work may lack this sense of personal
immediacy, and yet there is no doubt that Maxie Wander's work is intended for a male audience, too, and
that Christa Wolf wishes her works to change men's
lives as well as women's. Christa Wolf said in her
interview with Hans Kaufmann that modern literature
should address contemporary reality with "subjektive
Authentizität" in order to bring forth "neue Strukturen menschlicher Beziehungen in unserer Zeit" (p.
75). Maxie Wander's book does this on several levels:
within the lives of many of the women who speak,
between them and Maxie Wander herself, and between the
reader and all the participants in the text.

Now I will address stylistic and formal similarities between Guten Morgen, du Schöne and Christa
Wolf's work. Christa Wolf herself refers to these
interviews as "Vorformen der Literatur," some of which
approach literary forms ("Berührung," p. 213). [10] Her
judgement is based largely, I think, on the similarity
between the effect these texts have on the reader and
the effect she strives for in her own work: "das

Subjektwerden des Menschen." 11   At the same time,
there are certain stylistic similarities as well.
Internalized dialog between a female narrator and the
object of her reflection is characteristic of many of
Wolf's works: Christa T., "Unter den Linden,"
"Selbstversuch," Kindheitsmuster, and Kein Ort. Nirgends. These works might also be described as "self-
interviews" (reminiscent of Wolf's important "Selbst-
gespräch" in Lesen und Schreiben), and so it is perhaps not surprising that an intimacy of tone results
from these inner meditations which resembles that in
the Wander interviews. 12 In addition, the underlying,
usually unarticulated participation of Maxie Wander in
the interviews reminds one of the complex narrative
structure in Kein Ort. Nirgends. Just as it is often
difficult to be sure who is speaking in this text, it
is impossible to know in Guten Morgen, du Schöne which
parts Maxie Wander edited, and how. 13 There seems to
me to be a parallel reluctance to give the narrative
voice unqualified authority, and instead there are two
or more narrative perspectives. Through the nonau-
thoritarian quality of their narrative voice, both
Christa Wolf and Maxie Wander invite the reader to
participate subjectively in the text, to make judge-
ments on what is said, to relate what is said to
her/his own life and thought and thus to gain greater
self-knowledge and self-realization.

    A style and syntax typical of dialog evolve out
of the subjective meditations and exchanges with the
self which characterize Wolf's works. They often have
a fragmentary, tentative quality which is a result of
the speaker's desire to be as open and honest in her
discourse as possible. Myra Love has written that
"the discontinuity of Wolf's writing is . . . a tool
used in striving for 'subjective authenticity,'" 14 and
this is also true of the interviews in Guten Morgen,
du Schöne. The women who speak here often make leaps
in logic, as what they are telling reminds them of
related ideas and events. The result, as is the case
with Christa Wolf's narrative style as well, is usually an interlocking web. Even in narrations which
attempt to be chronological, like Katja's or Karoline's or Christa's, there are interwoven themes, key
concerns of the individual which are brought in again
and again and tend to disrupt (or better: to elaborate) the strictly consecutive narration of events.
The majority of the texts in Guten Morgen, du Schöne
start with a discussion of a central concern of the
speaker and only then do they begin to deal with the

events which are connected to that central concern. That is, these texts have something much like the web-like narrative structure that is characteristic of Christa Wolf's work, particularly Christa T., "Unter den Linden," and Kindheitsmuster. Lena's, Steffi's, Julia's and Petra's sections are good examples. This narrative structure is, of course, partly a result of the immediate, not easily controllable nature of oral testimony, as well as of the speakers' attempts to be complete and honest in what they say. Such subjective spontaneity also results in the most interesting and the most moving texts, in my opinion. In other words, the process of telling becomes much more important and more effective than the bare facts of what is told, that is, than a clearly organized narrative product.

The effect of the subjectivity of the Wander interviews is similar to that which Christa Wolf wishes to attain by means of what, in the Kaufmann interview, she calls her "'eingreifende' Schreibweise," which is not "subjektivistisch" but does presume "ein hohes Maß an Subjektivität" and "ein Subjekt, das bereit ist, sich seinem Stoff rückhaltlos . . . zu stellen, das Spannungsverhältnis auf sich zu nehmen, das dann unvermeidlich wird; auf die Verwandlungen neugierig zu sein, die Stoff und Autor dann erfahren" (p. 75). She describes the consequences of writing in this way:

> Man sieht eine andere Realität als zuvor. Plötzlich hängt alles mit allem zusammen und ist in Bewegung; für "gegeben" angenommene Objekte werden auflösbar und offenbaren die in ihnen vergegenständlichten Beziehungen (nicht mehr jenen hierarchisch geordneten gesellschaftlichen Kosmos, in dem Menschenpartikel auf soziologisch oder ideologisch vorgegebenen Bahnen sich bewegen oder von dieser erwarteten Bewegung abweichen). . . . (p. 75)

The key concepts which Christa Wolf identifies and values in Guten Morgen, du Schöne are articulated here in reference to her own writing: unreserved subjectivity and the resulting new vision of reality as an interlocking web of relationships instead of a hierarchical, ideologically organized universe of isolated individuals. This "subjektive Authentizität" aims for "die Hervorbringung neuer Strukturen menschlicher Beziehungen in unserer Zeit" (p. 75). The most effective of the texts in Guten Morgen, du Schöne also manifest this "subjective authenticity," e.g., those by Rosi, Barbara, Katja, Erika, and Lena. Certainly Maxie Wander seems to have exercised her editing principles according to its dictates. The "unreserved subjectivity" which Christa Wolf recognizes in the Wander interviews is closely connected to the "subjective authenticity" she advocates as the means of approaching reality as a writer, so that the process of demonstrating and exploring new and better human relationships becomes more important than the final literary product as such. The interconnectedness of unreserved subjectivity and subjective authenticity as an approach both to human relationships and to writing results, I believe, in the assertion of a new aesthetic ideal as well as a model for social dynamics in Christa Wolf's work. [15]

Now we must ask if the unreserved subjectivity that Wolf admires in Guten Morgen, du Schöne and her own subjective authenticity as a writer can accomplish what she claims: i.e., open up a new awareness of reality and serve as models for self-knowledge and self-realization which will ultimately change society. There is some evidence in Guten Morgen, du Schöne that women's refusal to separate their emotional life from their work and their social commitment has positive effects, both for the women themselves and for their society (for example, Erika, p. 152). We find indications that men, too, are changing--under pressure, for the most part--for the better. Karoline says of her husband:

> Richard hats schwerer als ich, der muß
> mit der neuen Situation zu Rande kom-
> men. Letzten Endes wird er sich in
> seiner Haut besser fühlen als früher.
> Ich hab ihn ja auch irgendwie unter-
> drückt, solang ich selber unterdrückt
> war. Jetzt muß er mir nicht mehr
> ständig was vorgaukeln. Jetzt hat er
> die Möglichkeit, ehrlich zu leben, mit
> mir gemeinsam und nicht mehr neben mir
> oder gegen mich. (p. 207)

We also find ample evidence that self-realization for these women does not lie in the rejection of committed subjectivity in favor of male values like "success" on the job (Margot) and in the sexual sphere (Petra, Barbara, Lena). Some of the women in Maxie Wander's book

discuss future alternatives to present social structures: the communal family ("Großfamilie," Uta),
women living together with their children (Barbara),
the elimination of the institution of marriage (Uta
and Steffi). Only Lena touches on the possibility of
lesbian love as an alternative to heterosexual relationships, although friendships among women are important to many of these women. So, on the whole, one
wants to say that Christa Wolf's claim is justified,
that women such as these in Guten Morgen, du Schöne,
who have combined subjectivity with critical reasoning
in the awareness that their self-fulfillment benefits
their society, are a potential force for social
change.

Nevertheless, some caution is also in order. The
women in Maxie Wander's collection are to some extent
a self-selecting group rather than any sort of representative sample of contemporary GDR women. As Maxie
Wander said, she did not seek such a sample, but
rather was merely interested in hearing how women
present their lives to themselves and others (p. 8).
Those women who were willing to explore intimate
aspects of their lives no doubt tended to be more
self-aware and interested in their self-fulfillment to
begin with. This might cause us to regard any impres-
sions gained from the interviews as unreliable or even
utopian in a negative sense. Christa Wolf sees in the
work a utopian spirit, but unlike those who have
criticized her own work as unrealistic and utopian,[16]
Wolf claims that what is at work in the oral testimony
collection is something positive: "der Geist der real
existierenden Utopie, ohne den jede Wirklichkeit für
Menschen unlebbar wird" ("Berührung," p. 209). If we
accept Wolf's conception of utopian as pointing beyond
itself by means of "Sehnsucht, Forderung, Lebensan-
spruch" and giving "ein Vorgefühl von einer Gemeinschaft, deren Gesetze Anteilnahme, Selbstachtung,
Vertrauen und Freundlichkeit wären" (p. 209), then not
only Guten Morgen, du Schöne but her own work as well
can be interpreted as positive utopian works with the
power to effect change.

Finally, we might ask whether an additional
criticism frequently aimed at Wolf's work might not
also be applicable to Guten Morgen, du Schöne. Some
critics have decried Wolf's identifying positive human
qualities, such as warmth and love, with women, and
negative qualities, such as one-sided rationalism and
selfishness, with men as traditional sex-role stereo-

typing. Gisela Bahr particularly criticizes "dieser
Rückfall in Gehabtes" in "Selbstversuch" and asserts
that it ignores the progress which has already been
made in breaking down such stereotypes in GDR society.[17] There is certainly the danger that categorizing
human qualities in a sex-related fashion can lead to
even greater alienation between women and men rather
than to increased understanding and acceptance of the
possibilities open to them all as human individuals.
This criticism has some validity for Christa Wolf,
whose work has generally tended to categorize human
characteristics and behavior in this fashion. And
Gisela Bahr is correct in questioning whether Wolf, by
seeming to link behavioral qualities to biology, does
not contradict the model of non-sex-specific differentiation she claims as her ideal. Even so, I agree
with Sara Lennox that Wolf has been much more concerned with working out general human possibilities
for differentiated self-realization than with re-
stricting any of these possibilities to one sex or the
other.[18]

A similar criticism cannot be made of the texts
in Guten Morgen, du Schöne, in part, of course, because they are not a conscious articulation of one
consistent attitude. Sexual stereotyping is still
present in GDR society, even in some of these women
themselves. But this is a matter of ingrained,
learned behavior and attitudes. Many of the women
interviewed have surmounted such stereotypical
thought. Rose, for example, scoffs at the "scientific" identification of such qualities as "Passivi-
tät, Abhängigkeit, Konformismus, Ängstlichkeit,
Nervosität, Narzismus, Gehorsam" as "typically" female, and ones like "Aggressivität, Gefühl für soziale
Rangordnung, größere Risikobereitschaft" as "typically" male. Her rejoinder: "Ich bin also ein Mann, dem
nur das Stückchen Schwanz fehlt" (p. 20) is one with
which most of her sisters in this collection would
agree in spirit, if not in style. Indeed, I believe
that this statement might be regarded as a somewhat
indelicate expression of the non-sex-specific differentiation that Christa Wolf is attempting to bring
about through her work. It may be that in the lives
of individual GDR women like some of those in Guten
Morgen, du Schöne, or at least in the best moments of
such lives, reality has achieved what literature has
only dared to project: the revolutionizing of human
relationships and the beginnings of the social changes
this will mean.

Westminster College, Missouri

Notes

[1] Christa Wolf, "Berührung," in her <u>Lesen</u> <u>und</u>
<u>Schreiben</u>. <u>Neue Sammlung</u> (Darmstadt/Neuwied: Luchter-
hand, 1980), p. 212. "Berührung" first appeared in
the 1979 Luchterhand edition of <u>Guten</u> <u>Morgen,</u> <u>du</u>
<u>Schöne</u>. Parenthetical page references in the text are
to the reprint in <u>Lesen</u> <u>und</u> <u>Schreiben</u>.

[2] For a negative evaluation of Wolf's subjectivity, see Hans-Georg Werner, "Zum Traditionsbezug der
Erzählungen in Christa Wolfs 'Unter den Linden,'"
<u>Weimarer</u> <u>Beiträge</u>, 22, Nr. 4 (1977), 60-72.

[3] Since the early days of the GDR there have been
legal guarantees of equal educational and training
opportunities for women, as well as of equal pay and
job advancement.

[4] <u>Guten</u> <u>Morgen,</u> <u>du</u> <u>Schöne</u>. <u>Protokolle</u> <u>nach</u>
<u>Tonband</u> (E. Berlin: Aufbau, 1980), p. 7. All page
citations from <u>Guten</u> <u>Morgen,</u> <u>du</u> <u>Schöne</u> in the text of
this paper refer to this edition (a reprint of the
original 1977 Der Morgen edition).

[5] "Die Dimension des Autors: Gespräch mit Hans
Kaufmann," in <u>Lesen</u> <u>und</u> <u>Schreiben</u>. <u>Neue Sammlung</u>, p.
95; all following citations from this text refer to
this edition, a reprint of the text in <u>Weimarer</u> <u>Bei-</u>
<u>träge</u>, 20, Nr. 6 (1974), 90-112.

[6] I owe this formulation to Ursula D. Lawson, in
a private correspondence.

[7] "Der Schatten eines Traumes," in <u>Lesen</u> <u>und</u>
<u>Schreiben</u>. <u>Neue Sammlung</u>, p. 246, p. 244.

[8] See related statements of Wolf's conviction
about women's ability to change society in her acceptance speech for the Georg Büchner Prize, October 1980
(Sonderdruck, Luchterhand), pp. 6-11.

[9] "Nun ja! Das nächste Leben geht aber heute an:
Ein Brief über die Bettine," afterword to <u>Die</u> <u>Günde-</u>

rode, by Bettina von Arnim (Leipzig: Insel, 1980). Reprinted in Lesen und Schreiben. Neue Sammlung, pp. 284-318.

[10] Irmtraud Morgner praised the interviews as models of realistic literature in her address to the Eighth Writers' Congress in Berlin, May 29-31, 1978, in Neue Deutsche Literatur, 26, Nr. 8 (1978), 27-32.

[11] "Lesen und Schreiben," in Lesen und Schreiben: Aufsätze und Prosastücke (Darmstadt: Luchterhand, 1972), p. 220.

[12] See Marilyn Sibley Fries' paper in this volume: "Christa Wolf's Use of Image and Vision in the Narrative Structuring of Experience." Fries refers to this aspect of Wolf's narrative style as her dialectical narrative structure, and points out the motivation of self-knowledge and honest self-exploration behind it.

[13] Christa Wolf describes how Maxie Wander prepared the texts: "ausgewählt, gekürzt, zusammengefaßt, umgestellt, hinzugeschrieben, Akzente gesetzt, komponiert, geordnet--niemals aber verfälscht" ("Berührung," p. 213).

[14] Myra Love, "Christa Wolf and Feminism: Breaking the Patriarchal Connection," New German Critique, 16 (1979), 45. The reference to "subjective authenticity" is taken from the interview with Hans Kaufmann, "Die Dimension des Autors," p. 75.

[15] Sara Lennox asserts in reference to Wolf's essay on Bettina von Arnim ("Nun ja! Das nächste Leben geht aber heute an") that "in the literary form given to love and friendship of these two women Bettina and Günderrode lie the beginnings of another aesthetic" ("Trends in Literary Theory: The Female Aesthetic and German Women's Writing," German Quarterly, 54, Nr. 1 [1981], 72.)

[16] For example, Hans-Georg Werner, p. 62.

[17] Gisela Bahr, "Blitz aus heiterm Himmel: Ein Versuch zur Emanzipation in der DDR," in Die Frau als Heldin und Autorin, ed. Wolfgang Paulsen, 10. Amherster Kolloquium zur deutschen Literatur (Bern/Munich: Francke, 1979), p. 227. Sigrid Damm and Jürgen Engler make the same point in their critique of the collec-

tion of sex-change stories in which "Selbstversuch" first appeared: "Notate des Zwiespalts und Allegorien der Vollendung," Weimarer Beiträge, 21, Nr. 7 (1975), 45 et passim.

[18] Sara Lennox, "'Der Versuch, man selbst zu sein': Christa Wolf und der Feminismus," in Die Frau als Heldin und Autorin, p. 222.

A New Look at Male-Female Relationships:
Plenzdorf's Legende vom Glück ohne Ende and
Ehlers' Hanna Mahler - Aufzeichnungen
einer jungen Frau

Ilse Winter

In GDR literature of the past thirty years one encounters a wide variety of emancipated women characters. Most of the works deal with typical problems which these women have to overcome on their difficult road toward self-discovery and self-realization. The conflict between career, on the one hand, and love or family responsibilities, on the other, the difficulties resulting from the woman's Doppelbelastung, and the struggle against traditional male prejudices are just a few of the problems which these characters have to face. In the recent past, however, several works have appeared which deviate considerably from the familiar patterns mentioned above. In the two novels which I am treating here, the central characters, female and male, attempt to realize a new kind of partnership between men and women. They question and ultimately reject conventional patterns of marriage and family life because such patterns constrict them as individuals. Instead, the central characters in both novels explore different kinds of relationships which offer each individual the chance to grow and develop fully. The interest in such "neue Lebensweisen" or "neue Lebensformen" which was expressed so consistently and urgently in Maxie Wander's Guten Morgen, du Schöne has become the central issue in Plenzdorf's and Ehlers' works.[1]

How can new patterns of life develop? What must and can women and men do to bring about a change in their traditional relationships? Who has to take the initiative? What difficulties and obstacles can be expected? These questions suggest some of the prob-

231

lems with which the two novels deal. Plenzdorf and Ehlers state clearly and unequivocally that new patterns of life can emerge only when a change in attitudes occurs, a change in attitudes--it should be emphasized--which women as well as men will have to undergo. As long as traditional patriarchal attitudes prevail, the conditions for genuine intimacy and partnership between men and women cannot develop.

Legende vom Glück ohne Ende illustrates this quite compellingly: the male character, Paul, undergoes the kind of change necessary for the realization of new patterns of life. [2] In less than a year he frees himself from his traditional male world view, which has trapped and stifled him and made him a model conformist. Until the day he falls in love with Paula, Paul leads a rather dull, yet exemplary life. After his studies in Moscow and his three years of service in the army, he is hired by an agency of the Foreign Ministry and trained for a career abroad. He marries a stunningly beautiful but rather stupid woman, lives in a modern apartment complex, from which he is chauffeured to work every day, and in his free time engages in activities which will promote his career. Since he is bright, adaptable, and charming, he is virtually assured favorable recommendations for ever higher positions within the system.

His initial reaction to the new love is cowardly. He feels guilty not because of his infidelity, but because he is afraid of being disgraced if his superiors discover his love affair. At first, he resorts to all kinds of tricks to avoid meeting Paula, and when she finally manages to corner him, he tells her quite bluntly that one cannot always have what one desires, that social obligations outweigh an individual's yearning for happiness. Later, however, when Paul realizes that his love for Paula is not a short-lived passion, but the most powerful and intense emotion he has ever experienced, he subordinates everything to his one basic need: to be together with the woman he loves. He leaves his wife and child, reports sick, and, ignoring all conventional proprieties, spends most of his time in front of Paula's locked door. (Paula refuses to see Paul or even speak to him after her small son has been killed in a car accident. Paula blames herself for the child's death; she believes that the tragedy occurred only because, in her preoccupation with Paul and her love for him, she neglected her children.)

When he reflects later on this time of radical change, Paul remarks: "Wenn ich mich selbst frage, dann habe ich vor allem gelernt, zu sein und nicht zu scheinen. Zweitens, Signale, die von anderen ausgehen, wenigstens zu empfangen. Und drittens, Signale, die von mir ausgehen, zu empfangen und zu entziffern" (p. 115). For the first time in his life, Paul follows the promptings of his emotions, and, in doing so, learns to acknowledge and appreciate the values by which Paula lives.

At first glance, Paula appears to be a composite of typical female stereotypes: she is very sensuous, uninterested in intellectual or cultural activities, and subject to spontaneous emotional impulses. She refuses to make "reasonable" decisions if such decisions violate her feelings. Although her doctor has warned her that she might not survive a third pregnancy, she refuses to practice birth control. She explains that she would not feel like a woman if she took the pill and that making love would be only half as enjoyable. She fails miserably in her one attempt to follow the dictates of reason instead of the heart: namely, to marry her wealthy admirer, Saft, and thus secure a carefree future for herself and her child. What elevates Paula above the stereotype of "Frau mit Herz" is her uncompromising capacity to believe in the truth of her feelings and to endure all consequences, however grave and painful. In the early stages of their love, Paul is scared by Paula's total commitment, but gradually he begins to shed his caution and his male habit of seeking compromise solutions. When, after weeks of waiting outside her door, he takes up the ax to gain entrance to Paula's apartment, he does not just smash the door--he shatters the last remnants of his old self, his dependence on success and approval by others, and, most of all, his conformism.

The nine months in which Paul and Paula live together are a period of uninterrupted bliss. Shortly after moving in with Paula, Paul gives up his prestigious career in order to take a position as handyman in the supermarket where Paula works as a cashier. In their desire to be with each other constantly, they transcend all limits of normalcy. The narrator in Plenzdorf's novel, an old neighbor who witnesses almost every phase of the love story at first hand, indicates Paul and Paula's new inseparability by writing their names together as one word. She reports:

> So haben Paulundpaula angefangen,
> miteinander zu leben. Sie sind von
> Stund an unzertrennlich gewesen. Den
> Fall, daß entweder Paul oder Paula
> allein auf der Singer oder sonstwo in
> Berlin zu sehen waren, gab es nicht.
> Es gab keinen Gang, den sie nicht
> gemeinsam erledigten. Das Bild, wie
> Paulundpaula zusammen aus dem Haus auf
> die Straße traten und meistens Hand in
> Hand oder Arm in Arm, hätte mit der
> Zeit zum Wahrzeichen der Singer werden
> können. Die ganze Singer lächelte,
> wenn Paulundpaula auf die Straße kamen,
> und alle sind gespannt gewesen, wie
> lang diesmal der Weg sein würde, den
> sie unmöglich getrennt zurücklegen
> konnten. Und alle haben den Kopf
> geschüttelt, wenn es wieder nur die
> drei Schritte bis zum Bäcker waren,
> aber alle haben Paulundpaula ihr Glück
> gegönnt. . . . Paulundpaula waren auch
> in ihrer Wohnung unzertrennlich. Sie
> haben auch da jeden Schritt gemeinsam
> getan. Sie sind zusammen in die Küche
> gegangen, um Salz zu holen oder Milch.
> Sie sind zusammen zum Regal gegangen,
> um ein Buch zu nehmen. Sie haben sich
> zusammen gewaschen, und Paula hat un-
> geniert gesagt, daß es für den einen
> noch lange kein Grund gewesen ist, auf
> den Korridor zu gehen, wenn der andere
> das Klo benutzen mußte. (p. 144)

Critics have often objected that the inseparability of Paul and Paula, their almost symbiotic
relationship, must be considered reactionary from an
emancipatory perspective because the couple seems to
relinquish its individuality rather than assert it.
This objection does have validity, but it may be
defused somewhat by pointing out that Plenzdorf is
primarily interested in tracing the development of his
male character, particularly Paul's transformation
from a model conformist and bureaucrat to an autonomous individual who no longer succumbs to norms or
pressures. With his deliberate decision to spend as
much time as possible with Paula, Paul challenges the
expectations which society places on male behavior.

In the context of the novel, Paul and Paula's inseparability should be seen as a gesture of protest and
defiance, an expression of strength rather than weakness. There is a similar instance of protest later in
the novel, when, after Paula's death, Paul refuses to
leave his infant son at a day-care center and insists
that the baby be with him in the supermarket at all
times. These and other examples illustrate one of
Plenzdorf's major concerns: the need for a reordering
of priorities, for building a society in which
emotional needs are fully recognized and taken into
account.

It is not surprising that Paul's new attitude
meets with severe disapproval on the part of the
authorities. To place personal interests above
official duties and the public interest is nothing
short of heresy. But Paul and Paula's neighbors and
colleagues from Singer Street and the surrounding
district react quite differently. That their reactions are so precisely described indicates that
Plenzdorf is not primarily concerned with depicting
the short happy episode of Paul and Paula's togetherness, but rather with the effects of their relationship on the community. When Paul starts working in
the supermarket, the whole character of the store
changes. Thanks to Paul's care, the shelves and the
merchandise are spotless, shopping carts no longer
have squeaky wheels, and all entrances to the store
(instead of just the customary one) are open. More
important than these external changes, however, is the
improvement on the human level. The cashiers and
saleswomen become friendly and helpful, customers and
employees start chatting together, elderly people and
children are made to feel welcome. This change in the
store's atmosphere is due not to Paul's efficiency,
but to his newly developed awareness of a basic human
need for warmth and closeness. The recognition and
acceptance of his own emotional needs have made Paul
more sensitive and caring; he can now demonstrate true
concern and understanding to his neighbors and fellow
workers.

Thus the love story of Paul and Paula is not a
private, but an altogether public affair--the entire
neighborhood is affected and influenced by it. One
testimony to Paul and Paula's impact on the community
is the numerous legends that spring up around episodes
of their love story. These legends spread rapidly and
are acted out enthusiastically by the neighborhood

children. Why do Paul and Paula become legendary figures, regarded with wonder and pleasure by almost everyone? Most people look at the couple as exemplary characters who embody qualities and realize a mode of life about which others can only dream. Especially for the women among Paula's colleagues and neighbors, it is truly miraculous to see a man give up a privileged position and change his male behavior patterns so radically. The popularity of the legends testifies to the power which the Paul and Paula story has over people's imaginations. The two lovers are regarded as audacious innovators or pioneers, demonstrating a male-female relationship which is totally free of manipulation, of any overt or secret attempt by one partner to direct or determine the other's actions.

Plenzdorf makes it quite clear, however, that Paul and Paula's union is exceptional, an ideal rather than an easily attainable reality. This awareness emerges in Paul's later relationship with Laura, which fails, largely because Laura still clings to traditional bourgeois views of marriage. She finds it intolerable that Paul should hold on to a position of such low prestige. She withholds her affection and threatens to leave him if he does not give in to her demands or live up to her expectations. Because she manipulates him in more or less subtle ways and tries to control his every move, she gradually alienates Paul and causes him to leave her and the children. It is no wonder that not a single legend is told about Paul and Laura. Their relationship is the norm rather than the exception; it lacks the uniqueness and radically new perspective of the Paul and Paula union. This legendary union became possible only because Paul was willing to reject most of his previously held beliefs, to shed his male values and behavior, and to become as spontaneous, open, warm, and caring a person as Paula. Plenzdorf suggests that such radical change of principles and goals is an absolute necessity before men and women can begin to share a life of genuine partnership and intimacy. He casts his male character as a role model who demonstrates that a man can, indeed, gain the respect and admiration of others, even though he lives and acts contrary to conventional standards of male behavior.

Plenzdorf's novel seems to suggest that a change in attitudes as experienced by Paul can be achieved only after a hard struggle. But is that always the case? Does an intimate partnership between a woman and a man have to come in the wake of a crisis? Must it be the result of a willed conversion?

Heinrich Ehlers, in his novel Hanna Mahler - Aufzeichnungen einer jungen Frau, has added two male role models to the growing body of works which explore alternate life styles for men and women.[3] Two of his male characters, Hanna's father Johannes and her friend and lover Paul, are very similar to Plenzdorf's hero in their relationships with women. They display warmth, gentleness, and unusual sensitivity in their dealings with others, and they do so because they never accept for themselves the role behavior expected of men. They are neither criticized nor ridiculed for their atypical behavior; on the contrary, they are well-liked and respected in their community. The central male character in Ehlers' book is Johannes Mahler. The novel, which could well be subtitled "Nachdenken über einen Vater," is essentially a love story between a father and his daughter. When Hanna is twenty years old, her father is stricken by a severe illness, and this illness leads her to reflect upon the years they have lived together and ways in which he has shaped her life.

Hanna's parents were divorced when the girl was six years old. For the next seven years she lived with her mother and had no contact at all with her father because her mother intercepted all letters addressed to the child. But since the relationship between Hanna and her mother deteriorated to point of open hostility over the years, the girl went to live with her father when she was thirteen's old. Alluding to the Joseph stories in Gene Hanna refers to the time spent with her mother as the seven lean years, a time of imprisonment during which she yearned for her liberation.

The major part of the novel deals with the following seven years, the "good years," as a calls them. In this period father and daughter discover each other and develop a relationship of standing and unconditional trust in and respect for other. Hanna emphasizes that in all these year father has never interfered with what she was because he respects her own judgment. Hanna in her notebook:

Die Tür zwischen unseren Zimmern
die ganzen Jahre nie geschlossen

sen. Das war möglich wegen einer Eigenart Mahlers: Er kümmerte sich nie
um den anderen, er guckte mir genauso
wenig auf den Tisch oder in den Schrank
wie ich ihm, obwohl er es sofort merkte, wenn etwas anlag, das seine Anwe-
senheit erforderte, wie ich es merkte,
wenn er den Kopf hob und Lust hatte,
etwas mitzuteilen. Unter dieser Be-
dingung hatte ich mehr Freiheit und
überhaupt mehr für mich allein als andere Töchter, denen die Mütter überall
hingucken, meine Schulkameradinnen
konnten von so etwas erzählen. (p. 59)

When Hanna reminisces about her early childhood,
she realizes that her relationship with her mother was
marked by a lack of physical and emotional intimacy.
Her mother regarded all bodily needs and expressions
as something secret, sinful, and shameful. Her father, however, has never attempted to suppress her
interest and pleasure in her own body. He explains to
her that she should be ashamed about lying and un-
cleanness, but about nothing else. There is no
barrier of inhibition and self-consciousness between
Hanna and Mahler. Even after their seven-year separation they do not find it difficult to re-establish the
former ease and naturalness between them. The morning
after return, Hanna, who is thirteen years old,
takes a bath in the presence of her father. Both she
and her recognize this as a symbolic act which
cleans Hanna of the maternal influence and restores
the former closeness between them. On occasions when
Hanna is distressed and miserable, she unhesitat-
ingly slips into Mahler's bed to be soothed and com-
forted by him. Yielding to her natural impulses and
growing up in an atmosphere of frankness and mutual
trust make Hanna more mature and self-confident than
others her age. For her, puberty is not a period
of stress and confusion. The transition from childhood to adulthood proceeds very smoothly, almost
effortlessly.

Hanna does not feel the urge to protest or
rebel against her father cannot be attributed to a
pliable, docile nature since she is not a meek or
submissive girl. She reacted violently against her
mother's attempts to mold and manipulate her; later,
when with Mahler, she antagonizes several of
her tutors and an army officer. Her anger and

238

rebelliousness can easily be aroused when men abuse their authority. Mahler, however, never acts authoritatively; he does not assume the patriarchal role of disciplinarian, critic, or guide. He treats Hanna as an equal, as a partner instead of a dependent. He does not hesitate to involve her in conversations which exceed her intellectual and emotional powers of comprehension. She is never asked to leave the room when Mahler has company, and even when her teacher stops by to discuss problems concerning Hanna, her father insists that she be present. As she reflects on the seven "good years" which she and Mahler shared, Hanna concludes that this period constituted the most durable bond imaginable between two people. They have become warm, intimate partners--yet their intimacy never develops into interdependence; they achieve a unique closeness without one of them enveloping the other.

It is her memory of this singular partnership which enables Hanna to cope with the crisis which occurs when she is twenty years old. Mahler falls ill very suddenly and, when he returns from the hospital, he is blind, suffers from temporary amnesia, and has difficulties expressing himself verbally. As Hanna begins to take care of her father, she realizes the threat to their relationship. Because he is so changed, she feels tempted to cling to the past image of her father, but she knows that such an attitude would mean to write him off. She also has to guard against the temptation of assuming the role of protector, nursemaid, or guide. Taking on such a role would reinforce Mahler's helplessness; it would reduce him to the status of a dependent and deny him the right to live his last years in dignity and self-respect.

The first months of readjustment are very difficult for both father and daughter. Hanna often despairs when she observes Mahler's depression, when she watches how he withdraws into himself or struggles in his attempts at simple communication. What helps Hanna to avoid the threatening estrangement is her tenacious desire to restore their former intimacy. She makes every effort to treat Mahler as a partner, although at first he insists that he is just a nuisance. She does not accept his blindness as an excuse to retreat from the activities of everyday life. Just as imperceptibly and tactfully as Mahler had guided Hanna through her period of readjustment seven years earlier, she now restores his self-confidence and willingness to participate in life. As the novel ends, Mahler and Paul (the father of Hanna's child) are engaged in a lively discussion concerning the baby, an indication that Hanna does succeed in rekindling her father's interest and belief in the future.

When Hanna returned to live with Mahler, Carola, a neighbor and friend, had shaken her head skeptically and said that such a relationship could not possibly work out. But Carola's skepticism was quite unwarranted. Father and daughter live in almost undisturbed harmony, not only because they share common interests (their love of books, music, and the countryside) but also because they reject the typical patterns prevalent in traditional families.

Looking back at the two novels, one is struck by the fact that only those characters who are willing to explore new ways of living together are able to find fulfillment and happiness. Carola's family life, Mahler's marriage to Hanna's mother, Paul's first marriage, and his later union with Laura are failures because, in these relationships, individuals feel restricted and confined by the roles they are expected to play. Paul and Paula, and Mahler and Hanna, on the other hand, live unhampered by the conventional behavior code of patriarchal society. Without surrendering their individual identity they are able to achieve a rare intimate togetherness. I am not suggesting that Ehlers' and Plenzdorf's novels are the harbingers of a new trend in male-female relationships, but they offer a refreshing glimpse of what a future might be like in which men and women are truly liberated.

Denison University

Notes

[1] Maxie Wander, Guten Morgen, du Schöne (Darmstadt: Luchterhand, 1978), p. 7.

[2] Ulrich Plenzdorf, Legende vom Glück ohne Ende (Frankfurt/M.: Suhrkamp, 1979). All future page references are to this edition. Plenzdorf's novel is an extension and variation of Heiner Carow's film Die

Legende von Paul und Paula for which Plenzdorf wrote the script; the film text was published by Suhrkamp in 1974. The characters of the two lovers, the plot, and the milieu are identical in the film and the literary version. The major difference is that the novel, unlike the film, does not end with Paula's death. The second part of the novel deals with Paul's grief over Paula's loss and his new relationship with Paula's Doppelgänger Laura.

3 Heinrich Ehlers, Hanna Mahler - Aufzeichnungen einer jungen Frau (Rostock: Hinstorff, 1980). All future page references are to this edition.

"Merkwürdiges Beispiel weiblicher Entschlossenheit"
--A Woman's Story--by Sarah Kirsch

Charlotte E. Armster

Great strides have been made in equalizing the
opportunities of men and women in the GDR. As an important aspect of socialist society, equal rights for
men and women were codified in the 1949 constitution,
and laws conflicting with this article were declared
null and void.[1] Statistics would seem to confirm the
overall emancipation of GDR women. For instance, more
than 85% of all GDR women of working age are either
employed outside the home or studying, and women make
up over half of the total labor force; nearly half of
the university students are women, and one third of
the working women are professionals.[2] It would seem
that Lutz-W. Wolff is correct when he maintains in his
afterword to the anthology Frauen in der DDR. Zwanzig
Erzählungen: "Die gesetzgeberischen, gesellschaftspolitischen und ökonomischen Maßnahmen der SED haben das
Leben von Millionen Frauen der DDR planmäßig und
schrittweise verändert und damit die Grundlage für
eine neue Beziehung der Geschlechter geschaffen."[3]

Data, however, present only a numerical picture.
The concept of equality involves more basic human
questions, for example, the questions of role expectation, gender awareness, self-realization, and self-
fulfillment. While no one disputes the factual evidence, it does not address these fundamental concerns.
Works of literature, in particular works written by
women about women in the GDR, can perhaps best investigate these questions, as does Sarah Kirsch's short
story to be discussed here.

"Merkwürdiges Beispiel weiblicher Entschlossenheit," first published in 1973, depicts a woman who,
although an integral and important part of the (male)

243

work world, is unfulfilled by her work.4 The very
first sentence of the text localizes the problem:
"Frau Schmalfuß war 28 und hatte immer noch kein Kind"
(p. 182). The modifier "immer noch" expresses both
urgency--at 28, her childbearing years are numbered--
and disappointed expectation. Whose expectation? The
statement is made by the third-person narrator, and it
is not immediately clear whose opinion it represents.
In the course of the narrative, the reader understands
that it reflects both Frau Schmalfuß' feeling and that
of society around her. The view of the narrator, on
the other hand, is less easy to pinpoint: is it one
of sympathy, ridicule, or a combination of both?

Frau Schmalfuß is a highly valued colleague at
her place of work and, with her many awards and com-
mendations proudly displayed, she is the picture of
self-confidence, reliability, and self-control. Her
professional success is, however, not matched in her
private life. She has never had a personal relationship with a man. The narrative voice suggests that
the reason for her being "unbemannt und noch ohne Kinder" (p. 182) lies in the absence of compelling physical attractiveness; we are told that the four beautiful attributes she possesses are spread so far apart
that no one has yet connected them together and thus
appreciated her beauty!

Frau Schmalfuß seeks self-fulfillment in her
work. She often takes on extra duties that her colleagues shun; she works overtime in the evenings and
on weekends. Moments of loneliness and a sense of
emptiness come over her occasionally--walking home
from work, in the shower, in "unbewachten Augenblik-
ken" (p. 182). Until now, however, she has quickly
suppressed and sublimated her momentary longings:
"Aber sie hatte sich fest in der Hand und suchte das
Glück in der Arbeit" (p. 182).

The overwhelming power of spring finally causes
her repressed emotional longings to come to the surface. One March day, while paying a charitable visit
to a colleague from work who has just given birth to a
child--she often makes such visits "im Namen des
Frauenausschusses" (p. 183)--, she is overcome by the
images of rebirth in nature: "die Schneeglöckchen
schaukelten, die Schwertlilien hoben die Erde an . . .
schwarze Wolken rasten im Wind" (p. 183). She pic-
tures herself pushing a baby carriage alongside these
images of wild, uncontrollable nature. It is inter-

244

esting to note that all of her fantasies take place outside of the work world, either in nature or at her home.

Schmalfuß' fantasy does not include a male figure (or partner, as it were), but rather only herself and her child. Her strong experiencing of spring makes her conscious only of her desire for a child; her repressed sexual needs, made obvious to the reader by the narrator's description, do not rise to the level of consciousness. She does not (consciously) seek to fulfill her need for human warmth and emotional bonding with another adult. She is unable to recognize in herself, either in her daydreams or in her emotions, evidence of this personal need. Her decision to pursue the idea of having a child evokes signs of her basic sexual drive; she experiences what the reader recognizes as standard erotic dreams. That her dreams might be erotic does not, however, dawn on her; she makes no attempt to understand the puzzling images and soon forgets them again. At no time does she seriously consider the possibility of finding a mate for a long-term relationship or marriage.

Schmalfuß has long since internalized the value of responsible and reasoned behavior as something necessary for the good of society; she has a strong sense of duty and is accustomed to subordinating her personal desires to societal goals. Thus she seeks to justify her wish for a child in terms of societal good. She reasons that her professional success obligates her to contribute further to society by having a child. And after all, she has a good job and a modern, pleasant apartment: the child would have a good home.

Having legitimized her personal desire, Schmalfuß casts around for a man, much as one might seek out a tool to do a certain task. She views the act of impregnation as a sort of service, a job like any other, and sets about determining the right person to fill the need and securing his agreement. She is evidently incapable of envisioning the arrangement she seeks in other than in terms of work; her efforts to attract her chosen father-candidate are carried out in the same rational fashion in which she would undertake any other assignment: "In den Tagen vor der Verabredung ging Frau Schmalfuß doch sorgenvoll ihrer Arbeit nach, unterzog den Kleiderschrank einer eingehenden Prüfung, brachte einen Rock in die Schnellreinigung,

kaufte einen roten Pullover" (p. 185). Thus she reduces the most intimate of human relationships to a
mechanical, practical procedure--controllable, calcu-
lable, and without emotional attachment.

Her innermost feelings about Friedrich Vogel, the
man she chooses, are never consciously realized. And
she is totally oblivious to the fact that Vogel finds
her attractive: "Sie ist wirklich eine schöne Person,
dachte er und sah sie von oben bis unten an" (p. 186).
It does not occur to her that her impregnation might
come about quite naturally as a love relationship.
Vogel, who under other conditions might willingly have
fulfilled her wish, is thunderstruck by her proposal
and retreats.

Unable to accommodate her emotional needs through
an arrangement with Vogel, Schmalfuß throws herself
into her work once more: "Sie kompensierte Traurig-
keit durch gewissenhafte Arbeit . . ." (p. 188), the
narrator tells us--until nature intervenes once more.
One summer afternoon, lying on the sofa under the
picture of an icebreaker that Vogel had given her,
tormented by the heat and the sound of water from the
fountains and sprinklers outside, her thoughts turn
once more to having a child; this time she envisions
kidnapping a baby. Again she avoids confronting the
source of her loneliness directly. Although a doctor
assures her that she can bear children, she makes up
her mind to adopt a child instead.

At this point, Schmalfuß begins to identify with
the virgin Mary--she, too, will have a virgin "birth"
by adopting a child. She organizes a trip with her
fellow workers to Dresden, to visit the art gallery in
the Zwinger; her undisclosed wish is to see Raphael's
Sistine Madonna. In the Zwinger, she makes her way
quickly past the other paintings: "Das waren Sta-
tionen auf dem Weg zum Ziel . . . Die Nackte, die den
Schwan küßt - Frau Schmalfuß ging schneller, um kein
Ungehagen zu spüren" (p. 191). Arriving at the
Raphael, she waits until she is alone, seeks out the
best viewing point and looks up at the madonna:

> Der Mantel von noch schönerem Blau als
> in ihrem Kalender. Die andere Frau,
> der alte Papst sanken in den Wolken da
> ein. Die Madonna war leichter, man sah
> jeden Zeh, obwohl sie das Kind trug.
> Sie sah freundlich aus, nicht so hei-

lig, fast eine Kollegin, die Frau mit
dem Kind. Ihr Mann war nicht auf dem
Bild, spielte keine Rolle. Frau
Schmalfuß erinnerte sich, in der
Schrift gelesen zu haben, daß es erst
eines Winkes von oben bedurfte, bis
Josef Maria mit dem Kind heiratete.
Heute wär sie allein geblieben, dachte
Frau Schmalfuß. (pp. 191-192)

Schmalfuß, like Mary, receives her child at
Christmas: "Mitte Dezember . . . durfte Frau Schmalfuß in Hinblick auf Weihnachten, Personalmangel im
Säuglingsheim und ihre eigene Hartnäckigkeit das Kind
entgegennehmen . . ." (p. 192). She thinks of herself
as a biological mother, drinks milk now instead of her
usual beer and asks herself "ob sie ihr ein Geschenk
bringen würden wie anderen Wöchnerinnen" (p. 192). At
the end of the story she is pictured tired and happy
after her first day of mothering. In a slightly dazed
condition she tries to follow a program on television
about a woman who takes her child to the day-care
center day in, day out, before and after work: "jeden
Tag zwei S-Bahn-Stationen auf der Hinfahrt, zwei S-
Bahn-Stationen auf der Rückfahrt, vier Treppen, vier
fremde Männer oder Frauen, die ihr helfen den Wagen zu
tragen. Manchmal reißen sich die Leute um den Wagen,
mitunter muß die Frau warten . . . Das würde sie alles
erfahren" (p. 192).

What are we to make of this "unusual example of
female decisiveness"--as I have translated the title?
The attitude of the narrator is often satiric, as
evidenced in quotations given above. The satiric
stance begins with the choice of names: Frau Schmalfuß (although one of her four beautiful physical
attributes, namely her legs, end "rechtwinklig in
langen, breiten, flachen [nicht platten] Füßen," p.
182) and Friedrich Vogel, whose name indicates his
intended function. We never learn Frau Schmalfuß'
first name; her relationship with others is always
formal.

Additional means of satire are the contrasting of
Frau Schmalfuß' thoughts with her actual feelings and
the simple recording of her thoughts as they contrast
with normalcy. The following excerpt offers an example of both:

Der Sohn oder die Tochter würde von ihr

247

erzogen werden, und sie erwog, dem Kind
eine glaubhafte Geschichte zu erzählen,
die Abwesenheit des Erzeugers zu begründen. Vielleicht war er einem Auto-
unfall zum Opfer gefallen? Oder hatte
ihn als Grenzsoldat eine feindliche Ku-
gel gefallen? Aber es gab ja viele Fa-
milien, die nur aus Mutter und Kind be-
standen. Und warum sollte Friedrich
Vogel nicht eines Tages--die Jugend-
weihe wäre der gegebene Anlaß--auf der
Bildfläche erscheinen und dem Kinde
eine wertvolle Armbanduhr schenken?
Ja, das war die Lösung. Denn Frau
Schmalfuß klopfte das Herz, wenn sie
daran dachte, den Kindesvater, wenn
auch mit Worten, unter ein Auto zu
stoßen . . . Sie hatte sich mit Friedrich Vogel dermaßen eindringlich beschäftigt, daß ihr ganz warm und eng in
der Brust wurde, wenn sie an ihn
dachte. (p. 184)

There is certainly sufficient reason to believe
that the narrator and, behind the narrative voice, the
author Sarah Kirsch find Frau Schmalfuß' behavior un-
natural and undesirable. But there may be extenuating
circumstances that mollify the criticism. After all,
what has caused Frau Schmalfuß to behave in this way?
It has been a frequent thesis of Sarah Kirsch, who denies any connection with the women's movement,[5] that
women cannot have it both ways, i.e., equality in the
professional sphere and a normal private life. Katharina in "Blitz aus heiterm Himmel" becomes emancipated only after she is changed into a man; only then
does she share things equally with her friend Albert
--but now the female side is lost, as is their old
sexual happiness.[6] And as Sarah Kirsch remarked in
her "Gespräch mit Schülern" in regard to the women she
interviewed for Pantherfrau who had achieved success
in their professional lives: "es geht aufwärts, aber
der Preis ist immer das persönliche Leben, eine Beziehung zu einem Menschen. Bei vielen geht es da ja
schief. Es funktioniert nur das eine."[7]

No matter how critical one is of Frau Schmalfuß,
it is, I believe, nevertheless possible to interpret
some aspects of her behavior positively. She has, for
example, not internalized a notion of her femaleness
in terms of maleness. Her perception of reality

excludes male dominance to a large degree. While this seriously affects her ability to form a relationship with a man, it also affords her a certain independence. She seeks fulfillment in her own way, not with and through a man, but through a child--a child that she wishes to have alone. For her, the child is not primarily the result of a union between woman and man; it fulfills her need for a human bond, and she wants it to be hers exclusively. Adopting the child, rather than being made pregnant, reduces the importance of the male even further. The female, in apparent control of her life, is a symbol of potency, however ignorant she is of her own needs. Her move toward self-determination and identification with motherhood is based on her strong gender awareness, which enables her to overcome role expectation--at least in regard to the societal expectation that women will marry and raise their children within the conventional family structure.

However fraught with unconscious psychological motivations her behavior is, Schmalfuß retains a measure of dignity. She has done what she could do to bridge the gap between the professional and private sphere. She does not resign herself to her situation and devote herself and her life exclusively to her work. The work world is not her salvation, from which she derives primary strength and support. The stereotypical role of self-sacrifice, discipline, and work achievement is broken and replaced by self-determination and self-fulfillment. She reconciles the split between the work sphere and the private sphere by establishing a human bond. She combines the two--in her own way. And thus the example of female decisiveness that Sarah Kirsch gives in her short story is indeed "merkwürdig"--it is both strange and unusual. Schmalfuß is not a heroine in the sense of being a model for others to follow. She is, however, not only a person to be scoffed at; we can sympathize with her as well.

Dartmouth College

Notes

[1] See Harry G. Shaffer, Women in the Two Germanies. A Comparative Study of a Socialist and a Non-Socialist Society (New York: Pergamon Press, 1981),

Ch. 2.

[2] These numbers have been rounded off for the sake of simplicity and are therefore only approximate. They have been taken from the Statistisches Jahrbuch der DDR 1980 (E. Berlin: Staatsverlag der DDR, 1980). Additional sources of information: Herta Kuhrig and Wulfram Speigner, eds., Wie emanzipiert sind die Frauen in der DDR? (Cologne: Pahl-Rugenstein, 1979); Harry G. Shaffer, Women in the Two Germanies. A Comparative Study of a Socialist and a Non-Socialist Society.

[3] Lutz-W. Wolff, ed., Frauen in der DDR. Zwanzig Erzählungen (Munich: Deutscher Taschenbuch Verlag, 1976), p. 250.

[4] Sarah Kirsch, "Merkwürdiges Beispiel weiblicher Entschlossenheit," in Frauen in der DDR. Zwanzig Erzählungen, pp. 182-192. Subsequent parenthetical page references are to this edition.

[5] See Sarah Kirsch, "Kunst und Alltag--alle Tage Kunst. Ein Gespräch mit Sarah Kirsch," in her Erklärung einiger Dinge. Dokumente und Bilder (Reinbek bei Hamburg: Rowohlt, 1981), p. 88.

[6] Sarah Kirsch, "Blitz aus heiterm Himmel," in Geschlechtertausch, ed. Wolfgang Emmerich (Darmstadt and Neuwied: Luchterhand, 1980).

[7] Sarah Kirsch, "Ein Gespräch mit Schülern," in her Erklärung einiger Dinge (Dokumente und Bilder) (Ebenhausen: Langewiesche-Brandt, 1978), p. 34; also included in the enlarged Rowohlt edition (Note 5), p. 29.

Social Change and Women's Issues in the GDR:
Problems of Women in Leadership Positions

Christiane Lemke

As part of the process of creating a new social
and political order in the GDR in the aftermath of
fascism and World War II, efforts were made to improve
the status of women and to integrate them as full
participants in socialist society. Changes in women's
roles have been greatest in the areas of education and
employment. In her book Guten Morgen, du Schöne
(1977), Maxie Wander recorded various ways of life of
women in the GDR. One of the women, Erika D., a
forty-one-year-old production assistant, divorced with
two children, is representative of the fundamental
changes that have occurred in women's social roles.
Erika D. was already married and had one child when
she started working at a radio station. She relates:

Und dann kamen die Frauenförderungs-
pläne. Mein Chef hatte eigentlich
keine Ambitionen, der sagte, das wäre
alles Quatsch, man sollte sich am Ar-
beitsplatz qualifizieren. Aber ein
anderer meinte, warum denn nicht, sie
fragt doch dauernd, und wir haben bloß
drei Frauen in der Abteilung. Um
Gottes Willen, rief mein Chef, in ihrem
Alter, hat sie denn überhaupt Abitur?
Nee, sage ich. Na, also, schreit mein
Chef, ist doch Quatsch. Der andere
blieb aber dran, und ich sagte wie
immer: Gut, mache ich. Ich wußte ja
gar nicht, was auf mich zukam.
Bin also zur Volkshochschule gewandert,
und dort traf ich eine Frau! Wir spra-
chen eine Stunde zusammen, dann sagte
sie: Es ist erstaunlich, was Sie alles

nicht wissen. Die Aufnahmeprüfung für
die elfte Klasse schaffen Sie nie. . .
. Abends habe ich zu meinem Mann gesagt: Ich habe keine Zeit mehr, ich muß
lesen. Da hat mein Mann nicht gefragt,
was ich lese und warum ich lese, er hat
nur dauernd gewimmert, daß kein Knopf
am Hemd war. Und hat ferngesehen. Und
ich saß in der Küche und hab studiert.[1]

In spite of all her difficulties, Erika manages to
finish school. Her grades in German are even excellent.

Aber was denkst du, zum Studium kam ich
nicht! Es kam nur ein Brief: Liebe
Frau D., Ihr Aufnahmegespräch und Ihre
schriftlichen Arbeiten haben leider
nicht den Erfolg gebracht, den wir
erwarten. Ihr Alter ist eigentlich
auch . . . Na, schönen Dank! Nun hast
du endlich den Beweis, du bist halt
doof. (p. 98)

But Erika doesn't give up. She applies again for
admission to the university and this time is accepted.
Her husband leaves her to marry another woman: "Paß
auf, der Mann war weg, und ein paar Tage später bekam
ich die Zuschrift: Sie sind immatrikuliert. . . . Kurz
und gut, dieses Studium wurde eine wunderbare Geschichte" (p. 103).

Erika is not an individual case. The opportunity
for women to change their social situation by means of
education and training is prevalent in the GDR. But
despite the progress made in the areas of education
and employment, women are still underrepresented in
leadership positions. The rise in the educational
level of women and their increasing percentage representation in the total labor force has not led to pro-
portional employment in leading positions. Although
women make up one half of the labor force in the GDR,
they hold only 30% of the leadership positions in the
economy and in society in general. This indicates
persisting differences in social status between men
and women.

As the following sectoral distribution of women
workers shows, both sexes still have preferences for
certain jobs and sectors of the economy.

TABLE 1. WOMEN IN THE GDR LABOR FORCE BY AREA OF
          EMPLOYMENT, 1955-1977 (in percent)

Branch	1955	1960	1965	1970	1975	1977
Industry	37.7	40.5	39.9	42.5	43.7	43.8
Handicrafts	34.3	33.6	38.0	40.1	38.7	38.5
Construction	9.0	8.6	9.7	13.3	14.9	15.8
Agriculture	51.3	45.7	47.8	45.8	42.9	42.9
Transportation	28.7[+]	32.3[+]	33.9[+]	25.5	27.3	27.2
Communication				68.8	70.5	71.1
Sales & Supply	59.0	64.6	67.2	69.2	71.4	72.6
Other prod. branches	59.4*	42.8	45.2	53.7	54.2	54.8
Non-prod. branches		64.2	68.0	70.2	72.3	72.8

Source: Herta Kuhrig and Wulfram Speigner, "Gleichbe-
         rechtigung der Frau - Aufgaben und ihre Rea-
         lisierung in der DDR," in their Zur gesell-
         schaftlichen Stellung der Frau in der DDR
         (Leipzig: Verlag für die Frau, 1978), p. 52.

         [+] Transportation and Communication are com-
         puted together

         * Other prod. branches and non-prod. branches
         are computed together

Women continue to be concentrated in such traditionally female fields as education, health, social services (non-producing branches), and sales, rather than
in heavy industry or construction.

    Women are slightly better represented in leader-
ship positions in those areas in which they predomi-

nate. In industry, every fifth leadership position is held by a woman; in agriculture, every sixth; in trade, every second; and in universities and colleges, every third; this includes top, middle, and low level positions.[2] In the region of Greiz, one of the industrial centers of the district of Gera, for example, more than half of the labor force is made up of women; their representation in leadership positions is 32%. In VEB Greika, located in the region of Greiz, 70% of the 5,000 employees are women, and 37% of the leadership positions are held by women. There is a great difference between the various levels of leadership, however. On the top level of management (factory directors) only one of the ten positions is held by a woman; none of the seven directors on the middle-management level is a woman; on the floor management level, on the other hand, six out of ten leadership positions are held by women.[3]

Sales and supply is one of the areas with a traditionally high rate of women employees. They make up slightly over 70% of the total employees in this branch of the GDR economy. In one firm, Wismut-Handel, 30.4% of the top positions (directors, head bookkeepers) were held by women in 1975, while 40.6% of the positions in middle-level management (branch managers) were held by women.[4]

The situation is worse in agriculture. In 1976, about 43% of the labor force consisted of women but only 16.2% of the leadership positions were held by women. Although this proportion has increased--in 1961 it was only 3.6%--it is still much lower than that of the men and lower than in other branches of industry.[5]

What are the reasons for the persisting differences in the employment of men and women in leadership positions? The requirements for attaining a position of responsibility are quite complex. They include professional training, political activity, and certain personal qualities, such as the ability to organize and plan, strength of character, authority.

In regard to job training, great changes have occurred during the past 20 years. The improved educational opportunities have led to a general rise in the level of education in the GDR. However, women workers are still less qualified than men, as the following table shows.

TABLE 2.   LEVEL OF TRAINING OF MEN AND WOMEN

| | 1971 | | 1977 | |
	Men	Women	Men	Women
University degree	6.7	2.7	8.9	4.4
Vocational college	9.5	6.3	10.7	12.9
Journeyman-master	5.2	1.0	6.0	0.6
Skilled workers	50.3	38.1	57.3	48.2
Unskilled workers	28.3	51.9	17.1	33.9
Total	100.	100.	100.	100.

Source: Wulfram Speigner, "Bildung für die Frauen und
Mädchen," in Zur gesellschaftlichen Stellung
der Frau, p. 222.

Differences in training alone, however, cannot
explain the lower representation of women in leadership positions; even in those branches or factories
where men and women have the same degree of training,
women still do not occupy half of the positions involving responsibility. The question remains why this
is the case.

Concerning political activity, all reports and
information published about women in leadership positions show that these women have at least one political function in the factory and/or in social and public affairs. The women's journal Für Dich and other
newspapers have recently published reports about women
in various leadership positions which illustrate this
fact. [6] However, the available information concerning
the political behavior and involvement of women indicates that the improvement in the educational level of
women and their greater involvement in work outside
the home has not led to an increase in political
activity comparable to that of men. Time-budget
studies indicate that women spend less time on public
and political activities than do men. They are also

less involved in political activities at their place of work and are less frequently members of the SED. Although the proportion of female party members has increased--in 1966, 25.7% of all members of the SED were women; in 1971, 28.7%; in 1975, 31.3%--in 1981 still only 33.7% of all party members were women.[7] Women's representation in party bodies is lower than in all levels of government; it also decreases with the importance of the office. Only in the Free German Labor Union (FDGB) and the youth organization (FDJ) are there more female members than male (FDGB: 50.7%; FDJ: 54.6%).[8] The small amount of time professional women in general spend in political and public activity, and their lower rate of membership in the SED may limit their professional advancement in a society in which a certain degree of activism in party, public, and mass organizations is required of persons in leading positions.

There is very little information available concerning the personal qualities of women in leadership positions. Reports dealing with women in such positions give no indication of differences in problems concerning authority and success that women might have as opposed to men. The author of an article which appeared in the journal Die Wirtschaft maintains that women are more emotional than men, due to their mother role. In his opinion, this can be very helpful in leadership positions, since this quality may enable them to be more receptive to social and personal problems at work. He does not indicate, however, whether his statement is based on surveys or is an outgrowth of personal opinion and stereotypes.[9] Whether women manifest the personal qualities needed to fulfill leadership positions depends not only on special management training but also on the social situation of women at work and off the job. Despite their assuming new roles in the economy, women continue to bear the traditionally female responsibility of caring for the home and family. The difficulty of carrying what has become known as the "dual burden" is confirmed by studies which indicate that most women do not feel they can work and take care of the home and family at the same time. Social conditions shape women's attitudes toward assuming responsibility at work, and many women tend not to accept responsible leadership positions. The dual burden explains to a certain extent this reluctance. Their professional advancement is hindered in a subjective way by the traditional conceptions of their roles in the home.

While younger women tend to accept leadership positions, marriage and especially the birth of children
diminish their willingness to accept positions of
responsibility.

Concern over the underrepresentation of women in
leadership positions has led to discussions within the
SED and the government. The SED communique "Die Frau,
der Frieden und der Sozialismus" (1961) initiated a
women's training and promotion campaign in the sixties. Various laws that have been passed since then,
for example, laws dealing with the educational system
(Bildungsgesetz, 1965), with youth (Jugendgesetz,
1964, revised 1974), with labor (Gesetzbuch der Arbeit, 1961; revised Arbeitsgesetzbuch, 1977), include
special provisions for the furtherance of women. The
discussion about inequality between men and women and
the underrepresentation of women in leadership positions has intensified in recent years. As already
mentioned, the women's journal Für Dich and other
journals and newspapers have increasingly published
interviews and reports on women in leadership positions.

Two different kinds of priority categories have
been set up to increase the number of women on all
levels of leadership positions. First, the factories
and companies themselves are requested to train more
women for and to promote them to leadership positions
and to change their attitude towards women in these
positions. Emphasis is put on better preparation and
training, starting already in the youth organiza-
tion.10   "Frauen fordern, um sie zu fördern" is the
slogan for this policy. Rudolf Fritsche, director of
Wismut-Handel, has complained that quite often women
are not given leading positions even though they are
qualified. In some cases the (male) directors are
still prejudiced against women in leadership positions; in other cases, the women themselves hesitate
to accept the position. They are afraid of the responsibility, and distraught or disorganized women
directors provide a warning example in support of
their reluctance to assume a responsible position.
Fritsche suggests that women should be encouraged more
than before and given preference when a new leading
position is to be filled.11

Another priority is to make it easier for women
to combine their jobs with family tasks. Party lead-
ers and factory directors are advised to keep in close

contact with those women who have recently married or borne children.[12] Facilities for shopping, child care, public transportation, and cultural activities are also to be improved. This seems to be a problem particularly in rural areas.[13]

The underrepresentation of women in leading positions is only one of the persisting problems involving the inequality of women in the GDR. Although their situation is much better than in the early years of the GDR and much better than in other socialist and western countries, the influence of economic, social, and educational policy seems to be limited. Official support is not enough to bring about a fundamental change in women's status. Broad public discussion of women's issues is needed, as well as the increased awareness and activity of the women themselves. The example set by women in leadership positions and the portrayal of women in GDR literature offer both men and women the opportunity to reevaluate the social status of women.

Freie Universität Berlin

Notes

[1] Maxie Wander, Guten Morgen, du Schöne. Frauen in der DDR. Protokolle (Darmstadt and Neuwied: Luchterhand, 1979), pp. 96-97. The original GDR version appeared in 1977 in the publishing house Der Morgen; a second GDR edition appeared in Aufbau Verlag in 1980. All page references in the text are to the Luchterhand edition.

[2] Presse-Informationen, published by the Ministerrat der DDR, No. 21, 20 Feb. 1979.

[3] Isolde Rudolf, "Frauen in leitenden Funktionen - wie sieht das im Kreis Greiz aus?" Neuer Weg, 34, No. 13 (1979), 537.

[4] Rudolf Fritsche, "Frauen und Mädchen langfristig für leitende Funktionen vorbereiten," Der Handel, 25, No. 12 (1975), 498.

[5] Klaus Fleischer et al., "Die Entwicklung der Frau in der sozialistischen Landwirtschaft," in Zur

gesellschaftlichen Stellung der Frau in der DDR, (Leipzig: Verlag für die Frau, 1978), pp. 145f.

[6] See, for example, "Porträt über eine sozialistische Leiterin. Ständig auf der Suche nach dem Neuen," Kooperation, 11, No. 3 (1977), 97; Ursula Half, "Mit Gefühl und Autorität," Für Dich, No. 26 (1979), 8f.; H. Straßburg, "Eine vom Bau," Für Dich, No. 26, (1979), 26.

[7] Gero Neugebauer, "Veränderungen in der Organisationspolitik der SED," in Der X. Parteitag der SED. 35 Jahre SED Politik. Versuch einer Bilanz (Cologne: Edition Deutschland Archiv, 1980), p. 123.

[8] Neues Deutschland, No. 174, 25 July 1980, p. 2.

[9] Günter Fischer, "Mein Leiter ist eine Frau," Die Wirtschaft, 35, No. 12 (1980), 23.

[10] See, for example, Rudolf, "Frauen in leitenden Funktionen," p. 538; Manfred Beier, "Frauen mit hoher Verantwortung," Presse-Informationen, No. 36, 23 March 1978.

[11] Fritsche, "Frauen und Mädchen," p. 499.

[12] Rudolf, "Frauen in leitenden Funktionen," p. 538.

[13] Robert Barthelmann et al., "Zur Qualifizierung der sozialistischen Leitungstätigkeit. Einige Aspekte der Förderung der Frauen," Kooperation, 11, No. 3 (1977), 132f.

Maternal and Child Health Care
in the German Democratic Republic[1]

Robert A. Greenberg

The GDR, like other socialist societies, expresses a strong commitment to maternal and child
health and social and family supports.[2] Article 35 of
the 1968 GDR constitution states that citizens have
the right to protection of their health through adequate living and working conditions and extensive
social services. In case of sickness or accident they
are guaranteed monetary benefits, free medical care,
and drugs. These constitutional rights are not only
clearly stated, they are honored. The health and
social services system is financed by a mandatory
social insurance tax of ten percent of an employee's
salary with a maximum limit of sixty marks per month,
an approximately equal amount from the employer, and
from general state revenues.[3]

All health and medical care facilities belong to
the state, and all people working in the health care
system are employed by the state, with the exception
of a small, steadily decreasing number of private
practices. (All private practices have to have been
established before 1950. They presently comprise 5.4%
of the physicians who are in practice outside of
hospitals.[4] Their income depends upon practice volume, but is heavily taxed so that great disparities in
physician income are avoided.) Throughout the entire
national health system the patient has free choice of
physician.

Ultimate control of the health and social services system rests with the National Ministry of
Health and Social Services. The intermediate administrative level is the county (Bezirk); the local level
is the district (Kreis).[5] The National Ministry of

261

Health and Social Services is responsible for the overall administration, planning, and financing of the system, for setting the standards for the training of health personnel, for setting priorities and managing the finances for medical research, and for establishing regulations related to actual medical care. (Regulations are published biweekly and sent to everyone in the health care system. They may be as specific as requiring patients with recurrent urinary tract infections to be periodically evaluated at regional specialty clinics.)

Examples of the responsibilities of the county health officers (Bezirksärzte) are planning the location of new medical care facilities and hospitals, assuring a rational distribution of resources, determining the county's need for various medical and dental personnel and then establishing the appropriate number of training positions in professional schools and universities, and planning the location of special institutions, e.g., infant day-care centers and special homes for the handicapped.[6]

At the local level, the district physician (Kreisarzt) is the chief health officer and responsible for all health and social service personnel. How involved this person becomes in the daily operation of clinics and practices depends on the administrative style of the Kreisarzt and the strength of the practitioners and clinic directors. The Kreisarzt assures that the Ministry's directives are instituted, presents the personnel and equipment needs of the various district facilities to the county administration, monitors the quality of services, assures that night and weekend call schedules are established, and serves as a mediator for solving problems that might arise between various health care providers or facilities. The GDR has clearly developed a complete state health care system.[7]

Tables 1-4 outline the organization of the GDR ambulatory (outpatient) health services, where, as in all health care systems, over 90% of patient care occurs.[8] This organizational plan has not, as yet, been completely implemented in all areas of the GDR. Although the facilities are for patients of all ages and with the variety of problems that patients bring to physicians, the specific services chosen for elaboration here are mainly those for mothers and children. The staff in the tables consists mainly of physicians. Depending on the size and scope of services in the facility, the staff also includes nurses, social workers, dental assistants, laboratory technicians, and a variety of other supporting personnel. The largest primary care outpatient facility is the district clinic (Kreispoliklinik).[9] There is approximately one such clinic per 50,000 people. It is

---

TABLE 1. DISTRICT OUTPATIENT CLINIC (KREISPOLIKLINIK)
1 PER 50,000 POPULATION

Staff	Maternal and Child Health Services
3 general practitioners	
3 general pediatricians	Well-baby clinics, day-care health programs, and sick care for infants and children
3 general dentists	
3 pedodontists	Dental care for children
1 obstetrician-gynecologist	Prenatal care
1 internist, general surgeon, otolaryngologist, ophthalmologist, and dermatologist	
2 physicians for children and youth	Kindergarten and school health programs

---

usually located in an urban area and serves as the basic care facility for the immediate neighborhood and as a consulting facility for smaller neighborhood units located throughout the city and for smaller clinics and practices in the outlying rural areas. (Clinics are also located in factories and in large

263

firms, making health care and occupational health programs very accessible to employees.)

When a pediatrician is present in a health care facility, the general practitioner is considered the primary physician for adults only, except during nights and weekends when the general practitioner-on-call will see children and refer patients to the pediatrician-on-call if necessary.[10] In rural areas where pediatricians may not be immediately available, the general practitioner may be more involved in the care of sick children over six years of age, especially if she or he has the interest. However, the official planning goal is for children's care to be supervised and, whenever possible, actually performed by a pediatrician. This is especially true of the well-baby clinics (Mütterberatung) where routine examinations and immunizations are given during the first three years of life. The pediatricians assigned to the Kreispoliklinik periodically visit the surrounding neighborhoods and hold well-baby clinics and consultation hours.

The general dentist manages the problems of adults; children are cared for by the general dentist when there is no pedodontist (Kinderstomatologe, a specialist in children's dental problems) available. Although presently some distance from its goal, the GDR plans for all children to be cared for by pedodontists. Much child dentistry will take place in day-care centers, kindergartens, and schools.[11] Since most children need some dental attention, providing care where they usually are seems quite rational. Children can be treated and then sent back to the classroom. (The Bezirk of Rostock has made considerable progress toward this goal; in 1976 approximately twenty percent of the pedodontists were working in school clinics with dental chairs and equipment located in the school. Another twenty percent of the pedodontists were in mobile units which go to the schools, a practical arrangement for rural areas with small schools some distance apart.)[12]

The Kreispoliklinik has a full-time obstetrician-gynecologist who cares for all pregnant women; even normal pregnancies are not followed by the general practitioner. The obstetrician-gynecologist visits rural or smaller urban clinics for prenatal sessions or, if the community is small, the patients are transported to the Poliklinik. All deliveries are in hos-

pitals.

The Kreispoliklinik has a number of other types
of specialists including the internist, who is usually
a sub-specialist-consultant. Unlike in the United
States, there is very little interest in developing
general internists.[13]

The physician for children and youth (Jugendarzt)
is usually a pediatrician, general practitioner, or
social hygienist (a physician who has specialized in
public health). As is true of all physicians working
in outpatient care, the majority of the Jugendärzte
are women.[14] These physicians are responsible for
preventive programs and routine examinations of children beginning in the fourth year of life and continuing through the eighteenth year (see below for details). They receive much of their specific training
while actually functioning in their role under the
supervision of an experienced Jugendarzt.[15] Although
these physicians are administratively part of an
independent department under the direction of the
district child and youth health officer (Kreisjugend-
arzt), their offices (Beratungstellen) are located
increasingly in the district clinic in order to facil-
itate access to consultants and laboratory services.
They conduct most of their activities in kindergartens, schools, and other special institutions for
children, however, and see children and parents for
special problems and counseling in their offices. The
Jugendarzt shares formal responsibility with school
officials and sanitation inspectors for hygienic
conditions in kindergartens and schools.

The next smaller unit of ambulatory health care
is the medium-sized outpatient clinic, which in rural
areas is called a Landambulatorium. They have several
general practitioners, general dentists, and usually a
pediatrician. They often hold their own well-baby
clinics. The obstetrician-gynecologist may visit
several times during the week. The dermatologist, the
otolaryngologist, and the internist visit periodically.

The smallest unit with full-time physicians is
the small clinic or practice (Staatliche Arztpraxis).
Only eleven percent of the doctors involved solely in
outpatient care are in such units.[16] Unit size varies
according to the needs of the community. A pediatrician is usually not stationed there permanently but

TABLE 2. MEDIUM-SIZED OUTPATIENT CLINIC
(LANDAMBULATORIUM)

1 PER 15,000 POPULATION

Staff	Maternal and Child Health Services
3 general practitioners	Occasionally sick care for children
1 general pediatrician	Well-baby clinics, day-care health programs, and sick care for infants and children
3 general dentists	Dental care for children
Part-time obstetrician-gynecologist	Prenatal care
Part-time consultative services by district specialists	

visits for the well-baby clinics. The general practitioner might see children when they are ill or patients might travel five or ten miles to see the
pediatrician in a larger facility. Distances to basic
services are relatively short in the GDR due in part
to the relatively high population density.

The basic health care facility, especially in
rural areas, is the community nurse station. The
community nurse or Gemeindeschwester is similar to the
public health nurse in the United States, but with
more varied responsibilities. [17] She is responsible
for approximately one thousand people of all ages in a
defined geographic area and is the key to rural health
care. She is the school nurse, health educator, and
occupational health nurse (e.g., for small agricultural cooperatives); she helps patients with financial
affairs, arranges funerals, provides first aid and
follow-up care for illnesses seen by doctors, does
home visiting, refills prescriptions, and performs

TABLE 3. SMALL OUTPATIENT CLINIC OR SMALL PRACTICE
(STAATLICHE ARZTPRAXIS)

Staff	Maternal and Child Health Services
1-3 general practitioners	
0-1 general pediatricians	Well-baby clinics, day-care health programs, and sick care for infants and children (by pediatricians if available; otherwise by general practitioner with additional experience)
0-3 general dentists	Dental care for children

TABLE 4. COMMUNITY NURSE STATION (GEMEINDESCHWESTER-STATION)

1 PER 1,000 POPULATION IN RURAL AREAS

Staff	Maternal and Child Health Services
1 community nurse	
1 part-time general practitioner	Well-baby clinics, day-care health programs, and sick care for infants and children (by pediatrician if available; otherwise by general practitioner with additional experience)
1 part-time general pediatrician (depending on need and local health plan)	

numerous other tasks. The scope of her medical practice depends upon her relationship with the physician
and upon her experience. In some communities, the
physician and nurse agree upon conditions when she may
even prescribe medications. The physician holds
office hours at the community nurse station several
times a week. A well-baby clinic, done by a visiting
pediatrician or the general practitioner, may be held
there if warranted by the number of patients in the
community and the distance to the physician's office.

In the GDR, responsibility for the health and
welfare of the population is clearly defined. In rural communities one of the practicing physicians has
this responsibility, although he or she may not actually provide all the services. This person is
called the Bereichsarzt. Under his or her supervision
are usually three to five community nurses. The
Bereichsarzt is ultimately responsible for such matters as sanitation in infant day-care centers, safety
in factories and agricultural cooperatives, and insuring that the elderly receive their complete social
services and that no one is in need of basic necessi-
ties.

In most of the fifteen counties of the GDR there
are sufficient numbers of primary-care physicians,
i.e., general practitioners, pediatricians, and obste-
trician-gynecologists.[18] This has been accomplished
in part by the state's fixing the number of training
positions for each specialty yearly in each geographic
area. When medical students apply for postgraduate
specialty training, they are counseled by a faculty
advisor to be certain their desires coincide with the
needed specialities.

Even rural areas have adequate health services.
The high population density and state control of
specialty distribution and location of practice positions in the GDR contribute to solving rural health
care delivery problems. The factors which have helped
attract physicians to rural areas include the following: financial incentives up to 250 marks per month
for practicing in rural areas--not an enormous amount
(approximately 20% of a physician's starting salary),
but it can be an inducement; relatively spacious
living quarters and access to skilled labor for re-
pairs and renovations, commodities very difficult to

come by in the GDR; an independence that is not likely
to be found in larger urban clinics, particularly in a
system so highly organized and regulated; a status in
a small community which is much higher than in urban
areas with multiple sources of care; shorter waiting
periods for consumer goods such as automobiles, which
ordinarily must be ordered several years in advance of
delivery; absence of professional isolation since
night call is shared among district physicians and
time is allotted for continuing education when possible; closer relationship to patients and an opportunity to understand the environment from which they
come; and industrialization of the agricultural cooperatives, a national economic goal that has improved
the quality of life in rural areas by stimulating the
development of local cultural and recreational opportunities.

    The obstetrician, the Gemeindeschwester, and the
Gesundheitsfürsorgerin (the health and welfare worker)
participate together in prenatal care. (The Gesundheitsfürsorgerin is similar to a social worker in the
United States but administratively belongs to the
medical care system, facilitating coordination between
health and social services. They often are nurses
with additional required special training in the
health and psychosocial problems associated with a
particular age group or disease.)19 The activities of
the Gesundheitsfürsorgerin for pregnancy include
visiting the homes of patients who are at high risk
for complications, investigating those who fail to
attend prenatal clinics, conducting health education
classes, counseling patients, and insuring that they
receive the appropriate social and financial benefits
associated with pregnancy and the birth of a child.
These benefits are considerable.20

    Patient participation in prenatal care is very
good. Ninety-five percent of pregnant women have more
than four prenatal examinations and 88% begin prenatal
care before the fourth month of pregnancy. Approximately 25% attend prenatal courses dealing with health
during pregnancy, preparation for childbirth, and
mothering skills.21 There are several reasons for the
high participation rate in prenatal care activities.
First, good health and the importance of medical care
are themes of GDR society, emphasized in the schools,
at work, and in the media. Prenatal clinics are

conveniently located, and working women are allowed paid time-off to attend, an important benefit since 85% of pregnant women are employed. Financial incentives also encourage attendance at prenatal clinics.[22]

Despite an active policy to encourage childbearing, the fertility rate declined steadily from 1965 to 1975.[23] A major increase in the rate of decline occurred in 1972, the year an extremely liberal abortion law came into effect.[24] However, since 1976 when even greater benefits for working mothers were instituted, the fertility rate has been increasing.[25]

Ninety-seven percent of babies are enrolled in well-baby clinics (Mütterberatung) in the first year of life, and 86.5% have their first examination at less than 21 days of age. All babies are visited at home by a Gesundheitsfürsorgerin or a Gemeindeschwester in the first weeks of life. Participation rates remain high throughout the three years of well-baby clinics, with 86.1% continuing to be seen regularly in the third year.[26] For several years over 96% of infants have been fully immunized by three years of age. The reasons for these high rates are similar to those listed for prenatal care--emphasis on the importance of health, financial incentives, convenient locations (e.g., day-care centers), and the vigorous outreach activities of the Fürsorgerin when necessary. Although the well-baby clinic may be held only one or two times a week when the physician is present, the Fürsorgerin may stay in the neighborhood or community most of the week and conduct classes for mothers and, together with the Gemeindeschwester, provide a continuous link between the family and the health care system. This is particularly important where chronic medical or social problems exist.

The day-care (Krippe) system, for which the Ministry of Health is ultimately responsible, is highly developed. In 1979 approximately 60% of children aged five months to three years were in day care, with enrollment preference given to infants of single and working mothers.[27] The centers are supported largely by the state with families paying no more than one mark per day.[28] There is usually one caretaker for four or five children. The fully qualified caretakers (Krippenerzieherinnen) complete three years of training in a school for allied health professionals (Medizinische Fachschule), in addition to ten years of basic schooling. (If the caretakers have not completed their training, they are enrolled in a work-study program with one day free each week to attend classes.) This profession is very popular and highly respected. The day-care facilities and programs throughout the GDR have great similarity. There are standard guidelines which describe the required physical facilities, staff, curriculum, and the regular formal evaluations of physical and psychosocial development. [29]

Each day-care center has a physician (Krippenarzt)--usually a pediatrician, but occasionally a general practitioner--who is responsible for the health of the enrolled children and for hygienic conditions. Fifty-eight percent of children under three years of age receive well-baby examinations and immunizations in their day-care centers.[30] This arrangement can be quite helpful for parents for whom it is inconvenient to miss work and for the physicians, who often receive valuable supplemental information from day-care center workers that might not be forthcoming from parents, e.g., information concerning behavior problems, social problems, or maternal-infant interaction problems. Parents are made aware of scheduled physician and Fürsorgerin visits and are encouraged to leave their questions with the day-care staff or to come themselves.[31]

In 1979 approximately 92% of children aged three years to six years and nine months attended kindergarten.[32] The Ministry of Education, which is responsible for the kindergartens, has established a unified curriculum which, like the day-care center guidelines, emphasizes education and developmental stimulation.[33] The elaborate health and developmental record begun in the day-care center is transferred with the child to the kindergarten and then on to the school, a continuity which facilitates early recognition and management of potential problems.

The preventive medicine program in kindergarten and during the school years is provided by the Gesundheitsfürsorgerin for children and youth and by the

271

Jugendarzt; they do not treat sick children, however.
School readiness examinations, designed to identify
children who may have subtle physical handicaps or
difficulty adjusting to school, are given twice in the
last eighteen months of kindergarten.[34] Practically
all pre-school children in the GDR are examined at
some point because some attendance in kindergarten is
compulsory during the year before school entry. Re-
ferrals are made for appropriate diagnostic studies
and treatment. Schools for children with special
needs are available throughout the GDR; however, access from rural areas may require busing or, rarely,
living-in.

Although the Gesundheitsfürsorgerin and the
Jugendarzt are available, when necessary, to consult
with teachers or children and their families, routine
examinations are performed on all school children
every three years. In addition, children must undergo
examinations prior to participation in certain sports,
in summer camps, and in the required part-time experience in industry. A final physical examination is
designed to assess ability to perform successfully in
the student's career choice. This examination is
particularly important for those planning careers that
will be physically demanding.

The GDR has clearly developed an impressive
health and social services system, exemplified by the
services provided for young parents and their children, even in traditionally underserved rural areas.
The country's morbidity and mortality statistics,
which were extremely poor in the early post-war years,
have rapidly become comparable to those of the United
States, but without the United States' marked regional
and socio-economic variations.[35] Still, some aspects
of the maternal and child health care system might be
improved. Care is fragmented between preventive and
therapeutic services, particularly in urban areas.
These are often provided at different locations, by
different people using separate medical records. This
can result in inadequate use of information and a
potential decrease in the quality of overall care.

There tends to be some duplication of responsibilities and perhaps excessive personnel in some
activities. For example, the well-baby clinics are
often attended by the physician, the special well-baby

272

Fürsorgerin, and the Gemeindeschwester. Although the latter two attempt to coordinate their efforts, their interests, education, and experience often overlap sufficiently to warrant only one of them being present. (The same criticism is appropriate for the prenatal clinics.) Also some of the tasks reserved only for physicians in the GDR might be transferred to the Gemeindeschwester, e.g., giving immunizations, performing routine physical examinations, and providing prenatal care to healthy women (especially after the first pregnancy). These might be done equally well, if not better, by a specially trained nurse and be less expensive for the health care system.

The frequency of routine physician examinations seems to be excessive. Although not all the well-baby checkups are received, particularly after the early months of life, the Ministry of Health requires monthly examinations for the first six months, examinations every six weeks for the next six months, every three months for the second year, and twice during the third year.[36] For the infant who is thriving there is evidence that this is excessive.[37] After infancy the most serious problems concern intellectual and psycho-motor development and behavior. Since the day-care center and kindergarten teachers routinely perform developmental and behavioral evaluations of their children, the need for physician examinations is further reduced. Standardization of forms and sharing information between different administrative units would diminish the frequency of examinations during the school years, a burden for physicians and families. Eventually the magnitude of required services may force such cost-benefit analysis.

The value of the elaborate pre-school programs as a social support and economic benefit for the family cannot be questioned. Their curriculum, however, needs to be evaluated. What are the long-term individual and societal effects of this highly standardized system, to which children are exposed during the most formative period of life? Some child-health professionals and parents in the GDR are asking this question.[38] However, if more children continue to participate, it will be difficult to find the appropriate comparison groups to answer it.

As might be expected in a state-controlled, prepaid, open-access health care system, some people complain of over-organization with a super-abundance

273

of regulations and administrators, excessive utilization, and failure of patients to assume financial and practical responsibility for their care. At the same time, however, GDR citizens take pride in what their society has provided for the welfare of its members, particularly its most vulnerable ones.

The University of North Carolina at Chapel Hill

Notes

[1] Since 1976 the author has spent approximately four months in the GDR studying the organization and delivery of maternal and child health services. He gratefully acknowledges the support of the International Research and Exchanges Board (IREX), New York, N.Y.

[2] Ministerium für Gesundheitswesen and the Akademie für Ärztliche Fortbildung der Deutschen Demokratischen Republik, Mütter-, Kinder- und Jugendgesundheitsschutz: Eine Sammlung von Rechtsvorschriften mit Anmerkungen und Sachregister (E. Berlin: Staatsverlag der DDR, 1978).

[3] Panorama DDR and Verwaltung der Sozialversicherung beim Bundesvorstand des FDGB, Sozialversicherung in der DDR (Dresden: Zeit im Bild, 1980), pp. 53-55.

[4] Institut für Sozialhygiene und Organization des Gesundheitsschutzes, Das Gesundheitswesen der Deutschen Demokratischen Republik 1980, Vol. 15 (E. Berlin: Nationales Druckhaus Berlin, 1980), p. 176.

[5] The GDR has 15 counties, 219 districts, an area of 108,180 km^2, and a population of 16,740,000 (Statistisches Jahrbuch der Deutschen Demokratischen Republik 1980 [E. Berlin: Staatsverlag der Deutschen Demokratischen Republik, 1980], pp. 1-6).

[6] Although there is considerable latitude for use of funds allocated by the Ministry to the counties for health and social service facilities, the overall goals for each planning period are established at the national level and must be the basis for decision-making.

[7] W. Kneist, "Aufgaben, Arbeitsweise und Organization des Kinder- und Jugendgesundheitsschutzes," in Kinder- und Jugendgesundheitsschutz, ed. Eva Schmidt-Kolmer and Rudolf Neubert (E. Berlin: Volk und Gesundheit, 1975), pp. 288-291, contains a complete listing of administrative responsibilities in the health care system.

[8] The tables have been modified from Kneist, p. 306.

[9] The Bezirkspoliklinik is larger but serves mainly as a referral and consultative facility.

[10] General practitioners like all physicians and dentists in the GDR receive four years of specialty training after completing the five years of medical school and a general clinical year; see: Akademie für Ärztliche Fortbildung der DDR, Weiterbildung des Arztes in der DDR (Berlin: VEB Kleinoffsetzdruckerei, 1975). General practitioners see 52% of all patients. Nine percent of these general-practitioner encounters are through house calls, and 90% of all house calls are made by general practitioners (Das Gesundheitswesen . . . 1980, p. 175).

[11] G. Reussel and K.-A. Schwelgengräber, "Die stomatologische Betreuung der Kinder in Kindergärten, Schulen, Krippen und Heimen," Stomatologie DDR, 24 (1974), 299.

[12] K.-A. Schwelgengräber, "Analyse zum Stand der Kinderstomatologie im kommunalen Gesundheitswesen des Bezirkes Rostock und Schlußfolgerungen für die weitere Entwicklung," Table 4, (unpublished article from the Bezirks-Jugendzahnklinik Rostock, 1976).

[13] This conclusion is based upon a number of interviews with internists in outpatient clinics and community and university hospitals.

[14] Medical school classes now have equal numbers of men and women, whereas in the recent past women comprised the vast majority of medical students.

[15] Kneist contains a summary of the contents of an ideal training program for the Jugendarzt, pp. 308-310.

[16] Das Gesundheitswesen . . . 1980, p. 176.

[17] C. Richter, "Die Gemeindeschwester in der DDR," in Die Gemeindeschwester, ed. Claus Richter (E. Berlin: Volk und Gesundheit, 1978), pp. 12-14.

[18] However, there is a need for more dentists in many areas. Since extensive fluoridation of drinking water is planned, this need may be considerably reduced in the future.

[19] "Qualifizierungsabschnitt A 4 - Gesundheitsfürsorgerinnen - Gesundheitsfürsorger," in Rahmenausbildungsunterlage für die Aus- und Weiterbildung der Werktätigen (Potsdam: n.p., 1971), n. pag.

[20] They include six weeks of paid leave from work before the estimated date of delivery and twenty weeks after; optional, unpaid leave for the first baby's first year of life (partial salary for this year with subsequent babies), with the woman's original position or a comparable one remaining open for her; one thousand marks for clothing and infant furnishings; generous financial support for single, employed mothers who must stay home because they are unable to find a place in an infant day-care center; progressive reduction, with the birth of each child, in the amount to be repaid on a 5,000 mark interest-free loan available to newly married couples under 26 years of age; ten marks per month for six months to mothers who breast-feed (two 45-minute, paid periods per working day are allowed for breast-feeding); and a number of other benefits (Sozialversicherung der DDR, pp. 18-23, and S. Akkermann and K.-H. Mehlan, "Law and Fertility in the German Democratic Republic," in Law and Fertility in Europe, ed. International Union for the Scientific Study of Population [Dolhain, Belgium: Ordina Editions, 1975], pp. 281-285).

[21] Das Gesundheitswesen . . . 1980, pp. 182-186.

[22] One hundred marks are given to women who attend prenatal clinics during the first 16 weeks of pregnancy; and 50 marks, to those who attend from the 21st to the 28th week (Akkermann and Mehlan, p. 282).

[23] Statistisches Jahrbuch 1980, p. 368.

[24] Mütter-, Kinder- und Jugendgesundheitsschutz contains the text of the abortion law, pp. 101-102.

[25] Since 1949 the population of the GDR has been generally decreasing (Statistisches Jahrbuch 1980, p. 353) due to both the low fertility rates and the high death rate associated with the relatively large number of elderly people in the GDR since World War II. War casualties and emigration prior to the closing of the GDR borders in 1961 contributed to this population age structure.

[26] Das Gesundheitswesen . . . 1980, p. 187.

[27] Das Gesundheitswesen . . . 1980, pp. 232-237. Ten percent of day-care children were under one; 44% were one to two; and 45% were two to three years of age.

[28] Akkermann and Mehlan, p. 286.

[29] Mütter-, Kinder- und Jugendgesundheitsschutz, pp. 257-322, and Pädagogische Aufgaben und Arbeitsweise der Krippen, ed. Eva Schmidt-Kolmer (E. Berlin: Volk und Gesundheit, 1976).

[30] Das Gesundheitswesen . . . 1980, p. 188.

[31] Employers must allow time for a parent to attend well-baby clinics if it is not possible to do so outside of regular working hours (Mütter-, Kinder- und Jugendgesundheitsschutz, p. 32). The day-care center personnel make an effort to keep the family informed of the health and development of the child and provide guidance for behavior management and developmental stimulation at home.

[32] Statistisches Jahrbuch 1980, p. 288.

[33] Ministerium für Volksbildung, Bildungs- und Erziehungsplan für den Kindergarten (E. Berlin: Volk und Wissen, 1975).

[34] The organization and content of the examinations given during the kindergarten and school years can be found in Kinder- und Jugendgesundheitsschutz, ed. Schmidt-Kolmer and Neubert, pp. 126-278.

[35] The infant mortality rate (deaths in the first year of life per 1,000 live births) in the GDR fell from 72.2 in 1950 to 12.9 in 1979 (Statistisches Jahrbuch 1980, app. I, p. 3, and Das Gesundheitswesen . . . 1980, p. 24). During the same period the rate

fell from 29.2 to 13.0 in the United States (Myron E. Wegman, "Annual Summary of Vital Statistics - 1979: With Some 1930 Comparisons," Pediatrics, 66 [1980], 823-833). Other morbidity and mortality statistics for the GDR can be found in Das Gesundheitswesen . . . 1980, pp. 7-167.

[36] Akkerman and Mehlan, p. 284. Given the propensity of GDR institutions to follow official policy, the potential for full compliance with these regulations exists.

[37] R. A. Hoekelman, "What Constitutes Adequate Well-Baby Care?" Pediatrics, 55 (1975), 313-326.

[38] The 1976 increase in the amount of time a working mother may spend caring for her newborn, with minimum financial sacrifice, reflects, in part, the concern for maintaining a strong maternal-infant bond. There has been a recent dramatic decrease in the proportion of infants in day care who are under one year of age--22.5% in 1975 to 10.3% by 1980 (Das Gesundheitswesen . . . 1980, p. 236).

Living Conditions in Rural Areas of the GDR

Ursula Koch

The traditional division of labor between rural and urban areas resulted, among other things, in inferior living conditions for small farmers and land workers in Germany. The transition from feudal times to the industrial age did not really change their situation: dependence on the feudal lord was replaced by dependence on the market. The technical, social, and cultural advancements that accompanied industrialization were achieved in the cities, not in rural areas.

One of the general goals of the GDR has been to bring the class allies--agricultural and industrial workers--closer together. As part of this plan, continuous efforts have been made to improve the living and working conditions of the rural population, and over the years, considerable progress has been made in bettering the objective conditions in rural areas. This study will investigate whether subjective changes have kept pace with these developments and whether consciousness and individual modes of behavior correspond to the objective advances.

As Rudi Weidig, one of the GDR's leading sociologists, states, sociological research on living conditions in this broad sense has scarcely been done:

> So wurden die verschiedenartigen Ver-
> mittlungen zwischen den . . . sozial-
> ökonomischen Verhältnissen und der Her-
> ausbildung der dem Sozialismus eigenen
> Art des gesellschaftlichen Lebens . . .
> sowie des individuellen Verhaltens noch
> kaum einer eingehenden Analyse unter-
> zogen.[1]

I will first describe some important developments in agricultural production and in the social structure of rural areas of the GDR. As a second step, I will show some data demonstrating changes in the life-style, consciousness, and behavior of the rural population. In addition, I will introduce passages from Ursula Püschel's book Unterwegs in meinen Dörfern, a GDR eyewitness report of life in the rural GDR.

The economic transformation of GDR agriculture took place in three major steps, the first of which was the land reform (Bodenreform) carried out by the Soviet Military Administration in the fall of 1945. At this time, farmland belonging to Nazi war criminals and all agricultural holdings over 100 hectares (ha. = approx. 2.47 acres) were expropriated and, for the most part, divided into small parcels of 5 to 10 hectares, which were deeded over to roughly 120,000 farm workers and landless peasants, 165,000 small land-holders, and 91,000 refugees and others. Table 1 shows the difference in the percentage of the total agricultural land made up of small and medium-sized farms after the land reform as opposed to before the war.

TABLE 1. FARMS WITH 0.5 - 20 HECTARES OF LAND

1939: 40.3% of all farmland

1951: 70.7% of all farmland

Source: Rainer Rilling, ed., Sozialismus in der DDR. Dokumente und Materialien (Cologne: Pahl-Rugenstein, 1979), I, 128.

In a drive to increase productivity, more than 800,000 farms were combined between 1952 and 1960 to form approximately 19,000 collective farms or Landwirtschaftliche Produktionsgenossenschaften (LPG); they represented about 85% of the cultivated land. Three types of collective farms were developed: Types I and II share only the fields or fields and machinery; Type

III, fields, machinery, and livestock. The following
table shows the continuous increase in the size of the
production units over the years.

TABLE 2. LPGs FROM 1952 TO 1975

Year	Types I/II		Type III	
	Number	Aver. Size (in ha.)	Number	Aver. Size (in ha.)
1952	1,740	109	166	175
1960	12,976	156	6,337	534
1971	2,664	243	5,663	838
1975	306	309	4,260	1,180

Source: Statistisches Jahrbuch der Deutschen Demokratischen Republik 1978 (E. Berlin:
Staatsverlag der DDR, 1978), p. 156

By 1967, industrial production techniques were in use
on a large scale in GDR agriculture. Specialized
service units, such as agrochemical centers and district workshops, supply fertilizers, agro-planes,
transportation vehicles, and harvesting equipment to
the collective farms in a given area. During the
seventies, several new types of production units were
founded; they combine a number of collective farms
under a cooperative council (Kooperative Einrichtun-
gen, Kooperative Abteilung Pflanzenproduktion, Kooperative Abteilung Tierproduktion). On the average,
these new units have a membership of 260 farmers and
workers, and an area of 4,200 hectares.[2]

Agricultural production in the GDR today is an
industrial type of enterprise. This has a direct
effect on personnel requirements (type and level of
qualification) and on general living conditions, such
as work time, leisure facilities, health care, and
schooling in the country. Most of the small farmers,
land workers, and refugees from the East (Umsiedler)
who received parcels of land during the land reform
had grown up under capitalist (and in some of the
eastern areas rather feudal) conditions. To be a

281

farmer had traditionally only required that one owned a piece of land--it did not presuppose that one had specific qualifications. And landless laborers hadn't had access to schooling. As late as 1960, only about 10% of the agricultural labor force had some kind of vocational training.

Today's industrialized farming, with its high level of mechanization and complex planning, cannot do without a well-qualified work force. The GDR has systematically furthered the education and training of the rural population. This development is reflected in the following table:

TABLE 3. QUALIFICATION STRUCTURE OF FARM POPULATION (in % of total farm employees)

Year	Total	University Degree	Technical School	Master	Skilled Worker
1963	1,028,927	0.4	1.6	2.8	13.3
1970	886,624	0.8	3.2	5.3	48.3
1977	770,133	1.8	5.3	6.6	70.0

Source: Statistisches Jahrbuch der Deutschen Demokratischen Republik 1980 (E. Berlin: Staatsverlag der DDR, 1980), p. 167

Women and juvenile agricultural workers receive special attention in the GDR. As shown in Table 4, the number of female agricultural workers has steadily declined in recent years. GDR specialists at the Institut für Ökonomik der Landwirtschaft und Nahrungsgüterwirtschaft attribute this decline, among other things, to the rise in the average age of female employees. They state, too, that problems concerning housework, the care of children and the elderly in rural families still remain. The general level of training of women is considered satisfactory. In 1979, 84.7% of the female agricultural workers had some vocational training. In 1963, only 8.5% of the women surveyed had received vocational training; in 1970, 49.3%. In agriculture as well as in other sectors of the economy, the ratio of women to men in management positions or with degrees in higher education remains low. [3]

The percentage of juveniles in the agricultural sector (12.2% in 1979) is lower than the percentage of juveniles in the industrial sector (14-16%). Considerable care is being devoted to attracting juveniles, as well as women, to agricultural professions. Every LPG must establish special development plans for these

TABLE 4: PERCENTAGE OF WOMEN AND JUVENILES AMONG AGRICULTURAL EMPLOYEE

Year	Women	Juveniles
1965	45.5	7.2
1970	44.8	7.2
1975	43.5	9.9
1979	43.3	12.2

Source: Statistisches Jahrbuch der DDR 1980, p. 164

two groups: a Frauenförderungsplan and a Jugendförderungsplan. According to the 1977 LPG statutes (the statutes are the legal basis for the cooperatives as differentiated from nationalized enterprises), annual plans are to be set up, and the LPGs must give an account of their progress. [4]

The conditions of both work and leisure time in rural areas are supposed to approximate those in the city, characteristic differences (between the ways of life in the city and country) notwithstanding. The GDR claims to have established--for the first time in German history--an economic situation in which the rural inhabitants' social well-being and chances for improvement no longer depend on the size of their land holdings.

In keeping with the concept of the unity of social and economic policy, plants (Betriebe) play a

283

highly important role in promoting various aspects of the social well-being of their employees. In this sense, in spite of their differing form of organization--cooperative, rather than state-owned--LPGs are "plants": they have the same obligation to provide for the well-being of their workers. As stated by legal experts at the Karl-Marx-Universität Leipzig: "Sowohl die LPG Pflanzenproduktion als auch die LPG Tierproduktion haben den Schutz der Gesundheit, das Recht auf Freizeit, Erholung und Urlaub, Freistellung von der Arbeit, Unterstützung bei Krankheit und im Alter . . . zu gewähren." [5]

In regard to physical working conditions, all plants are obligated to work toward the elimination of heavy labor and the reduction of noise and dust levels. In cooperation with communal authorities, the plants maintain health care programs and manage company-owned housing. They are responsible for transportation. Plants cooperate with local schools in holding regular courses for school classes (Patenklassen). They actively promote the continuing training and education of their employees; for example, employees' positions are kept open for them while they are on leave for further training. The plant organizes sports activities, vacations, rehabilitation programs; it encourages participation in cultural events and appreciation of the fine arts.

The means to finance these various programs are budgeted in the plant's consumption fund (betrieblicher Konsumfonds). Table 5 gives a breakdown of the money expended in 1975 by six companies with a total of 40,000 employees; 1,374 marks per employee were paid out. This example is taken from industry, but the obligations of the LPGs are analogous. The needs addressed by these expenditures are not considered "private" needs, although they of course greatly influence individual well-being. The expenditures are thought of as part of the workers' wages (though not paid out in money); the percentage of the wages they represent rose from 18.7% in 1970 to 21.5% in 1976. In addition to the above benefits, members of the LPGs get land for their private use. They can use machines and tools belonging to the LPG to work this land, even after they retire.

Rural health care has been totally reorganized in the GDR. Health care facilities include hospitals,

TABLE 5. COMPANY CONSUMPTION FUND

Expenditures	Percentage of entire fund	Marks per person
Physical working conditions	38.4	527.70
Education/child care	13.9	190.99
Nutrition	10.8	148.40
Culture, sports	9.9	136.03
Housing	8.9	122.29
Recreation	6.5	80.31
Health care	4.2	57.71
Protection of the environment	3.3	45.34
Other	4.1	56.33
TOTAL	100.0	1,374.07

Source: S. Stötzer, "Die Befriedigung materieller und geistigkultureller Bedürfnisse der Werktätigen in volkseigenen Kombinaten und Betrieben der Industrie der DDR," Wissenschaftliche Zeitschrift der Karl-Marx-Universität Leipzig, Gesellschafts- und Sprachwissenschaftliche Reihe, 25, No. 5 (1976), 406.

polyclinics, ambulatory facilities, doctors' practices, and nurses' stations. At present there is one medical doctor for approximately 520 inhabitants. It is important to mention the cooperation between the LPGs and health authorities. The manager of Produktion und Arbeitsvorbereitung in the LPG is also responsible for arranging prophylactic health checks and vaccination against tetanus before spring work in the fields begins. Infant mortality, usually taken as an indicator of the quality of health care, used to be extremely high in rural areas, for example in the area of Neubrandenburg. By 1976 Neubrandenburg had arrived at a mortality rate lower than the GDR average, which in itself has been greatly reduced since the war, as shown in the following table.

TABLE 6.   INFANT MORTALITY GDR - NEUBRANDENBURG

| | Deaths per 1,000 live births in | | | |
	1949	1952	1960	1976
GDR	78.3	59.1	38.8	14.0
Bezirk Neubrandenburg		108.0		13.1

Source: Statistisches Jahrbuch der DDR 1978, p. 351

Low infant mortality means not only a good health care system, but also peaceful living conditions and the training and care of mothers.[6]

   With the modification of working and living conditions in rural areas, the question of food service has become more and more urgent. Given the number of women working and the introduction of shift labor on the LPGs, the traditional means of food preparation (e.g., the housewife's cooking a warm meal for the family at noon) presents problems. Of all household chores, meal preparation was found to take up the most time: an average of 15.4 hours per week in 1972.[7] In order to enable all members of the family--including the women--to spend their free time participating in cultural, social, or sports activities, an effort has been made to remove meal preparation from the private sphere.

   An example given in the study prepared at the Wilhelm-Pieck-Universität Rostock is the VEG (Volkseigenes Gut) Friedländer Große Wiese, in which 248 of the 436 employees are women. Together with other neighboring VEGs and LPGs they founded an inter-enterprise cooperative for meal preparation. Two main difficulties had to be overcome. First of all, since the kitchens of the member enterprises were scattered throughout the area, there were problems of coordination and transportation. Also, some of the kitchens did not meet the standards set for modern canteens. Secondly, as the authors report, not all the members of the cooperating plants wanted this sort of food of the cooperating plants wanted this sort of food service:

> Nicht alle Beteiligten waren von vorn-
> herein zur kooperativen Zusammenarbeit
> bereit. Es kam darauf an, die Bereit-
> schaft jedes einzelnen für die Lösung
> der objektiv herangereiften Aufgaben
> durch beweiskräftige Analysen zu errei-
> chen. Es galt, Betriebsegoismus, Be-
> strebungen der Taktik der Rückversiche-
> rung und des Zweifels am Gelingen zu
> überwinden. Dieser ideologische Prozeß
> mußte planmäßig geleitet werden.[8]

In the end, experience with the new catering system was satisfactory, but it also became clear that in the long run it was not to the advantage of the VEGs and LPGs to provide meals themselves. A new kind of coop- erative plant (VEB Gesellschaftliche Speisung) was founded instead, following the example of several ur- ban catering services.

On the whole, traditional differences in rural and urban living conditions have been overcome. Machines have done away with most of the hard physical labor connected with farming, and there is no longer the threat of financial ruin because of bad weather or crop failure. All farmers and LPG employees work a 5-day week and have paid vacations, all receive pen- sions, etc. In the past, leisure time was a rare blessing in rural life. Today, as a consequence of the 8-hour workday, there is time for the various cultural activities that have become part of rural life. Former "leisure time" activities, such as child care and housework, have been subsumed under working activities: there are day-care facilities for child- ren and paid household days off from work.

Inequalities in living conditions still exist, however, in regard to housing: housing in rural areas tends to be older than in the cities, and there is a lack of modern conveniences, such as indoor plumbing and bathing facilities.[9] And in spite of the good educational facilities in the country, differences in formal education still exist between industrial and agricultural workers. Table 7 shows the proportion of employees in industry and in agriculture with univer- sity (Hochschule) and technical school (Fachschule) degrees.

287

TABLE 7. EMPLOYEES WITH UNIVERSITY AND TECHNICAL
SCHOOL DEGREES IN 1979 PER 1,000 EMPLOYEES

Degrees held	Per 1,000 employees in industry	in agriculture
University	35.6	24.2
Technical School	79.9	61.0

Source: Statistisches Jahrbuch der DDR 1980, p. 99

In her book, Unterwegs in meinen Dörfern (1980),
GDR writer and art critic Ursula Püschel, who comes
from a rural background herself, describes a visit she
made to a LPG in Berlstedt am Ettersberg; her impres-
sions and conversations with agricultural workers and
others offer an interesting glimpse into life on a
LPG. [10]

One member of the LPG describes the effects of
the many changes in living and working conditions on
the mentality of the workers; he makes a distinction
between the older members and the younger ones:

> Solche Eigentumsmentalität, sagt K.H.,
> ist verbreitet bei Leuten über fünfzig.
> Jüngere interessiert das nicht mehr.
> Sie interessiert allerdings auch
> anderes nicht--da fällt um halb fünf
> der Hammer, dann ist Feierabend. Bei
> Menschen mit genossenschaftlichem
> Denken kann man mehr herausholen. Wenn
> ein Gewitter am Himmel stand, gingen
> sie aufs Feld, egal wann. . . . Nun
> müsse man andere Stimuli ansetzen, auch
> materielle. (p. 94)

In the past, people who milked cows didn't need a
school diploma in order to do their hard physical
labor. Today milkers write scientific papers on
milking problems as part of their training. Ursula
Püschel reports on a graduation thesis prepared by two

288

Püschel reports on a graduation thesis prepared by two young milkers on the LPG:

> Beim Reden über die Milchgewinnung wird
> mir die Hausarbeit für den Facharbei-
> terabschluß rübergereicht: "Milchgewin-
> nung, Behandlung und Kontrolle in in-
> dustriemäßiger Produktion im Melkka-
> russell". Ich finde darin Wissenschaft
> handlich, auf die Arbeit im Berlstedter
> Melkkarussell bezogen und mit eigenem
> Standpunkt dargelegt. Am Ende stehen
> drei Verbesserungsvorschläge, einer
> bezieht sich auf die Quetschgefahr,
> wenn Kühe das Melkkarussell betreten.
> Man lernt mehr, als man braucht, sagen
> sie. Das zahlt sich aus--die Bewegung
> des Geldzählens. Und vor allem: Man
> weiß mehr. (p. 106)

The **Melkkarussell** is a merry-go-round-like turning assembly, onto which the cows step in order to be milked as the carrousel turns, and then step off again. Thus milking is not physical work anymore, but rather a matter of getting many hundreds of cows through this merry-go-round line without slowdowns or accidents.

Among the cultural activities on the LPG visited by Ursula Püschel is the village band, in which LPG members play the various instruments. Here is a partial listing of the complement:

Trompete	Diplomlandwirt
Trompete	Zahnarzt . . .
Flügelhorn	Traktorist
Flügelhorn	Lagermeister
Flügelhorn	Elektromechaniker
Schlagzeug	Brigadier Pflanzen
Schlagzeug	Brigadier Tierzucht
Baßtuba	Technologe
Posaune	Architekt
Baritonhorn	Kranfahrer
Tenorhorn	Lehrling. . . . (p. 133)

A professional musician from the Weimar Staatskapelle is the band leader, coming to the village in his free time. Ursula Püschel records his remarks:

> Haunstein, im stillen Glanz von Zu-

friedenheit, sagt mir über seine Arbeit
hier: Dazu kann einen niemand zwingen,
das kann man nur machen, wenn man
Freude daran hat, sonst funktioniert es
nicht. Was man hier für falsche Töne
in die Ohren kriegt, ist nicht zu
sagen. Aber das ist nicht wichtig.
Hier kommen Leute zusammen, die den
ganzen Tag gearbeitet haben. (p. 135)

Younger LPG members have become accustomed to the
diversity of cultural activities available and take
advantage of them; older LPG farmers tend to stick to
the land, working their private plots during their
leisure time and after retiring. Ursula Püschel
reports a conversation with a 75-year-old farmer and
his wife about their retirement activities:

Sie haben gesagt, wenn Ihre Frau
sechzig wird, dann soll sie nicht mehr
arbeiten, dann soll sie was haben vom
Leben.
Also dann soll sich die Frau Ost
und West ergründen. Im Westen leben
ihre Geschwister.
Was denn--alleine?
Ich kann doch nicht weg. Daß ich
vier Wochen verreise, das geht nicht.
Das Pferd ist da, Ziegen sind da,
Hühner sind da, Enten sind da, Kar-
nickel, Schweine . . .
Die von der LPG haben och alle
Urlaub.
Hmm. . . . Meine Plantage, da muß
ja auch was gemacht werden. Da ist
oben Obst und unten Kartoffeln oder
Rüben. Drei Morgen, hundert Zentner
Kartoffeln, vierhundert Zentner Rüben.
Seine Frau: Was, hundert Zentner
Kartoffeln?
Na, dies Jahr nicht, aber im all-
gemeinen. (p. 52)

The improvement of living conditions in rural
areas in European countries is not only a question of
Christian ethics or socialist morality. In the years
to come the very existence of the agricultural sector
will depend more directly on the degree to which it
proves itself capable of participating in the achieve-

ments of society. Working hours, vacations, housing, wages, health care, and cultural life will influence the worker's decision to take a job in agriculture. These issues will be just as important for production as the level of mechanization and automatization.

Land reform and continuous organization have established the basis on which GDR farmers and planners have built up a new quality of life and production in rural areas. Karl Marx used the term "Idiotismus des Landlebens" to describe the isolation, monotony, and underdevelopment of rural life. [11] That is no longer true today in the GDR. GDR farm workers share the advantages, and the disadvantages, of highly industrialized production conditions.

Fachhochschule Ostfriesland

Notes

Ich danke Margy Gerber und Gordon Tracy für ihre Hilfe! U.K.

[1] Rudi Weidig, "Zur Dialektik der Entwicklung von Sozialstruktur und sozialistischer Lebensweise in der DDR," Deutsche Zeitschrift für Philosophie, 28, No. 1 (1980), 5.

[2] Heinz Heitzer, GDR. An historical outline (Dresden: Zeit im Bild, 1981), p. 222.

[3] Christa Bednarek, Harry Reimann, and Hellmut Stegmann, "Das gesellschaftliche Arbeitsvermögen in der Landwirtschaft der DDR," Sozialistische Arbeitswissenschaft, No. 6 (1981), p. 432. See Christiane Lemke's article "Social Change and Women's Issues in the GDR: Problems of Women in Leadership Positions," included in this volume.

[4] "Beschluß über die Musterstatuten und Musterbetriebsordnungen der LPG Pflanzenproduktion und LPG Tierproduktion vom 28. Juli 1977," Gesetzblatt der DDR, Sonderdruck Nr. 937, dated 16 Sept. 1977.

[5] Richard Hähnert, Wolfgang Schneider, and Erich Siegert, "Rechtssubjekte und subjektive Rechte im LPG-Recht unter den Bedingungen des Übergangs zu industriemäßigen Produktionsmethoden in der Landwirt-

schaft," <u>Wissenschaftliche Zeitschrift der Karl-Marx-Universität Leipzig</u>, Gesellschafts- und Sprachwissenschaftliche Reihe, 30, No. 3 (1981), 250.

[6] See Robert A. Greenberg's article "Maternal and Child Health Care in the German Democratic Republic," included in this volume.

[7] Reinhold Anders, Robert Barthelmann, and Renate Kruse, "Grundsätze und Erfahrungen bei der Organisation der Gemeinschaftsverpflegung im Gemeindeverband Ferdinandshof," <u>Wissenschaftliche Zeitschrift der Wilhelm-Pieck-Universität Rostock</u>, Gesellschafts- und Sprachwissenschaftliche Reihe, 27, No. 10 (1978), 691.

[8] Reinhold Anders et al., p. 693.

[9] See Rainer Rilling, ed., <u>Sozialismus in der DDR. Dokumente und Materialien</u> (Cologne: Pahl-Rugenstein, 1979), II, 47.

[10] Ursula Püschel, <u>Unterwegs in meinen Dörfern</u> (Munich: Damnitz 1980). Subsequent page references will appear in text.

[11] Karl Marx, Friedrich Engels, "Manifest der Kommunistischen Partei," <u>Marx-Engels-Werke</u>, IV (E. Berlin: Dietz, 1972), 466.